TROUT
STREAMS
of
Central New York

TROUT
STREAMS
of
Central New York

J. MICHAEL KELLY

Burford Books

Printed in the United States of America.

10 9 8 7 6 5 4 3 2 1

Library of Congress Cataloging-in-Publication Data
Kelly, J. Michael, 1949–
    Trout streams of central New York / J. Michael Kelly.
        pages cm
    Includes index.
    ISBN 978-1-58080-178-2
    1. Trout fishing—New York (State)—Guidebooks.   2. Trout fishing—
New York (State).   3. New York (State)—Guidebooks.   I. Title.

    SH688.U6K453 2015
    799.17′57097471—dc23

                                                        2015028664

DEDICATION

To Dad, who taught me the best way to fish,
and the right way to live.

Contents

Acknowledgments ix

Introduction xi

Part I: Waters Quick and Cold

CHAPTER ONE	South of the Flower City 3
	Monroe County 6
	Ontario County 13
	Livingston County 19
	Yates County 27
CHAPTER TWO	Trout in the Heartland 31
	Onondaga County 32
	Cayuga County 61
	Madison County 75
	Cortland County 94
	Oswego County 110
CHAPTER THREE	Trout Waters of the Southern Tier 123
	Steuben County 124
	Chemung County 139
	Schuyler County 144
	Tompkins County 147
	Tioga County 153
	Broome County 159
	Chenango County 163

Part II: Tactics for Taking Central New York Trout

CHAPTER FOUR	Of Worms and Rainy Days 169
CHAPTER FIVE	Spin Fishermen I Have Known 175
CHAPTER SIX	Hatch-Matching Made Easy 181
CHAPTER SEVEN	Down Below with Nymphs and Wet Flies 185

CHAPTER EIGHT   Streamers and Big Trout Are Like Bogie
                      and Bacall 191

CHAPTER NINE   Filling Up Your Fly Box 197

CHAPTER TEN   Hail to the Natives 203

CHAPTER ELEVEN   Fishing the Rainbow Run: Somewhere Today,
                      Elsewhere Tomorrow 209

CHAPTER TWELVE   Trout-Fishing Manners and Ethics 215

APPENDIX I   Stocking Quotas for Central New York Trout
                      Streams, 2014 219

APPENDIX II   Central New York Trout-Fishing Regulations 225

Index 231

Acknowledgments

Any friend or relative who has seen the sagging bookcases in my living room knows I am not kidding when I say I have never met a fishing guidebook that I didn't like. Those shelves hold a grand total of more than 750 volumes, on every topic from birding to the Bible, but roughly two-thirds are about hunting, fishing, and related subjects. I was surprised, just now, when I counted exactly 73 guidebooks telling me and other readers of the fishing that awaits us in various parts of the world. Some of these tell-alls have kept me on the trail of trout in Montana, Michigan, Pennsylvania, and other places where I have actually fished and caught something, with the guidebook's considerable assistance. A few of my other guidebooks are about the fishing opportunities in California, Iowa, and other states that I have yet to see except from the window of a passenger jet.

Since my wife is always after me to donate a few copies of this or that to the local library or even a neighborhood garage sale, I have been compelled to admit that I love fishing guidebooks, even those that I don't ever get to read completely, because they take me to places I have never been before. I'm sure Chickie was not surprised, therefore, when I told her I had decided to write a guidebook of my own, one that would give long-overdue credit to one of the most underrated trout fishing regions in the eastern United States.

It couldn't have happened without Chickie's unconditional support. Peter Burford, my publisher, made my task much easier than it otherwise might have been, just by being the all-around good guy that he is. One of these days, I'm going to have to take him trout fishing.

Special thanks are due my wife's co-worker, Jodi Saurini, a computer wizard who helped me over several technological hurdles during the preparation of this book. Finally, my gratitude goes to the many fisheries biologists and technicians in the Department of Environmental Conservation's Region 7 and Region 8 offices who fielded every question I had for them with just the right mix of enthusiasm and patience. Readers should be pleased to know that these dedicated professionals love Central New York's trout fisheries nearly as much as I do, which is to say, one heck of a lot.

Introduction

The Beaverkill River in Sullivan and Delaware Counties is one of a very few New York trout streams known to anglers around the world. Another is the West Branch of the Ausable River, which flows through the long shadows cast by Whiteface Mountain in Essex County. Both rivers came by their celebrity status many decades ago, and whether they still deserve the accolades thrown their way depends on who is asking, who will answer the question, and how the fish have been biting lately.

I wish I could say that all trout streams whose names are spoken in reverential tones are as good as advertised. However, in all honesty, a river's reputation frequently has more to do with sentiment than science, and most waters flowing through the Catskills and Adirondacks have never lacked for champions to sing their praises. Their most ardent fans were those outdoors writers who, beginning in the 1920s and continuing for several decades thereafter, filled the pages of sporting publications and the New York newspapers with exciting accounts of their weekend trout-fishing adventures. Metaphorically speaking, many hook-and-bullet scribes were deskbound dreamers each Monday through Thursday. Lucky for their readers, they frequently managed to sneak out of the office after the Friday lunch hour. If these refugee writers could sail through a couple of busy intersections in the big city, they might cover the remaining distance to a favorite Catskill boardinghouse in a couple of hours. That would give them a chance to be on the upper Beaverkill or one of the big pools below the village of Roscoe before the Friday-evening mayfly hatches commenced. After that, they didn't have to head home until Sunday afternoon.

Back at the office, the trout-fishing oracles often managed to sprinkle their fishing reports with anecdotes about their most recent Upstate adventures. Of course, a bit of name-dropping always added spice to the story. In the 1920s and '30s—sometimes recalled by angling historians as the Golden Era of Fly Fishing—some of the better-known outdoors writers were generous souls and willing to offer their fellow typewriter-punchers a tactical tip now and then. Often, the advice was proffered over a half-empty but quickly refillable beer mug or shot glass at the Antrim Lodge, which was strategically located near the junction of the Beaverkill and Willowemoc Creek. Those who lacked the critical information about hatches and flies when they entered the taproom generally managed to acquire it before closing time, provided they made proper use of their drinking money.

SECONDHAND REPORTS WERE BETTER THAN NONE

In this subculture, fishing writers who seemed to have things all figured out teamed with less knowledgeable scribes to get the word out to everybody's readers. Gradually, generations of New York City–area fly fishers who had never set eyes on Cairn's Eddy on the Beaverkill or Edward Ringwood Hewitt's gin-clear pools on the Neversink River read so much about them that they never felt the need for a proper introduction.

The Catskill waters were, indeed, very pleasurable to fish, but as writers like Ray Bergman, John Alden Knight, and Red Smith touted favorite regional streams, they apparently forgot a few other choice spots whose reputations lagged only because they were located just a little too far away from Manhattan.

I am convinced some of those slightly remote rivers and creeks were every bit as good as the famed streams north of the city boroughs—and still are.

The most prominent example of overlooked and underrated trout fishing, in my view, is that vaguely defined tourism region referred to as "Central New York." Draw an imaginary circle with a radius of just 100 miles from downtown Syracuse. The trout waters in that circle are second to none, if you consider them in their totality. Central New York's sparkling streams include meadow brooks you can explore while wearing wet sneakers, and rivers that are too wide to cover with even a perfectly executed double-haul cast. Many of these forgotten waters are packed with trout, even today. Some are crowded with anglers, too, but the majority of the streams are lightly fished and convey the wonderful sense of peace that comes with simply having a few pools to yourself.

If we generously considered Central New York to include a block of 18 counties whose combined boundaries stretch across a map from Greater Rochester to metro Utica and from the brushy backwoods of the Tug Hill Plateau south to the fertile dairy farms in the Susquehanna Valley, we'd have encircled what is arguably the most underappreciated trout fishing region in the state—if not the entire East. This area, which includes sprawling suburbs and dense forests as well as skyscraping cities, is drained by dozens of major rivers and creeks and at least as many jump-across rills that support brown, rainbow, or brook trout. Yet even today Central New York waters are seldom considered as vacation destinations, despite the fact that many offer the potential for big hatches and big catches to those who explore them.

Now, I freely admit to taking my own shot, now and then, at fishing the trout waters of the Catskills and Adirondacks. They deserve the attention outdoors writers give them, but each year along the Beaverkill I get into friendly conversations with anglers who have downstate addresses. I also share a piscatorial tale or two when I go fishing and camping with my family in New York's North Country. It simply amazes me, during these encounters, how few state residents seem to have heard of Nine Mile Creek, Chittenango Creek, Oriskany Creek, and other excellent trout fisheries in the heart of our state.

LOW ON ANGLERS, NOT ON FISH

With the notable exception of Nine Mile, which offers well-worn paths along both banks as it meanders from Otisco Lake to Onondaga Lake, most of the better streams in the Rochester, Syracuse, and Utica metropolitan areas are lightly trod. The opening day of trout season, April Fools' Day, usually lures an impressive crowd of bait drowners to area streams, but most of those casual sportsmen are through for the year once they've hooked a couple of the trout deposited in roadside pools by Department of Environmental Conservation tanker trucks.

Speaking of hatchery trout, the DEC's network of publicly funded fish farms annually pumps about 250,000 speckled beauties into Central-region streams. Another 75,000, give or take a few, are stocked in Onondaga County creeks by the county-owned hatchery located on the banks of Carpenter's Brook in Elbridge. The yearly exodus from cement rearing ponds into more natural settings begins in late March and continues into early June. Many regional trout waters are planted with fish several times each spring. A few creeks have annual stocking quotas of 10,000 or more fish a season, and some of the same streams' allocations include generous

Bud Eberlin of Weedsport fishing Nine Mile Creek in the early season.

numbers of fat, 12- to 15-inch-long two-year-old browns, along with the 8-inch "catchable" trout that say good-bye to hatcheries after only a year or so of high living.

As you would suspect, most anglers target the two-year-olds, and not long after the hatcheries began stocking such fish in the late 1990s conservation officers and DEC biologists were swamped with complaints about "truck followers." These greedy folks could be found throughout the state, parked each morning at hatchery entrances. They waited for workers to load their tanker trucks with fish, then followed the vehicles to favorite stocking locations. When they had their limits of trout—preferably plump two-year-olds—these lazy "sportsmen" went home, only to return on the next stocking day. Since trout stockings invariably take place on weekdays, fishermen who had to wait until Saturday to stretch their lines complained about streams being "fished out."

SPREADING THE WEALTH

After looking into the situation, then–DEC Region 7 fisheries manager Les Wedge and then–Region 8 fisheries manager Bill Abraham petitioned their Albany higher-ups to change regulations in Central New York. The creel limit was left at five trout a day, but of the five, only two could be longer than 12 inches.

Most anglers seemed supportive of the change, which basically spread the wealth (bigger browns) among more anglers. It became routine, on many streams, to catch browns measuring between 11 and 13 inches that had several hook marks on their jaws. In the past, such fish were dumped in a wicker or canvas creel. As fishermen became more aware of the two-over-12 rule, some found it easier, and more sportsman-like, to set free any trout of debatable length. The subtle change in attitude brought to mind the slogan coined by the famed angler-author Lee Wulff decades earlier: "A good game fish," he wrote, "is too valuable to be caught only once."

Some of the biggest beneficiaries of the revised creel limits were the more popular streams in Central New York, and the anglers who fished them frequently.

I should emphasize, however, that some of the region's top trout waters aren't stocked at all. For instance, it has been more than two decades since any hatchery fish took a swim in Oriskany Creek between Solsville and Oriskany Falls. The fishing in that stretch, for browns running between 8 and 14 inches, is outstanding with bait, lure, or fly. Anglers who pile up frequent-fisher points on Oriskany Creek know its shaded banks and spring seeps assure them of lots of action even in July and August. But most fishermen in the region will never know, because they don't try this prime fishing hole much, if at all, after the first four or five weeks of the trout season. There are so many other regional streams flowing under the radar, for one reason or another, that even well-traveled fishing fanatics who live in Central New York should be able to find a personal honey hole or two in this book.

RIVERS NEED FRIENDS, TOO

Not all streams in the region are ignored by anglers, and a few are in need of gentle treatment by conservation-minded fishermen. Two prototypes come to mind. At one end of the spectrum, I can and will identify some traditional early-season spots that hold stocked or even wild fish in April but seem barren of trout by mid-June. Ironically, some of these "marginal" trout waters may shelter wily browns weighing 5 or even 10 pounds all season, even though rising water temperatures and low dissolved oxygen levels cause small trout to vacate the premises. You won't catch numbers of trout in these creeks during the midseason, but you do stand a chance of nailing a genuine trophy when conditions are right. Just remember, the more big ones you release now, the more will be waiting to challenge your skills in the years ahead.

xvi   TROUT STREAMS OF CENTRAL NEW YORK

At the opposite end of the habitat spectrum but just as susceptible to greedy fishermen are the native brook trout streams, which—depending on the location—may be in robust condition or in imminent danger of being swept from the landscape. Central New York has many waters populated by wild natives. Most such trickles hold few, if any, trout longer than 7 or 8 inches, and these sparkling little jewels are so hard up for calories that they eagerly feed on anything drifting past their hidey-holes. They are notably easy to catch after a spring or summer downpour raises and muddies the water they call home. We can fish for these beautiful little char without guilt, but conscientious anglers will think twice before creeling a brace of brookies, let alone keeping a limit. Since *Salvelinus fontinalis* is New York's state fish, we will take a closer look at the health of brookies in a later chapter.

Meanwhile, permit me to take you on a journey through Central New York's trout country, and to share some tips for catching a few in pools along the way.

I have the distinct impression that avid readers of fishing guides purchase volumes such as this one with the aim of becoming better, more knowledgeable fishermen. To them, there is no such thing as too much information. Among other things, they yearn to know the number of trout stocked in a given stream, as well as the timing and volume of aquatic insect hatches, and, of course, whether that water is generally accessible to the public or can be fished only with permission of adjoining property owners.

This book will, I hope, give you a great deal of such valuable knowledge, and tell you how to learn even more on your own. Assuming most anglers would be likely to test my recommendations pertaining to nearby streams before planning day trips or expeditions to more distant places, I divided my 18 counties into commonsense geographic areas. These groupings are called "South of the Flower City," which covers trout waters in the Rochester area; "Trout in the Heartland," about Syracuse-area streams; and "Trout Waters of the Southern Tier," which focuses on trout fishing in or near counties close to the Pennsylvania border.

You will quickly realize that I am not afraid to compare one creek with another. However, I've resisted the temptation to rely mainly on statistical analyses for rating trout waters. Figures lie, after all, and yes, liars figure. Instead of doing lots of math ratios, I've called my trout streams as I've seen them. I take such liberties because I have fished some of these waters for 30, 40, even 55 years. If I didn't know those streams by now I wouldn't dare to write a book about them or their neighbors. In some cases—but not all—I have backed up my opinions about certain spots by bringing other anglers into the discussion. Their declarations may influence readers slightly, significantly, or not at all when they venture forth to explore previously unknown waters just a few miles from their homes, but I am confident the ensuing arguments at local diners and tackle shops will be based more on facts and less on rumor than was the case in the recent past.

Although I am first and foremost a fly fisherman, I am not a fly-fishing snob. In my opinion, fly rodders inherently are no more effective or ethical than the bait dunkers and spin doctors. I believe in following fish and game laws to the spirit, not just the letter. Anglers who have complaints about certain regulations are welcome to voice those misgivings and work to change them. Meanwhile, however, they should play by all the rules, not just the ones they agree with. If you break the laws you don't like, why shouldn't I do the same? Anarchy does not bode well for anglers.

In the same vein, where the law permits, there is nothing morally wrong with keeping a couple of trout now and then to share with your family, friends, or neighbors. Just remember that your good judgment is critical in such matters. Some streams can easily afford to give up a few fish and some cannot. If you are a beginner, know that your experience will eventually tell you whether an individual brook or river is loaded or not. Until you can say for sure, it is best to err on the side of caution.

A welcome sign at Onondaga Creek.

During my 55 or so trout seasons, I have practiced fly, bait, and spin fishing with zest, and will continue to do so in accord with water conditions, regulatory parameters, and my physical health. Most fly fishermen I've known or observed in action were conscious of the ethical issues that swirl around the currents of cold, swift streams, but I have seen the same love of sport and concern for the preservation of trout among those who specialize in bait and spin fishing, too. Consequently, this book is aimed at all avid anglers, as long as they believe in fair play and high ethical standards.

The book is divided into two main sections. Part 1 features descriptions of nearly 140 trout streams in Central New York, identified and located with the help of DEC biologists and many dedicated anglers whom I count as friends. After you have finished taking notes on part 1, get yourself a fresh legal pad and dig into part 2, which is all about methods for catching trout in these featured streams. I am absolutely positive that you will find much of value within these pages.

PART I

Waters Quick and Cold

CHAPTER ONE

South of the Flower City

MONROE, ONTARIO, LIVINGSTON, and YATES COUNTIES

We can reasonably debate whether the Catskills or Central New York has the better trout fishing, but there is not a sliver of doubt which region is doing a better job of promoting its outdoor assets. As evidence, consider the nicknames of the communities engaged in the epic struggle for anglers' spending money. The village of Roscoe, which straddles the banks of the Beaverkill in Sullivan and Delaware Counties, routinely refers to itself as Trout Town, USA.

On the other hand, Syracuse, although surrounded by beautiful trout streams in Onondaga County, is known far and wide as the Salt City. Not exactly designed to lure trout anglers to town, is it? The nickname harks back to pioneer days, when the salt boiling industry was a leading employer along the shores of Onondaga Lake. As for Rochester, several sources tell us that its nickname, the Flower City, stems (excuse me) from an annual Lilac Festival.

Why aren't these great cities and counties using high-visibility advertising campaigns to draw trout-fishing tourists to their local creeks? Something like "New York's Trout Central" might remind visitors of doubled-over fly rods and singing reels. It's not too late, and hopefully tourism experts will soon appreciate that the area economy can net many millions of dollars by hooking up with trout fishers.

Perhaps a new book will give the promotion of regional trout waters a jump start. The chapters and essays in this volume, *Trout Streams of Central New York*, cover approximately 140 streams with year-round, resident populations of brown, brook, or rainbow trout. With a couple of exceptions (Little Sandy Creek, to name one), I did not include Lake Ontario tributaries, because most of them do not have year-round trout populations, other than the juvenile steelhead that smolt and swim down to the lake when they are about 8 inches long. You will note that the exceptions to the "no tributary" rule are either tributaries of tributaries, or take in the upper reaches of a feeder creek, where a high waterfall or some other natural barrier keeps steelhead and salmon separated from resident brown and brook trout. I also decided to write sparingly, if at all, about Finger Lakes tributaries that greet spawning rainbows in April but do not hold fishable populations of trout—of any species—throughout the year. Of course, I made room for spawning streams that are worth trying between rainbow runs. Some of those places, such as Owasco Inlet, are among the state's most productive and versatile trout fisheries.

Even after eliminating many steelhead and Pacific salmon spawning streams that spill into Lake Ontario, and the inland streams that beckon to spring rainbows but nearly go dry in the summer, I did not come close to running out of rivers, creeks, and brooks to write about. Brawling creeks and rivers abound in these pages, but you will also learn about plenty of small, weed-choked streams that are so flat and glassy, you might want to toss a rock at the water before casting, to make sure the surface hasn't turned to ice.

The book you hold is what I would immodestly describe as a comprehensive guide to trout streams in an 18-county region of New York. Although the region's cold-water fishing hatches more fans each season, prospects vary considerably from one county to the next.

In fact, two of the counties reviewed—Monroe and Seneca—have only two streams that the DEC recognizes as trout water. Another, Wayne County, has no streams within its boundaries that currently support trout year-round.

Monroe County has two fairly large trout streams, one of which is dominated by steelhead spawning runs from Irondequoit Bay. The other, Oatka Creek, is one of the state's top brown trout fisheries and as such merits thorough discussion a few paragraphs from here.

The Seneca County trout streams are Canoga Creek, which empties into Cayuga Lake in the Canoga Marsh Wildlife Management Area, along Route 89, and Reeder Creek, which is on the east side of Seneca Lake. Each has its followers, but in terms of productivity Seneca County's duo doesn't come close to the Monroe County trout streams. For now, let's give both Canoga and Reeder Creeks an honorable mention and get back to a couple of larger, more accessible streams.

Canoga Creek has a small population of wild brook trout, which is augmented by an annual stocking of about 200 brookies from the state hatchery system. However, the creek is of limited value even to local anglers, since the most trout-friendly segment, upstream from Route 89, is posted, and permission from the landowner is required for fishing. Downstream from Route 89, the creek runs through the Canoga Marsh Wildlife Management Area and is open to the general public. While the marsh might not be quite as fishy looking as the water upstream from Route 89, it can be productive, especially in the first month or two of the season.

Reeder Creek, which flows along Route 121 (Yale Farm Road) north of the Seneca Army Depot before taking a steep drop downhill to Seneca Lake, is one of a dozen or so small tributaries that see minor runs of spawning rainbow trout each spring, but it's the only one I'm aware of that has some wild brown trout in its upper end. Pay heed to landowner rights by asking permission before trying your luck.

Wayne County is a good place to fish for warmwater species in the summer, but has no trout streams aside from a few Lake Ontario feeders that attract spawning salmon, steelhead, and brown trout during the cold months of the year. Pete Austerman of the DEC Region 8 fisheries unit led a survey crew that recently electrofished three small streams in Seneca County as part of the Eastern Brook Trout Joint Venture. Although Mudge Creek, Sodus Creek, and Little Glenmark Creek had formerly been stocked with brook trout, the state workers did not find any natives and do not consider the trio of streams to be trout water.

There are no ifs, ands, or buts regarding the other counties that Rochester-area anglers would consider worth a visit on Saturday morning.

The Flower City area had a rich angling heritage long before the 1990s, when the ESLO Derby and other troll-for-cash trout and salmon contests drew thousands of fishing boats to the city's waterfront. I wonder how many of the sportsmen who competed for big-bellied king salmon and steelhead in Lake Ontario's spacious fishing grounds knew that a regional resident named Seth Green had invented a heavy, multiple-lure rig for trolling deep in New York lakes in the 1800s? Surely, they must have known, too, that Green was the very same man who, in 1864, designed, built, and operated the first commercial-scale fish hatchery in the United States, in Caledonia, on the border between Monroe County and Livingston County.

Maybe they just never heard of Green. One of the reasons modern fishermen don't know much about the history of their sport is that they are doing a heck of a lot of fishing, but not enough reading. The situation reminds me of the poacher who took a game warden out on a lake in his fishing boat and, after a long gab session, grabbed a stick of dynamite from his vest, lit it, and tossed it overboard. Aghast at the blatant violation of the law (and all the fish that were floating to the lake's surface) the warden began reciting those violations, chapter and verse. Meanwhile, the poacher lit another stick of dynamite, set it on the warden's seat, and said, "Are you going to keep talking, or do you want to fish?"

These days, the game warden in the joke would be replaced by a librarian, who would respond to the explosions by asking, "Didn't you read the fishing regulations guidebook at all?" The poacher would respond, "Who has time to read anything these days?"

And then both the poacher and the librarian would resume taking "selfies" with their smartphones.

RANKING OUR TROUT STREAMS

If money or reputations were at stake, comparing one trout water to another would be a fool's errand, for the quality of the fishing in any river or stream can be ruined overnight by flood, drought, pollution, or other calamity. At the same time, Mother Nature's recuperative powers are simply amazing, and a year or two of light fishing pressure might be all the help a once-famous creek needs to flow down the comeback trail.

Just for fun, I consulted with DEC biologists and some well-traveled fishing buddies to come up with the graphics you will see throughout this guide. The ranking system rates streams, in ascending order, from 1 to 5. Taking into account factors including accessibility for fishing, trout abundance and size range, natural reproduction and stocking rates, year-round water temperatures, and trout food supplies, I ranked 72 of the more than 130 streams discussed between these covers.

You'll read here about many creeks and brooks that got 2s or 3s; none that netted 0s and a few 4s. Only a handful of waters clearly deserved 5s, but maybe your favorite is among them. Overall, I'm a tough grader, but the more I know about Central New York's trout waters, the better I like them.

I hope to see you on the water one day soon.

MONROE COUNTY

By some random act of nature, Monroe County has only two year-round trout streams within its borders, Oatka Creek and Irondequoit Creek, and even these two fishing holes must be marked with asterisks to denote special circumstances. Oatka Creek is arguably one of the 5 or 10 best inland trout waters in Central New York, if not the entire state. Unfortunately for tourism promoters, the creek actually is shared by three counties—Wyoming, Genesee, and Monroe. Irondequoit, in contrast, is an important Great Lakes tributary, and steelhead swim up it in tackle-smashing gangs, but its headwaters hold some of the prettiest wild brown trout you or I will ever see. Another unusual attribute of Irondequoit Creek is its special-regulations section in Powder Mills Park, which includes a county fish hatchery. The hatchery, operated to sustain park fishing programs for kids, senior citizens, people with disabilities, and others who might benefit from extra rod-and-reel time, is a valuable recreational asset for eligible Rochester-area residents.

OATKA CREEK

RATING: ★★★★ (4 stars)

NOTEWORTHY: Oatka has one of the more dependable Hendrickson mayfly hatches in the region.

BEST TIME TO FISH: The last week of April and first week of May are Hendrickson times.

As just mentioned, the bragging rights to Oatka Creek are shared by three counties, but there seems to be no doubt that the best trout fishing on this regionally famous stream flows within Monroe County. The lower end of Oatka, from its junction with the Genesee River in Scottsville upstream to the mouth of Spring Creek in Caledonia, teems with brown trout, stocked and wild. However, even its loyal regulars are prone to complain about Oatka's high degree of difficulty—which, I must admit, has also left me scratching my head more than once. Yet the Oatka veterans understand that the challenges posed by the stream's multiple hatches of aquatic and terrestrial insects, heavy fishing pressure, and treacherous wading are also some of its most persuasive charms.

Countless authors of books about fishing have urged readers to observe the water carefully before making their first cast in a new or unfamiliar pool. However, based on the behavior of Oatka Creek anglers, I am convinced patience is very overrated, as virtues go. Popular pools, such as those in the parks at Garbutt and Scottsville, fill up in a hurry at prime times. When the Hendricksons, March browns, and *invaria* sulfurs are on the water, you cannot expect to have first crack at a pet pool, even if you arrive an hour ahead of the hatch du jour's anticipated starting time. In this atmosphere, you may just have to rely on personal experiences or the generosity of other anglers—a slim possibility at best, until you get to know a few of the Oatka gang—to solve that old riddle: "So what are they taking?" Remember to ask the guy whose rod is bent, not the fellow who is rummaging through a fly box and trying desperately to capture a flying insect for comparative purposes. Don't forget, either, that attaining a hookup with one of Oatka's fussy feeders all on your own is a proud achievement. Maybe you can bring it to the net the next time you're in town.

The creek's winding route through Monroe County begins in one park setting and ends at another. The first place I'm calling to mind here is the junction pool where Spring Creek, having just exited the DEC hatchery grounds in Caledonia, mixes with Oatka Creek. The blending of quality and quantity (Spring Creek's icy and bubbling currents with Oatka's depth and flow volume) creates an instant attraction for trout and fisherman, alike. That other park setting I was thinking of is the one in Scottsville, just upstream from the creek's junction with the Genesee River. In between these two idyllic places, visiting anglers will find streambanks with well-worn paths and some other areas that are heavily posted by private landowners or fishing clubs. Like most trout waters that have no nearby equals, Oatka Creek is coveted by all sorts of anglers, and the DEC has tried to accommodate the demands of each archetype by rewriting certain clauses in New York's environmental conservation laws. Special regulations are rampant here, and the angler who has never fished Oatka before should keep handy an up-to-date version of the state's *Freshwater Fishing* regulations guide.

As of late 2014, the special regulations in force included the presence of a year-round no-kill (catch-and-release) zone from Union Street in Garbutt upstream for 1.7 miles to the Wheatland Center Road. Only artificial lures or flies may be used in this stretch. There are also seasonal no-kill rules in force from October 16 through March 31 in two areas. One is from the Bowerman Road crossing in Scottsville upstream for 1.4 miles to Union Street, and the other is from the Wheatland Center Road upstream for 2.5 miles to the mouth of Spring Creek. The two sections with no-kill regulations from mid-October through March are subject to a reduced creel limit—two trout of 12 inches or more apiece—during the state's general trout season, April 1 through October 15. These sections are also for users of artificial flies and lures, only.

Finally, sections of Oatka Creek not mentioned already are currently open all year, even to occasional bait dunkers like you and me. The daily creel limit is five trout, only two of which may be more than 12 inches long.

Watching for the Hendrickson hatch on Oatka Creek.

Admittedly, this is a regulatory hodgepodge, but the restrictions and exceptions add up to plenty of opportunities for all sorts of fishermen, and most of all for fly fishermen. I'd say that spin fishers have it made on Oatka Creek, too, since the no-kill and year-round rules beckon to them as much as the most ardent of feather flingers. However, there must be some sort of taboo on the sharing of trout water by spinning enthusiast and long-rod expert, because such a mix is seldom seen.

Why that is, perhaps you can tell me someday. There's room for all, if each is generous in spirit. Meanwhile, Oatka Creek will remain one of the better fly-fishing waters in the Empire State. Here's why:

- **Trout and plenty of them.** If you feel like explaining the economics of catch-and-release trout fishing, buy another copy of this book and highlight the next couple of sentences. Before implementing the smorgasbord of rules now in place for Oatka, the stream received an annual stocking of approximately 10,000 brown trout a year, including around 1,500 two-year-olds that averaged about 14 inches long. Now the fish that used to be destined for frying pans around the Rochester area are recycled, and more than once, in some cases. Surveys of anglers by DEC Region 8 fisheries biologist Brad Hammers's crew indicate that a significant number of "stockies" are caught and let go multiple times in the special-regulations sections of Oatka Creek before they are finally removed from the creek by angling, predation, or other causes. That means trout fishermen visiting the stream get more bites for their bucks, and so do other sportsmen, whose license fees support state fish and game programs.

- **Big ones, little ones, short ones, long ones.** Some anglers like streams that hold only big trout, or at the least many big trout. To my way of thinking, the ideal stream is one whose feature attraction is trout of all sizes. Such a stream is in robust health, for it boasts the habitat and food supply that will shelter and sustain several year-classes of trout, from 3- or 4-inch fingerlings to five- or six-year-olds that top the 18- or even 20-inch mark on a measuring tape. Usually, the majority of trout turned up by electrofishing survey crews in such a stream will range between 9 and 12 inches, but experienced anglers will hook plenty of bigger fish, too. That is a pretty good description of Oatka Creek's fishery.

- **Bugs by the bazillions.** And that's just the *good* bugs. Actually, while Oatka has its share of mosquitoes, deerflies, and biting midges (no-see-ums), the creek is deservedly known for its seasonal sequence of mayfly hatches, starting with the early- to late-April emergences of size 18 through 20 Blue-Winged Olives and Blue Quills and ending up with various sulfur-colored species in early to mid-June. The most prolific hatches are the Hendricksons (*Ephemerella subvaria* and *E. invaria*), which coat the surface of the creek in the last week or two in April and, some years, the first week of May as well.

Hendricksons have a reputation for being midafternoon critters, and in the Catskills many fly fishers sleep in while the hatch is in progress, in expectation that the big bugs (a size 12 or 14) won't be floating down feeding lanes before 2 PM. However, that rule of thumb does not apply everywhere, and quite a few Oatka regulars will swear that midmorning is not only a great time to float a Hendrickson dry, but even better for going subsurface with a nymph or emerger pattern. My favorite time is during a post-emergent spinner fall. My favorite time of day for Hendrickson is from around 6 PM until dark, when the biggest trout in the stream will be looking for the daily spinner activity.

After the Hendrickson hatch has concluded for the year, there may be a week or so of rather slow action on the creek, but the brief lull is followed by daylong but low-intensity hatches of size 10 March browns that will frequently draw splashy rises in the riffle areas. Some of the rises will signal the hunger of 15- or 16-inch trout, but even bigger browns can be taken in the creek's choppy water by ace nymph fishermen. A popular local pattern during the hatch is Spencerport fly tier Carl Coleman's March brown nymph, a heavily weighted and lacquered fly that sinks like a stone. It's a staple in local fly boxes, but I am among the successful users who think the fly imitates a small crayfish even better than it mimics a nymph.

Following the March browns, which continue to show sporadically until June 20 or thereabouts, fly fishers can look forward to hatches of size 16 and 18 sulfur-colored mayflies, along with low-volume but productive caddisfly emergences through June. After that, ants, beetles, and other terrestrial insect species trigger decent surface action around any of Oatka's many bank-shading willow trees.

To get to the creek from the Rochester area, take Route 490 south to West Chili. At the bottom of the exit ramp, turn south onto Union Street and drive about 5 miles to a T-intersection. Turn left onto North Road, and proceed about 2 miles to Scottsville. Route 383 takes you west from there, and closely parallels the creek. Access points to investigate include, from east to west, Bowerman Road, the Oatka Creek Park on Union Street, the crossing at Wheatland Center Road, and the Route 36 bridge, which is just downstream from the Spring Creek junction pool.

IRONDEQUOIT CREEK

RATING: ★★ (2 stars)

NOTEWORTHY: Essentially, a feast of steelhead with wild browns for dessert.

BEST TIME TO FISH: Late April, for if the browns aren't hitting, the chromers might be.

My memories of Irondequoit Creek are fond ones, focused mainly on a Saturday morning when I hooked—and lost—what might have been my biggest steelhead ever, before accepting a couple of gorgeous foot-long brown trout as consolation prizes. That was more years ago than I care to admit, but the story is not atypical of this stream, which is managed by the state for lake-run steelhead but still serves as home for wild browns of respectable size.

DEC biologist Matt Sanderson, who oversees Irondequoit for the Region 8 office, said a scientific survey of the Powder Mills Park stretch of the stream revealed relatively poor habitat overall but better living conditions and higher numbers of trout than in the Woolston Road area.

Older surveys, said Sanderson, showed good numbers of wild brown trout and also turned up an occasional wild brook trout. A more recent sampling of Irondequoit for the multistate Eastern Brook Trout Joint Venture did not show any brookies to be present, but the Region 8 office still hears from anglers who claim to be catching natives now and then. If *Salvelinus fontinalis* has a natural redoubt in Irondequoit Creek, the location is undoubtedly in the headwaters upstream from Powder Mills Park.

My encounter with a steelhead in the 10- to 12-pound class occurred in that upstream sector, between Railroad Mills and Fishers, two small communities south of Bushnells Basin in the town of Victor. Because there is no natural barrier to stop them, steelhead and chinook salmon are both able to reproduce in these headwaters, but browns hold their own. I was dunking night crawlers and spawn sacs one April day when a huge steelhead, a darkly colored male that was on the verge of performing its mating duties, inhaled a worm. Although I bore down on my 8½-foot fly-bait rod as hard as I could, that big fellow broke me off and was last seen heading downstream for parts unknown. After that incident, I caught several suckers as well as a couple of nice browns.

Although this book focuses on resident trout populations, I do not wish to discourage anyone from fishing for steelhead, and Irondequoit Creek has its share of big ones. In fact, it has almost as many steelhead as anglers at times! The crowded conditions are at their worst on weekends from mid-March through April, when the fish hustle upstream through pocket water in Penfield, Perinton, and Pittsford townships. As the big 'bows finish spawning and gradually return to Lake Ontario, the native browns often go on a bit of a feeding binge, as if they were aware that the competition was gone until next year.

One pleasing aspect of Irondequoit Creek, at least for small-stream fanciers, is its cozy contours. The lower end of the creek, downstream from Powder Mills Park, averages only about 20 to 30 feet across but contains some 4- to 6-foot-deep pools. In the suburban headwaters, the wild browns await their autumn spawning rituals in numerous pools that are only 10 to 15 feet wide. It's hip-boot water, and in most spots wading isn't really necessary.

Because much of the creek is bordered by steep rip-rap or clumps of alders and willows, it is difficult for fly fishers to tackle, although each spring seems to draw more of them to Irondequoit's crowded steelhead runs. The stretch above the county fish hatchery could be fished with floating flies before the spawning rainbows have said "Sayonara," but anglers determined to succeed with the purist approach will need to cast in cramped quarters. Along with dry-fly patterns, streamer flies and single-hook spinners will work well in Irondequoit's upper reaches, as long as the visiting angler is willing and able to adjust to the surroundings.

ONTARIO COUNTY

One of the more underrated fishing holes in the Finger Lakes region is Naples Creek, the main tributary of Canandaigua Lake. We will be looking into the attributes of this stream in a chapter devoted to the rainbow trout spring spawning run, but in the meantime, why don't you and I explore some of the other cold-water streams that flow within Ontario County? They aren't spectacular, exactly, but they do have assets worthy of a trout fisher's attention.

Naples Creek, itself, has more going for it than the average angler appreciates. That spring rainbow run—which is constantly touted by outdoors writers from throughout New York and a few other states besides—is the main reason for the countless cars parked along village streets on April Fools' Day, but not the only one. Keep reading!

NAPLES CREEK

RATING: ★★★ (3 stars)

NOTEWORTHY: In addition to its heralded spring rainbow run, Naples and its tributaries hold plenty of other trout.

BEST TIME TO FISH: May is the time to try for a Central New York slam, which consists of catching three species of trout in a day.

In addition to big, lake-run rainbows and thousands of juvenile 'bows, Naples Creek and its tributaries shelter a fair number of brown trout and, in some of its headwaters, a healthy population of wild brookies, too. Anglers who relish solitude and therefore can barely tolerate the crowds of fishermen who gather around the man-made plunge pools and other stream improvement structures in the early days of a new trout season would be astonished at the mixed bag of opportunities that await them in May or June. The spawning rainbows may linger into the last week of April or even later, but most of the anglers who pursue them are long gone by then. Low, clear water gives inexperienced visitors the false impression that few trout are available to be caught, but in a sense the season is just starting.

The real mystery about Naples Creek is where it begins. Some fishermen contend Naples starts just outside the village, where it is joined by Eelpot Creek. Others argue that Eelpot Creek actually isn't a tributary at all, but merely the upper end of Naples Creek. To me, a careful look at any

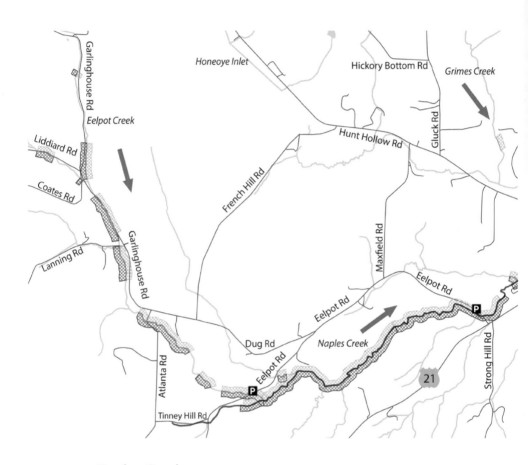

Naples Creek

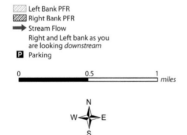

Left Bank PFR
Right Bank PFR
Stream Flow
Right and Left bank as you
are looking *downstream*
P Parking

0   0.5   1
                          miles

N
W   E
S

map of the watershed affirms that the stream flowing from the hills off Garlinghouse Road is in fact the same one that winds from there past the trailer park, then slides under Route 21 before picking up the volume of two bona fide tributaries, Tannery Creek and Grimes Creek, in the space of about 50 yards. It's all Naples Creek to me!

Regardless of that minor but persistent dispute, the main stem of Naples Creek *below* the junction with Grimes Creek is known for its large brown trout as well as its spawning-run rainbows. My best brown from Naples, by far, was a 21-inch hooked in a riffle just upstream from the Grimes junction pool. Other anglers have told of even longer browns caught downstream from the Route 245 bridge, which is beloved by many rainbow chasers, too. The Naples Creek watershed has other locations that deserve attention in spring or summer, especially after heavy rain showers have stirred the appetites of local trout.

As evidence of the rich sport that awaits Naples Creek anglers after the spring rainbow run has ebbed, consider the reports filed over the years by my longtime friend, the former Region 8 fisheries manager Bill Abraham. Like my late father, he loved both trout fishing and golf, so much so that he and a couple of his buddies enjoyed an annual outing that put them in proximity to both good trout streams and interesting golf courses. The golfing is always fun, but some of the trout waters have produced

A central New York "slam"—brown, rainbow, and brook trout.

better than others. One of the best trips of all began with a short drive north from Abraham's Wayland-area home to Naples Creek. During that Memorial Day weekend junket, he and one of his trout-seeking pals each caught their limit of rainbows. In those days, the creel limit in the Finger Lakes tributaries Abraham oversaw was no more than three 'bows, each one 15 inches or better.

"There are always a few spawned-out rainbows that hang around in the creek," Abraham said. Browns too big to fit in an average creel thrived downstream from the village of Naples, and wild brook trout held sway in two tributaries, Grimes Creek and Tannery Creek, the retired fisheries boss informed me. The following information will help fishermen zero in on those resident trout that share the water with the giant rainbows of Naples Creek.

GRIMES CREEK

RATING: ★★ (2 stars)

NOTEWORTHY: This scenic, fast-flowing tributary—which slips under a bridge on Route 21 (Mark Circle) in downtown Naples—is overlooked by most anglers.

BEST TIME TO FISH: Early April, when spawning rainbows, browns, and even brookies can be found in the creek.

Although it has some of the coldest, clearest water in the Naples Creek watershed, Grimes Creek doesn't get much attention from the vast majority of the anglers who cross over it during the early part of the trout season. Limited access is the main reason. The problem is that the DEC has acquired public fishing rights on approximately two-thirds of a mile of creekbank, most of it below an impassable waterfall. The pool at the base of the fall is about 7 feet deep and can be counted on to hold some nice trout—browns as well as rainbows—year-round. Other pools between the falls and the mouth of Grimes Creek are typically less than 2 feet deep and are challenging to fish most of the time. The section of the creek referred to here is about 15 to 20 feet wide in most spots, hemmed in by bank cover and treacherous to wade.

Now and then a wild brook trout takes a leap of faith into the falls pool, but most of the natives that remain in the creek live upstream from the cataract, as do many wild browns. Driving upstream along Quick Road, you will get tempting glimpses of Grimes Creek, but only a small segment of the stream is open to public fishing. Posted land is the trend here, but it never hurts to ask permission from a landowner or two.

TANNERY CREEK

RATING: ★★ (2 stars)

NOTEWORTHY: In this tumbling tributary, brook trout live where rainbows don't.

BEST TIME TO FISH: Spring thunderstorms cause trout to lose their inhibitions.

Three species of trout are in residence at Tannery Creek, which joins Naples Creek about 150 feet upstream from the latter's merger with Grimes Creek, on Mark Circle in the village of Naples. Rainbows are present all year. While the spring and late-fall action features fair to excellent opportunities for 'bows that weigh in excess of 3 pounds, the months of June through October find deep pools occupied mostly by 8-inchers, though summer anglers are sometimes rewarded with a bonus 12- or 14-incher. Try drifting a caddis larva pattern if you seek the nicer fish.

Although few of the rainbows caught in Tannery Creek between spawning runs will top the 15-inch minimum creel length, the smaller trout give themselves a good accounting while on the hook. Just be sure to check and recheck the special regulations section on "Finger Lakes Tributaries" in your state *Freshwater Fishing* booklet. As this book was written and sent to press, Finger Lakes feeder streams in DEC Region 8 had a one-rainbow limit in place. As a result of that restriction—the limit used to be three rainbows a day—you should notice an improved catch rate in the next several years, for the trout you catch and release are essentially being recycled for re-catching and re-releasing.

Tannery Creek is about 8 to 10 feet wide in most spots. Public fishing signs are visible on the banks from the creek mouth upstream to an impassable falls just outside the village. Above the falls, you have a good chance of encountering native brookies where the creek flows through the Hi Tor Wildlife Management Area, for a distance of about 1 mile. It's accessible from Naples via East Hill Road.

RESERVOIR CREEK

RATING: ★★ (2 stars)

NOTEWORTHY: Fish it early for big, really big 'bows and later in the season for wild brook trout or browns.

BEST TIME TO FISH: After a spring shower raises the water level.

Reservoir Creek usually doesn't fish as good as it looks, and that's a shame, for this brook—which crosses Route 21 just south of the Naples village line—is simply gorgeous. It has numerous knee-deep pools, short stretches of pocket water, and innumerable undercut banks. As my pal Mike Brilbeck and I scouted the creek one late-March afternoon, we were astonished by the size of the rainbow trout that had swam up from Canandaigua Lake on their spawning mission. We saw dozens of rainbows more than 2 feet long, and a couple (literally, for they were building a spawning redd) appeared to be nearly 30 inches from stem to stern.

The following week, one day after the season had opened, we did not find a single spawner. That comes as no surprise to readers who have spent many days trying for Finger Lakes rainbows. It's the nature of the beast, here today but gone tomorrow.

Anglers who revisit Reservoir Creek—the one that borders the public golf course on the outskirts of Naples—in late April or early May stand a good chance of finding a few late-running rainbows, as well as an occasional wild brown or native brook trout. If nothing else happens, anglers who creep along the steep banks of Reservoir Creek will creel a happy memory. That, plus a golf ball or two. Many balls launched from the practice range land in the brook or on its banks.

More Ontario County Trout Streams

While the annual presence of spawning rainbows is an extra-added attraction, Ontario County has a trio of first-class trout streams that are full of brown trout and, in one case, a bunch of native brookies, as well. Funny, but the locals hardly ever mention the following fishing holes!

Mud Creek, also known as Ganargua Creek, is a small-to-medium stream that flows northward through the town of South Bristol. It has excellent cover and temperatures that remain trout-friendly all year. The trout in residence are wild browns of a respectable size. Best of all, the state-owned Stid Hill Multiple Use Area tucks around a 2-mile stretch of the creek. To find Stid Hill, take Route 21 north out of Naples, and bear left on Route 12, also called Bristol Springs Road. Follow that one for about 8 miles to Bristol Springs. Then take Route 64 north for approximately 2 miles to South Bristol and the WMA. Ultralight spinners or live bait will do quite nicely on this stretch.

Another stream with built-in access is **Honeoye Inlet**, which flows into the south end of Honeoye Lake. DEC biologist Pete Austerman likes this stream for its combination of wild browns and brookies. The browns turned up by Region 8 electroshockers in 2012 included some longer than 14 inches. Most such fish like to hang out in the deep, shaded pools found throughout the inlet.

You can seek permission to fish from individual landowners or simply walk along the creek where it passes through the Honeoye Inlet WMA, which is visible from East Lake Road south of Honeoye Lake.

Another stream that Austerman pointed out is **Mill Creek**, which flows north from South Bristol into the village of Honeoye. Its deep pools and runs are home to some nice wild browns. Unfortunately, access is very limited and out-of-towners should plan on knocking on a door or two before fishing in sight of any NO TRESPASSING signs.

One more stream in Ontario County has acquired an enthusiastic following among trout anglers in the Canandaigua area. That would be Canandaigua Outlet, which is not classified as trout water. Most years, it gets too warm to hold trout by mid-June or so.

The DEC stocks the outlet between Shortsville and Phelps with nearly 8,000 browns, including about 300 two-year-olds.

"It is very popular among the local anglers," said Austerman. "There's quite a bit of open, informal access, and people in the area seem to like fishing close to home."

He called it "a classic put-and-take situation."

LIVINGSTON COUNTY

If you love small streams that harbor wild trout and seldom are visited by hatchery tankers, be sure to follow up on your reading of this book by taking a familiarization tour of Livingston County. Those who live within reasonable driving distance will put some of these waters in their little black books of "secret" stops, I promise. That's truly ironic, for the one famous stream that stores most of its treasures within the county is anything but hidden from the outside world.

I'm thinking here of Spring Creek in Caledonia. This is a place where anglers with steady nerves and polished fly-fishing skills duel daily with wild trout that happen to live on the grounds of a Civil War–era fish hatchery. Every serious fly fisher should make a pilgrimage to this weedy, crystalline stream at some point in life, just to test his mettle. Livingston County also embraces two high-quality streams—the Cohocton River and Mill Creek (not connected in any way to the one in Ontario County)— which spend only a brief time within its borders before wandering off in other directions. These streams provide very good fishing at times, but many anglers with mellow temperaments will like, most of all, the county's assortment of streams that hold native brook trout, wild browns, or rainbow trout. The following assessment will help you fill out your own list of favorite fishing holes in one of New York's prettiest counties.

SPRING CREEK

RATING: ★★★★ (4 stars)

NOTEWORTHY: Although it flows through a fish hatchery, Spring Creek is populated by some of the wildest trout you will ever encounter.

BEST TIME TO FISH: Late October and early November is the trout spawning period and also when fishing pressure tends to be light.

Sometimes I have to pinch myself to be sure it wasn't just a dream, but I once had a heck of a day on Spring Creek. In less than four hours, I caught 13 brown trout from that mesmerizing stream. Readers who have fished the spot a few times will whistle softly when that bottom-line figure registers. Getting into double figures is easy on many Central New York trout waters, but Spring Creek is not one of the pushovers.

The biggest fish I brought to net that day was only 14 inches long, but I reeled in a couple of foot-long brownies, too. Each trout, regardless of size, was stream-bred and wild as wild can be. Best of all, only a couple of the fish I tangled with that afternoon hit beneath the surface. Dry flies, mostly *Ephemerella dorothea*s that I imitated with a bright-yellow-bodied Comparadun pattern on a size 16 hook, accounted for an even 10 of my lucky 13.

The author casts on Spring Creek at the hatchery grounds in Caledonia.

That was a red-letter day, for I feel pretty good about my skills whenever I manage to hook two or three trout from the creek. After all, most of the time it is as transparent as a brand-new picture window, and it is fished constantly by Rochester-area anglers. Spring Creek, which is about 25 to 40 feet across in most spots, runs through the grounds of the state hatchery in Caledonia, in northern Livingston County. Fish culturist Seth Green built the facility in 1864, and it has been operating ever since. It's the oldest trout hatchery in the United States, and today the DEC uses it to raise 13- to 15-inch, two-year-old brown trout for stocking throughout the state.

The trout that tuck themselves into the shade beneath wads of weeds in Spring Creek have no trace of fish-farm innocence and are rarely easy to catch. Remember how your father or grandfather or other trout-fishing mentor had to remind you now and then that "if you can see the trout, they can probably see you, also" and schooled you to wear drab clothing and stay back from the bank as you fished? Well, that wise advice goes double when applied to Spring Creek. Stealthy movements, tiny flies, and gossamer leader tippets, 6X or finer, are part and parcel of fishing this stream.

DEC Region 8 fisheries biologist Pete Austerman doesn't think heavy fishing pressure or extreme water clarity are the only factors that make Spring Creek trout so difficult to catch.

"As the name implies, Spring Creek is a spring-fed stream with cold water all year long," he said. "It is also very productive and therefore supports a high biomass of trout."

Spring Creek trout have no problem finding enough to eat, Austerman said. The rich supply of mayflies, scuds, and other aquatic life makes it possible for trout to feed unmolested when the hatchery is closed. Fishing hours on the approximately half a mile of stream on the hatchery property are from 8 AM to 4 PM daily, year-round. That regime effectively preserves any trout inclined to stuff themselves on the sulfur hatches that are so thick most evenings in late May and June.

Fortunately for anglers, there is an intimate section of Spring Creek just below the hatchery grounds that is not off-limits after four o'clock. Known as "The 900" because it is just 900 feet long, this water is almost as full of trout as the fish factory it adjoins. It is just a short walk from a marked parking area to The 900. That ease of access virtually guarantees somebody will fish this water almost every day of the year. The 900 traffic usually peaks during the sulfur hatch in June, but it is also appealing to anglers who react to a midwinter warming spell by doing a little trout fishing. The water temperatures in January or February are in the mid- to high 40s, easily tolerable to trout. I have done a few winter trips to Caledonia, myself, and more often than not I have seen rising trout on these occasions.

Be sure to wear chest- or waist-high waders no matter when you visit The 900, for there are certain spots where you must maneuver through water with a soft, silt bottom to get into a good casting position. Don't wear wading gear of any kind when you fish on the hatchery grounds, as all wading is forbidden there. You must fish from the bank, where you will be forced to perfect your roll cast and tower cast. Once you see how clear and smooth Spring Creek is, you'll realize that the no-wading rule makes good sense. One obvious reason for the rule is the impact booted feet would have on the weed beds that bloom all summer before shrinking in the winter and early spring. When the weeds are thick, they are cursed by many an angler, for they result in frequent hang-ups and a need to check your hook for bits of vegetation every now and then. On the other hand, when weeds are sparse, the trout at Caledonia usually respond by gathering in dense schools, where a cast that spooks one fish may scare the entire group.

Anglers who fancy king-size trout might want to explore other Central New York streams, for the brown trout hiding in the shadows and under weed mats at Spring Creek seem to max out, with few exceptions, at about 16 inches, and the typical catch consists of fish in the 7- to 14-inch range.

A lovely little wild brookie.

As with brook trout in most other small streams, the occasional native found here will seldom be more than 9 or 10 inches long.

To reach Spring Creek from Buffalo, Rochester, or Syracuse, map a route to the Thruway and take that toll road to the Route 390 exit. Go south on Route 390 to the Scottsville exit, then turn onto Route 251 and drive into the village of Industry. Cross the Genesee River, then turn right onto River Road, which goes into Scottsville. In that village, go left onto Route 383 and drive approximately 3 miles to the intersection with Route 36 in the adjoining villages of Caledonia and Mumford. The hatchery sign will be on your right.

SPRINGWATER CREEK

RATING: ★★★ (3 stars)
NOTEWORTHY: A small stream with a diverse trout population.
BEST TIME TO FISH: Late April should find this almost-famous stream in prime condition.

Like Naples Creek and Owasco Lake Inlet (about which, more to come), Springwater Creek historically had a strong run of spawning rainbow trout during the first few weeks of New York's trout season. Sadly, this gathering of the fishes is not nearly as big a deal as it once was in some streams, but the DEC is trying to rectify the situation by adopting and enforcing stricter regulations in the western Finger Lakes (Canadice, Canandaigua, Hemlock, Keuka, and Seneca) and their tributaries. The changes are clearly explained in the "Finger Lakes and Tributary Regulations" page in the state's *Freshwater Fishing* guide, which is supplied at no cost to anyone purchasing a New York fishing license.

One tributary that figures to be positively impacted by the changes is Springwater Creek, which is the major spawning stream for the rainbows in Hemlock Lake. The new rules include a daily creel limit of three trout or landlocked salmon from the DEC Region 8 tributaries, and only one of those three fish may be a rainbow.

I am convinced, personally, that this measure will lead to an expansion of the rainbow trout population in both Hemlock Lake and Springwater Creek. That expansion likely will encourage anglers to explore other streams in the Hemlock watershed, not for rainbows, but rather for the wild brook trout that thrive in several area streams.

Ultimately, it seems to me, the new regulations will be treated as a de facto catch-and-release edict by most anglers. Fishermen who used to regard the daily limit of three rainbows of 15 inches or longer will not keep the first 16- or 17-inch rainbow they land. It is far more likely that any rainbow shorter than 20 inches will be returned to the water immediately, and as anglers get into that habit on Springwater Creek and other tributaries, the no-kill cult of sportsmen will grow and spread through the region. That trend will gain speed as tributary anglers notice their daily catch rates are expanding.

The scenario I am predicting is exactly what happened on Lake Ontario feeder streams a few years ago after the DEC reduced the tributary creel limit to one steelhead per day, and it should unfold in similar fashion on most regional rainbow streams.

In 2014, while I was fishing on Oatka Creek, I bumped into a couple of sportsmen who have spent many early-season outings on Finger Lakes tributaries. They said the fishing in Springwater Creek that spring was the best they had seen in many years. Few anglers kept any rainbows, but most enjoyed reeling and releasing some nice spawners.

Springwater regulars consider 5-pound rainbows to be exceptionally nice fish, though 2- or 3-pound specimens make up the majority of the springtime catch. Trout of that size might bore anglers who are used to taking much larger trout in Catharine Creek and some other tributaries, but I wonder, what's wrong with tying into 16- to 19-inch spawners on a routine basis?

That's how the creek was in its "good old days," and if DEC biologists are right about the impact of the revised regulations, well, happy days are here again!

Springwater Creek is about 6 miles long, an average of about 10 feet across, and has many pools that are between knee-deep and waist-deep when it is flowing at normal spring-season levels. It can be reached by taking U.S. Route 20 west from Canandaigua to Lima, and following Route 15A south (which becomes East Shore Road) from there down to the south end of Hemlock Lake and the hamlet of Springwater.

This is an easily wadable stream with lots of bend pools and undercuts to hide big rainbows and the wild brook trout that thrive in the main stream and a network of ice-cold tributaries. It is an ideal bait-fishing spot but can also be explored with streamer flies and single-hook spinners. The bait and hardware will work best with ultralight tackle, with 4-pound test guaranteed to produce more bites and strikes than the heavier line favored by most of the fishermen who are seeking the local rainbows.

Springwater Creek is crossed near its lower end by Kellogg Road and is closely shadowed in its headwaters by Pokamoonshine Road. Some area residents refer to the upstream reaches as Pokamoonshine Creek. From

Kellogg Road down, and also from Kellogg Road to Depot Road, the water is open to public fishing, except for a couple of small private properties. Even at locations where there are POSTED signs, it is sometimes possible to obtain permission.

CANASERAGA CREEK

RATING: ★★ (2 stars)

NOTEWORTHY: Overlooked because one of the state's better streams is a tributary, this one deserves a peek on your way to or from Mill Creek. Note, also, that this is not the same creek that flows north from Chittenango.

BEST TIME TO FISH: At night, from mid-June through August.

The other Canaseraga Creek, which is crossed by a bridge on Route 13 just east of the village of Chittenango in Madison County, flows through mucky farmland that is perfect for growing onions. This one grows trout—not a whole lot of them but some beauties. Twenty-inchers live in this creek, which runs through the Rattlesnake Hill Wildlife Management Area in northern Allegany County and then picks up the currents of Mill Creek and Little Mill Creek in Dansville before heading north to a junction with the Genesee River near Mount Morris.

Canaseraga Creek is known for its abundance of 10- to 12-inch brown trout, like this one, and also has a healthy population of brookies.

Canaseraga Creek is populated mainly by pike and bass below Dansville, but some shockingly big brown trout are reported now and then at tributary mouths, spring seeps, and other places where the stream temperature gets a boost.

These areas, just barely cold enough to hold stocked or wild browns during the summer months, can be fished with some success after dark. A black beadhead Woolly Bugger will work as well as any other fly or lure, but if you're a spinning specialist, toss a shallow-running stickbait about 4 inches long.

More Livingston County Trout Streams

Some surprisingly fine small-stream trout fishing is available in Livingston County, especially in its southeast corner, where native brookies can be caught with regularity. Give the county's legendary water quality some credit. Hemlock Lake, which is connected with several brook trout streams, has supplied Rochester residents with drinking water for decades.

Reynolds Gulf Brook empties into Hemlock Lake's southeast corner and is paralleled by Reynolds Gulf Road. About 10 feet wide in most places, it has plenty of small brook trout to complement the rainbows that spawn on its gravel. It flows through woodlands and is well shaded. Another good one that's close by is **Green Gulf Brook**. It has brookies, 'bows, and browns, all of them wild. Green Gulf has an impassable falls about a mile upstream from its mouth. Many, though not all, of the brookies live above the falls.

One more brook trout stream close to Springwater is **Pardee Hollow Creek**, which flows south to the upper reaches of the Cohocton River instead of going north to Springwater Creek. It's a pretty little run, with numerous woodland pools that are somewhat reminiscent of the small brook trout streams found in the Catskills, of all places. Several other trout waters are also worth a few hours of your time if you happen to be visiting or passing through Livingston County.

Little Dansville Creek and **Little Mill Creek** are two streams known mainly for their wild brown trout. Of the pair, you'd likely assume that Little Dansville is the one that flows through the village of Dansville. Well, never assume anything, for Little Dansville Creek begins in Nunda, about 15 miles west of Dansville, and never comes close to its namesake community.

Little Mill Creek, on the other hand, joins Mill Creek (not the one from Ontario County) at Dansville. Like Little Dansville Creek, Little Mill Creek holds some handsome browns, but it also has a robust population of wild brookies. Both creeks can be fished effectively with flies, but not in every spot. One great way to check out these and other minia-ture trout waters is to fish upstream using one method and downstream with another; for example, up with spinners and down with dry flies. If nothing else, this versatile approach should get you an A for effort when you look back on your performance. That attitude, in turn, will boost the your confidence and help you slow down a bit and stop worrying about the exact shade of a hatching fly or whether your spoon or spinner is too small to fool local trout.

One last Livingston County water that merits a shout-out is **Sugar Creek**, a spring-fed stream located near Ossian. You can find it off Linzy Road. It is populated by both stocked and wild browns; access is avail-able for about a mile's worth of streambank within the Rattlesnake Hill Wildlife Management Area. Permission to fish is usually granted by land-owners at stocking locations, and anglers embarking on a trip on an unfa-miliar part of Sugar Creek can save themselves some effort by asking DEC fisheries personnel in Avon (585-226-2466) for a list of recent stocking sites. It's going to be a relatively short list, because Livingston County's better trout waters have an abundance of wild fish and therefore do not require much stocking.

YATES COUNTY

You wouldn't expect the smallest of Upstate counties to have an abun-dance of trout streams, and it doesn't. However, Yates County does have a couple of cold-water options for fishermen in quest of speckled beauties. One of these, the Keuka Lake Outlet, connects Keuka Lake with Seneca Lake. The result of that unusual linkup is a sort of seasonal doubleheader. In early spring and often in November and December, too, the outlet is populated by spawning rainbows from Seneca Lake. Landlocked salmon are also frequent visitors in the autumn months. In May and June, mean-while, fishing for brown trout can be quite good, thanks to annual stock-ings in the outlet by the DEC. Water temperatures are tolerable enough to permit some trout to hold over from one year to the next, but the majority of brown trout that wind up being creeled are current-season stockers, including two-year-olds that average around 14 inches long. The "twos," as some anglers call them, are stocked at the rate of about 400 a year. The remaining stocking quota consists of 8- to 9-inch browns.

Undoubtedly, the most unusual and most appreciated aspect of the Keuka Outlet is its easy access. An old railroad bed now serves hikers, bicyclists, and, yes, trout fishermen. Locals know that well-beaten path as the Keuka Lake Trail, and they talk about it with pride.

KEUKA LAKE OUTLET

RATING: ★★★ (3 stars)

NOTEWORTHY: As this place is anything but remote, don't complain about the lack of solitude. This is a very social fishing hole, and anglers mingle with hikers, bikers, joggers, and, at least a couple of times a day, their fellow fishermen.

BEST TIME TO FISH: Late April through May.

If it doesn't make you feel self-conscious, one of the better ways to get a spot on the Keuka Outlet that you can call your own is to put your bare-minimum tackle requirements into a backpack and then pedal or hoof it, on bike or in boots, on the adjacent trail. A four- or five-piece pack rod would be perfect for such an outing, whether you prefer spinning or fly fishing.

The outlet runs approximately 6 miles from Penn Yan on Keuka Lake east to Dresden, where it empties into Seneca Lake. Between its beginning and end, the stream flows over several waterfalls, which block upstream migrations of rainbows from Seneca Lake but do not necessarily prevent stocked browns from moving downstream if they feel like it. Much of the outlet is about 50 feet wide, and the stream has an assortment of pools, eddies, and runs, all of which seem well suited to fly fishing. If the trout aren't biting, you can enjoy some fair bass fishing for smallmouths that average 12 to 14 inches.

About half of the outlet, the 3-mile stretch from Dresden upstream to Cascade Mills, is visited by spawning rainbows, some of which can weigh up to 8 pounds. From there to Penn Yan the fishing is for browns and smallmouths.

To find the rainbows—and maybe an occasional holdover brown trout or even a landlocked salmon—take U.S. Route 20 to Geneva and then follow Route 14 south along Seneca Lake's west shore and into Dresden. There, turn right onto Route 54 and look for trail markers. Alternatively, you can fish downstream from Penn Yan to tackle the best brown trout water.

One of the outlet's functions, in addition to providing good fishing opportunities, is to control water levels on Keuka Lake, especially during heavy rain and runoff currents. That is accomplished by the use of flood-gates. If the water is too high, the gates can be opened to draw levels down; conversely, if Keuka Lake is unusually shallow, the gates can be closed to allow less outflow than normal. Either way, the drawdowns and refills seldom affect angling outcomes.

FLINT CREEK

RATING: ★★ (2 stars)

NOTEWORTHY: Along with wild browns, this stream is home to a nonmigratory strain of rainbow trout, which is unusual in New York.

BEST TIME TO FISH: Late May, when the water levels are still up and people are mowing lawns and doing other yard work around the creek.

When you add up the positives and negatives about Flint Creek, it will strike you as a tantalizing prospect. So near, yet so far! By this, I mean that this stream looks like a good fishing hole, but no part of it—zero, zip, nada—is marked with public fishing rights signs. Much of the creek, however, is posted with signs that warn would-be anglers not to try it, no matter what "it" might be. That's why I would advise you to eyeball Flint Creek from your car, perhaps when you are in the neighborhood anyway, and put on your best smile before popping the big question to those folks you will find mowing or raking or planting in yards near the creek. The question, obviously, is whether there is any chance you can get permission to do some trout fishing in this stream.

DEC officials insist that many property owners in rural areas like central Yates County do, on occasion, grant permission to polite, cheerful anglers who are looking for a spot to fish. Sadly, many fishermen are shy about asking strangers for anything, and more than a few trespass without permission, and litter streambanks with discarded lure packaging and plastic or paper beverage containers. It is much easier to say "thanks anyway" after getting a thumbs down than to get caught sneaking along a streambank that's bordered by warning signs.

Now, you wouldn't want to make a long drive to Flint Creek only to discover that the landowners are really steamed about getting some attitude from a foulmouthed angler the last time they gave someone the opportunity to wet a line in their backyard. So why not just do a little fishing in Naples Creek, where access is extensive, or some other area fishing hole one Saturday morning, and save an hour before or after to scout for go-aheads on Flint Creek?

Focus your scouting on the 6 miles of the stream visible from Italy Valley Road, as that is where the rainbows reside and also happens to hold a fair number of wild browns. Most of the stream is less than 20 feet wide, and has some nice pools interspersed with gravel- and cobble-bottomed riffles. It holds fish enough to encourage some sly anglers to save one or two pretty rainbows for the landowner's breakfast.

Flint Creek can be found by taking County Road 18 east out of Naples. Look for well-defined pull-offs, especially those near bridge crossings or bank-stabilization projects, for such good works hint that it's not unusual in these parts for landowners and fishermen to be friendly.

This may be as good a time as any to make a suggestion about footgear for small to medium-size trout waters. I used to carry both hip boots and chest waders when I was exploring unfamiliar waters, but find myself using waist-highs more and more often. They are stockingfoot style, weigh very little, and—once fitted with a sturdy set of suspenders—very comfortable.

CHAPTER TWO

Trout in the Heartland

ONONDAGA, CAYUGA, MADISON, CORTLAND, and OSWEGO COUNTIES

Back in 1991, when fate (and a couple of wise editors) saw fit to give me my dream job as the full-time outdoors writer for the *Post-Standard* in Syracuse, I could scarcely believe my good fortune. For one thing, I was making a rare move from one Syracuse newspaper, the afternoon *Herald-Journal*, to another—the morning *Post*. The plan put together by editors of both publications was to groom me as the successor to Bob Peel, the long-time hook-and-bullet columnist for the *Post* who was fighting a coura-geous battle with cancer. It was a worrisome scenario, from where I was sitting. Although both dailies were owned by the wealthy Newhouse clan, their reporters were encouraged to keep fraternization between the two papers to a minimum and to scoop the competing newsroom at every opportunity. I was especially concerned that the sports department I was joining would give me the cold shoulder, even though Bob and I were good friends and I had read his columns and features since my college days.

I also wondered how much of a rope the *Post-Standard* editors would give me. Who would edit my stories? Would they dictate contents, or advise me about taboo subjects?

Well, it turned out that Dave Rahme, the *Post-Standard* sports editor at the time, was an avid outdoorsman. He put me at ease about five minutes into our first conversation.

"I think you should just make your own schedule," he said. "You've been around this place long enough to know what's going on, and I can tell you know a lot more than I do about the fishing and hunting in Central

New York. So, you come up with the story ideas, let me know a week or two ahead what you're going to write about, and get outdoors as much as you want."

Was that the description of a dream job, or what? I accepted the position immediately, and vowed to see that Dave and whoever might succeed him someday would never regret the degree of trust they put in me.

I also found time for a heck of a lot of fishing. I figure I averaged about 250 days (or parts of days) on the water, year after year. Although I fished for and wrote about numerous species, from bullheads to muskies and bass to walleyes, trout were then and remain today my favorite fish. Consequently, I cast flies, retrieved spinning lures, and drowned night crawlers in cold-to-the-touch streams at every opportunity. I wound up spending 16 years as the outdoors writer for the Syracuse newspapers.

Upon retiring from the news business in 2007, I fished for trout harder and more often. I wet my line in awe-inspiring rivers in Montana, Michigan, and Pennsylvania. Enjoyable as those trips were, I was always grateful to pull into the driveway when each journey was done. For the farther I traveled, the more firmly I believed that some of the finest trout fishing anywhere was just down the road from where I lived. Hopefully, readers will give these Syracuse-area streams a try, and treat them with the respect and affection they deserve.

ONONDAGA COUNTY

If you are a trout fisher who lives in Onondaga County, you might have had trouble keeping a straight face a few pages back, when I characterized some regional streams as underfished. Yet it's true, with one prominent exception. Nine Mile Creek has deeply worn footpaths along most of its length, and state surveys confirm its brown, rainbow, and brook trout are pestered by extraordinary numbers of fishermen. A dozen or so Onondaga County streams, however, seem to be overlooked once the opening-day commotion is finished, and in the prime months of May and June I often have long stretches of water, heavy hatches of mayflies, and fine fishing all to myself.

So why, you might wonder, would I want to alert guidebook readers to the potentially superb opportunities in my own backyard? Well, it is a sad fact that good trout streams anywhere, and especially those that flow through urban and suburban neighborhoods, need the help of able public officials and civic leaders. As long as fishing holes like Limestone Creek and Geddes Brook are underappreciated by local anglers and governmental agencies, they will also be in constant danger of being damaged or

Fishing the rock abutment at Nine Mile Creek.

destroyed by industrial pollution, agricultural runoff, unchecked urban sprawl, and other modern menaces.

Onondaga County government leaders, in my opinion, have not fully realized the worth of the cold-water gems that twist and tumble through local suburbs and countryside. Some of the better trout streams in the state, Nine Mile Creek being an excellent example, are within a half-hour drive from downtown Syracuse, and more than a few resident anglers make it a point to spend their lunch hours with fly or spinning rods in hand. Thanks to the efficiency of a vintage 1930s hatchery operated by the county parks department on Carpenter's Brook in Elbridge, more than 70,000 trout are deposited in local waters each spring. In some instances, those fish are the frosting on the cake, in that they augment preexisting populations of wild trout. Certain other waters would have little to offer if not for the local hatchery's annual output. Yet on at least two occasions, budget problems have led county legislators to seriously consider shutting the hatchery down. Woe to Syracuse-area sportsmen if that calamity ever occurs!

Why Location Really Does Matter

As things stand, Onondaga County waters are stocked solely by the local fish farm, and at 100 percent of their estimated carrying capacity, based on

DEC biologists' recommendations. Although Monroe and Essex Counties both raise trout to supplement state stocking programs, Onondaga is the only county in New York that cranks out all the trout its waters can handle.

The fact that it has its very own taxpayer-supported fish hatchery puts Onondaga County at or near the top of any New York angler's must-see list, but the county's geographic location may be even more enticing. Syracuse is wrapped around the intersection of Interstate 81 and the state Thruway. If that's not the "Heart of New York," as some recent marketers have dubbed the spot, what is? The long and the short of it is, no matter where you live in the Empire State, you can get to either I-81 or the Thruway, and from that point you are off and running to the Syracuse area's trout attractions. It's a day trip at worst.

Any trout fisherman who uses either of those car paths to take a cross-state journey will heed his GPS unit's advice by driving through the Salt City. Yet you'll see nary a billboard with a word or picture pertaining to trout fishing. Thruway rest stops might have a short stack of brochures on Onondaga's fishing waters, but these subdued sales pitches don't exactly shout *Come and get it.*

I shouldn't complain about the lack of publicity focused on streams like Nine Mile Creek, Butternut Creek, and Fabius Brook, which are my home waters, after all. But as you continue to read about them, you will see that the trout streams of Onondaga County are numbered among those fisheries that need intervention occasionally, to gain protection from expanding suburbs, farming operations with fertilizer runoff problems, and faltering municipal sewage treatment facilities.

NINE MILE CREEK

RATING: ★★★★★ (5 stars)

NOTEWORTHY: Big springs near Marcellus Falls make Nine Mile the best (and coldest) trout stream in Onondaga County.

BEST TIME TO FISH: Mid-May to mid-June, when "the sulfurs" are hatching.

In the "heartland" area of New York—which I have somewhat arbitrarily declared to consist of Onondaga and four other counties (Cayuga, Cortland, Madison, and Oswego)—there are dozens of good trout streams. Nine Mile Creek is one of the most productive but also one of the most threatened of the whole bunch.

Since I am a lifelong resident of the town of Marcellus, through which Nine Mile flows, I take great pride in the creek, but I also worry about its

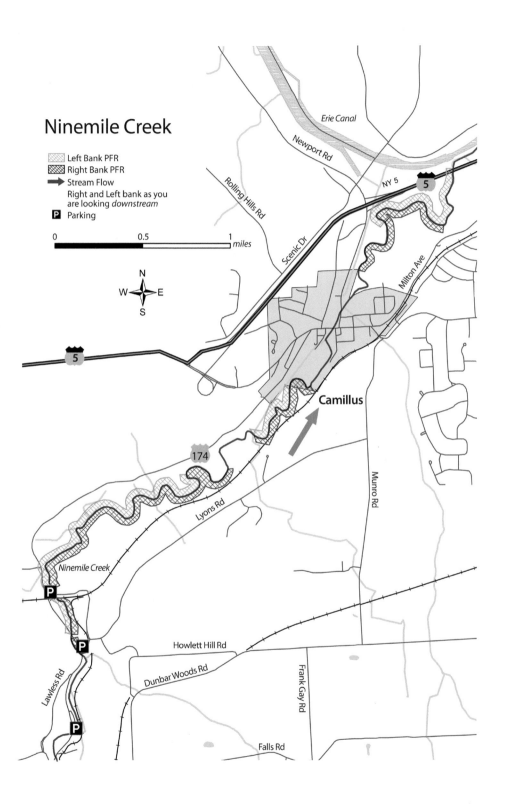

Ninemile Creek

- Left Bank PFR
- Right Bank PFR
- → Stream Flow
  Right and Left bank as you are looking *downstream*
- P Parking

0   0.5   1 *miles*

N
W—E
S

Erie Canal

Newport Rd

Rolling Hills Rd

Scenic Dr

NY 5

5

Milton Ave

5

174

Camillus

Lyons Rd

Munro Rd

Ninemile Creek

P

P

Howlett Hill Rd

Frank Gay Rd

Lawless Rd

Dunbar Woods Rd

P

Falls Rd

long-term prospects. My father introduced me to what is now my home water when I was 10 years old. He carried me on his back across a side channel of the creek to get within a rod's reach of a small eddy. I still remember the halo-framed spots and the clean scent of the brook trout I caught in that place.

Several years after catching that 9-inch native, I hooked and landed my first really large trout. It was a hook-jawed old brown that measured 21¾ inches long and weighed 4 pounds and 2 ounces a couple of hours after I removed it from the deep pool under Montague's bridge. I was 13 at the time, and I hooked the fish in mid-August, after a quick downpour had given the creek a bit of fresh color. The following week, a photo of me and my trophy appeared on the front page of the *Marcellus Observer*.

My family history is full of trout-themed vignettes because we happened to live close to the creek and the fishing was good enough to supply many Friday meals for our Roman Catholic household—Mom, Dad, and seven kids. Marcellus was and is a small town where little things are sometimes done up big. However, some of the happenings in the village I grew up in really were important precisely because they involved the creek, which played a critical role in the local economy.

Nine Mile Creek on a misty day.

You've Come a Long Way, Baby

Today, Nine Mile Creek is a wonderful trout stream, with only a modest amount of commerce along its banks, but for more than a century the creek supplied water to power the machinery and convey raw or treated waste products created by mills of wide description. Most of these factories and shops offered steady employment for multiple generations of immigrants from Scotland, Ireland, and elsewhere. The creek suffered from pollution but its trout—all brookies for eons and a combination of the native species and imported brown trout beginning about 1900—somehow managed to survive. Nine Mile seemed to shrug off the haymakers men threw at it, whether the blows came in the form of dyes hosed off the wood floors in the Marcellus woolen mills, or raw sewage leaking from creekside septic systems.

Paul Sheedy of Camillus fishes along a concrete abutment on Opening Day on Nine Mile Creek . . .

. . . with a nice reward a couple of hours later.

The knockout punch was a mammoth fish kill that occurred in 1963 and suffocated virtually all of the trout then living in the creek between Marcellus Falls and Camillus, a serpentine current path about 6 miles long. Thousands of trout and nearly as many white suckers, carp, and other fish were strewn along the creek that fateful day. A majority of the victims were brook trout, but most of the large fish decaying in the shallows were browns. The biggest of them all was a 29-incher, found about half a mile downstream from Marcellus Falls by George Arthur, an avid trout fisherman who was the athletic director at Marcellus Central School.

The Vanishing Brook Trout

Although no conclusive report ever appeared in the local papers, persistent rumors pointed to a tree-spraying contractor who, it was said, rinsed his empty chemical tank along the creek with the aid of a power hose. Some people blamed the local industries that were still active along Route 174, which paralleled the creek, but in those days nobody worried about having "closure" in the matter. Fishermen simply wanted their beloved Nine Mile Creek to teem with trout once more.

Approximately one year after the fish kill, the creek was reseeded with both browns and brookies, many of them fitted with shiny metal jaw tags. Anglers had a choice between jotting down the tag numbers and notifying state fisheries biologists, or contacting the county hatchery in Elbridge. Either way, officials could tell whether the restocking program was a success.

At first, there were cheers all around, as the stocked trout found plenty to eat and quickly grew the round bellies that are proof positive of an abundant food supply and a rapid rate of growth. In the next summer or two, my friends and I had a blast catching football-shaped trout, including brookies that grew to 14 or 15 inches long. But after that, the pseudo-natives from the hatchery seemed to be less and less common. My angling diary, maintained for more than 30 years, was full of brook trout data during the creek's recovery period, but by 1970 or so my favorite fish were much scarcer than they used to be. Although I yearned for the gorgeous natives of old, it was clear that brown trout were taking over the neighborhood. My father, who grew up fishing for wild brookies in Nine Mile Creek and greatly admired their beauty, never quite reconciled himself to their passing. For my part, I had few natives to logs in my diary pages, although the hatchery crews dutifully released 4,000 or so brookies in the stream's cold currents year after year.

What caused the brook trout's demise in Nine Mile Creek? I have been asked that many times, and I have what I believe to be a plausible theory. Namely, survival of the native char was threatened from the moment bigger, more aggressive brown trout were introduced in the stream. When browns and brookies started over from scratch—that is, following the 1963 fish kill—the relatively delicate natives likely were doomed.

The data scribbled into my fishing diary confirm my suspicions that the naturally reproducing population of brook trout in Nine Mile Creek was greatly diminished by the end of the 1970s.

Rainbows from Who Knows Where

These days, Nine Mile is mainly brown trout water, although stocked brookies are common in the week or two following a visit by the county hatchery truck. Amazingly, the wild and holdover browns share the faster stretches of the creek with *wild* rainbows. I caught one rainbow near the Martisco railroad crossing a few years ago that measured 20 inches long, and clearly was not a hatchery fish. Rather, it could have been a twin of any of the big 'bows that spawn in tributaries of the Finger Lakes. I believe, and several DEC experts concur, that Nine Mile's crop of silver streaks is rooted in Skaneateles, Cayuga, or Seneca Lake, and it is entirely plausible that they got from point A to point B by riding a wave of high water during an exceptionally rainy spring season. They swam downstream through the Seneca River, made a right turn at Onondaga Lake, and then swam up my favorite creek. Once they cleared a waist-high dam at Amboy, they had clear swimming to the base of Marcellus Falls.

The alternative theory, which suggests that stocking trucks fueled the rainbow run, is not supported by the facts. Although the Marcellus Park section of Nine Mile is stocked with a few dozen rainbows annually to serve as fodder for the Marcellus Optimists Club's youth fishing derby, the 'bows I've reeled in miles downstream from that spot do not resemble the hatchery specimens. The ones I'm talking about come in all sizes, now, and appear to represent at least four year-classes, in fisheries science parlance.

Nine Mile Creek is the outlet of Otisco Lake, a water supply reservoir located in southwestern Onondaga County in the towns of Marcellus, Spafford, and Otisco. After it passes over or through the 12-foot-high dam at the north end of the lake, it winds through the towns of Marcellus and Camillus before emptying into Onondaga Lake in the town of Geddes. Stocked heavily with about 25,000 browns and brookies each spring, it also has an abundance of wild trout. The creek, although less than 40 feet across in most places, is capable of growing browns as big as 12 pounds. If you don't believe that, check the photo of that monster and numerous 4- to 8-pound whoppers displayed in The Wayfarer, a trout-oriented tackle shop that until recently operated just north of the railroad underpass on Route 174. Most, although not all, of the "hero shots" that cover the shop's Wall of Fame depict browns caught in Nine Mile.

The snapshot monsters would have a huge wow factor no matter where they were hooked, but a more typical Nine Mile catch for a skilled angler would consist mainly of 9- to 12-inch browns, with a bonus bite every so often by one that's 14 or even 16 inches long. True giants swim in the creek's deepest pools. Unfortunately for you and me but luckily for Nine Mile's potbellied browns, the parking areas and footpaths along the banks are pounded by trout-fishing traffic. The bigger fish are extremely wary, seldom seen and inclined to feed mostly at night, when few anglers are about. After a comprehensive study of angler effort and expenditures in New York's counties, Cornell University researchers found that the creek was one of the most heavily used trout waters in the state. Fishermen spent an estimated 56,284 "angler days" on Nine Mile in 2007, alone.

If fishing activity was measured on a "acres of water" basis, Nine Mile would be considered even more crowded, for the creek is less than 30 feet wide in many spots, while the most hard-hit of Catskill trout waters are three or four times that big, on average.

Sulfur Hatch Is a Main Event

Nine Mile is a busy place for several reasons, starting with its proximity to Syracuse and its obvious abundance of trout. The least of its attributes is its population of aquatic insects, which is merely average compared with the teeming swarms of bugs that hatch almost throughout the season in other blue-ribbon rivers. Instead of reasonably robust numbers of this mayfly and that one, Nine Mile is home to large numbers of one mayfly, plus a few of these and some of those.

Specifically, my backyard creek's one truly heavy mayfly hatch is the *Ephemerella invaria*, which locals commonly refer to as the Light Hendricksons or sulfurs. These bugs, imitated by a variety of fly patterns wound about size 14, light-wire hooks, often are so profuse from about May 20 to June 15 that trout come to anticipate their daily dance on the creek's surface. Pale-yellow Comparadun patterns and rusty-brown nymphs tied on size 1X-long hooks work very well when the sulfurs are on, but my go-to fly for the hatch is an emerger pattern made of rusty seal fur or angora goat hair, with wood duck or pheasant fibers for tails and legs. Most critical, however, is the tuft of dun-colored hair from a snow-shoe rabbit's foot to mimic a mayfly dun's unfurling wings.

Later in the season, around the last week of August, you won't want to miss the *Isonychia bicolor* emergence; and small blue-winged olives (sizes 18 and 20) also stir some surface feeding on rainy days through September. One of my better catches from Nine Mile consisted of three wild browns taken one evening during a sporadic hatch of *Isonychia*. Using a dun variant nymph that I copied from the late Art Flick's *New Streamside Guide*, I landed and released just three browns, but they measured 15, 16, and 19 inches and came stubbornly to my net in ascending order of size.

The inclination of its medium- and even large-size browns to feed at or just below the surface when a hatch is in progress certainly doesn't do anything to diminish Nine Mile Creek's fan base. However, the trait that keeps anglers coming back throughout the season is its reliably cold water temperatures. Even during the dog days of August, when most other streams south of Canada are so warm that their trout must huddle around cool springs and tributary mouths or perish, most of Nine Mile's browns remain hale and hearty. With cold water guaranteed, the creek beckons to shrewd anglers all season long.

The best way to understand and appreciate Nine Mile is to think of it as a creek that's upside down or backward. Most trout streams in New York—or elsewhere, for that matter—originate as cold headwaters trickles, which join up with other rivulets until they have attained their maximum size. Stream flows like these widen and warm as they near their junction with other, downstream tributaries, which derive their volume from surface water runoff. These flows are wider and warmer than the headwaters, and therefore less likely to hold large numbers of trout, especially during the hot summer months.

This is not the case in Nine Mile Creek, however. At first, as it flows north from Otisco Lake, it's a warmwater stream, although just cool enough to sustain stocked trout until mid-June. From its spillway at the north end of the lake, the creek parallels Route 174 as it ducks under bridges at Sevier Road, Schuyler Road, and U.S. Route 20. It slips beneath the Lee-Mulroy Road and then flows along South Street and into Marcellus Park and the village of Marcellus. The park is an overlooked resource. It is stocked in April and early May in this section, and a series of deep plunge pools and other stream improvement structures have made it one of the more popular spots on the entire creek. However, the stretch warms up rapidly and is seldom worth fishing after June. If this were all Nine Mile

Creek had to offer, it would not be visited by more than 300 anglers on an average Saturday in April. But there's much more to this water than you can glean from a highway map.

The Spring Is the Thing

From the dam at Otisco Lake all the way downstream through the village of Marcellus via Route 174, the creek temperatures climb into the mid- or high 70s through most of the summer. But as you drive in a northerly direction after exiting Marcellus and pass the crumbling remains of the old Crown Woolen Mill on the your left and then head downhill toward the former Martisco Paper Company building, a dramatic change takes place. Within a distance of 300 yards or so, at least half a dozen large limestone springs bubble up along the edges of Nine Mile Creek. The springs roughly double the volume of the creek, and the water is extremely cold. Fishermen who park their vehicles along the road just upstream from the Martisco mill and walk along the road shoulder can see some of the springs, which have temperatures in the high 40s or low 50s year-round. There many other springs between the paper mill and the village of Camillus, and they assure anglers that Nine Mile's trout will be vigorous and hungry even when long hot spells have put the residents of other streams in jeopardy. I can remember many days in July and August when air temperatures were in the mid-90s but the shady side of the creek was the coolest place around, next to a workplace with top-notch air-conditioning!

Paul McNeilly fishing the Martisco Railroad culvert pool on Nine Mile Creek.

Nine Mile from Marcellus to Camillus is a pretty stream to fish from April Fools' Day through the end the season on October 15, and extremely productive whether you prefer fly, lure, or bait. From the frothy pocket water just downstream of Marcellus Falls to the tree-lined bends and gentle glides in the boggy woods between the railroad culvert and the village of Camillus, Nine Mile is stuffed with trout that will test an angler's skill and patience.

Intense fishing pressure makes the happy chore of catching a few Nine Mile trout more difficult than it would otherwise be, but the fish are never really scarce. If you are not getting at least one or two trout per hour of effort, you simply need to brush up on your techniques, starting with the way you approach the stream. Like trout in all hard-fished waters, those in Nine Mile Creek become experts at hiding, and are fussy about what they eat. You cannot walk right up to a good-looking pool with the sun at your back and your boot soles scraping and thumping on slippery rocks. Rather, a successful angler on this creek and other popular streams is a master of the arts of concealment, himself. The standard advice for dealing with wary trout is centuries old but as valid today as it ever was. Simply move quietly and slowly, and stay in the shadows instead of casting your own dark shape on shallow water. Use polarized lenses, not to see trout, necessarily, but to discern the contours of the creek bottom and calculate how to take your next step without disturbing the water. These preventive measures will put nice fish on your line, one day after another, no matter where you do your trout fishing.

In March, 2015, the DEC announced it had established a no-kill (catch-and-release) trout fishing zone on Nine Mile Creek, from the dam at Amboy downstream to the mouth of the creek on Onondaga Lake. Previously, the creek had been governed by standard trout fishing regulations, including a creel limit of five trout per day, of which no more than two could exceed 12 inches in length. Like most other no-kill areas in New York, the one on Nine Mile will be open to angling year round. However, unlike other catch-and-release sections in the state, bait fishing will not be prohibited in the Nine Mile Creek no-kill. Other catch-and-release areas are open to the use of flies and artificial lures, only.

GEDDES BROOK

RATING: ★★★ (3 stars)

NOTEWORTHY: Flows through a shopping center but fishes better than it looks.

BEST TIME TO FISH: Right after a May downpour.

When I was a youngster, the man whom I was fated to succeed as the *Syracuse Post-Standard* outdoors writer ran an annual fishing contest during the first week of the trout season. Bob Peel, also known as Rod Hunter, called it the I Beat Rod Hunter contest, and he kept it simple, offering a yellow badge with those very words to anyone who submitted a trout bigger than his best catch of the week. It sounds a little hokey compared with today's high-pressured fishing derbies and tournaments, but area anglers were proud to catch a trout larger than Bob's, and many wore fishing caps or raincoats festooned with several of those badges.

One multiple winner was Tony Kowalski—Big Tony to his friends. The Solvay angler and Bob had a great time matching catches in the 1960s and '70s, and one usually needed a 16-incher or better to top the other. Hundreds of eager anglers joined in the fun over the years, but few beat Bob as often as Big Tony did. Peel prowled the banks of many streams in search of his winners, while Kowalski's ace-in-the-hole was a dandy spot just a short drive from his own neighborhood—Geddes Brook.

Trout Fishing Good, Bad, and Ugly

Because Geddes is a tributary of Nine Mile Creek, a gorgeous stream, anglers who try it for the first time can scarcely believe their eyes. In sharp contrast with Nine Mile, Geddes is downright ugly. It is urban fishing at its worst—and best—for if you can avert your eyes from the plastic trash bags, discarded car tires, Styrofoam packing blocks, and countless other sorts of litter, you will see a stream with enormous potential.

Geddes Brook is only about 8 miles from my home but I paid little heed to its cold, clear water and mix of wild and stocked brown trout for many years, until one hot and humid summer afternoon in the late 1990s. When the phone rang, my son Sean was on the other end of the line. He was hoping I might recommend a spot where he could take advantage of the downpours that had just swept through the Syracuse region. Nine Mile Creek was roaring and the color of coffee with cream, and Skaneateles Creek didn't look much better, he said.

I suggested he dig a can of worms and drive over to the old Fairmount Fair shopping center to give Geddes Brook a try. To be honest, I told Sean, I did not know much about the brook, other than the fact it had some trout in it and tended to rise quickly following a summer storm but usually cleared in a hurry, as well. It was tough to fly cast in some stretches and impossible in others, I warned. Of course he went fishing anyway.

At about 6 PM my phone rang again.

"Hey, Dad," Sean shouted in my ear. "You better get over here and fish this creek you told me about."

He had creeled a limit of five browns, all between 11 and 13 inches long, in less than two hours of fishing. A couple of his fish came from the alder-choked stretch that runs through the Fairmount Fair shopping center property, but the rest of Sean's keepers and several more trout he caught and released were hiding beneath cut banks farther downstream, about midway between the villages of Camillus and Solvay.

Sean assembled another nice mess of browns the next day. The day after that I tussled with a few Geddes Brook trout, myself.

We agreed the only thing wrong with this productive trout water was the view. For sheer homeliness, Geddes Brook outdoes even Logan Branch, a spring creek in Bellefonte, Pennsylvania, that is lined by billboards and at one point disappears beneath the floor of a quarter-mile-long, rusty-looking factory. Fortunately, just like Logan Branch, Geddes Brook fishes much better than its Plain Jane looks would suggest.

This junk-filled stream, no more than 10 or 15 feet wide in most sections, has its beginnings just upstream from Shove Park, a Town of Camillus facility that is close to the dense housing developments and clusters of retail stores, car repair shops, garages, and restaurants on busy West Genesee Street. Open to the public, Shove Park is a good spot to try bait or spinning lures on the first day of the trout season and again during the Orchard Fish and Game Club's annual fishing derby, held in May. Outside those two events, fishing at the park is poor, due to low water and very limited bank cover.

Fishing is noticeably better after the brook glides behind Holy Family Catholic Church, shortcuts through a miniature golf course, and pours out of a culvert pipe beneath Onondaga Road. From the culvert pool, which is barely big enough to hold a rising brown trout or two during the evening sulfur hatch in late May, the brook continues east along the back side of several large department stores and then turns left to pass through three culvert pipes. Fish there, as I sometimes do, and you may or may not catch anything but you will certainly cause at least one motorist to pull over by your spot. Usually, this driver will ask, incredulously, "Are there any fish in this creek?" Now and then, the car will be occupied by an elderly sportsman who is thrilled to see that somebody else recognizes what Geddes Brook *could be*, rather than what it once was.

Perhaps that older gentleman donated his sweat equity to the cause in the late 1980s, when local Trout Unlimited volunteers built a series of stream improvement devices and planted thousands of willow shoots along the creek's bank. The wood-and-wire structures have mostly collapsed after a series of floods, but the willows have formed a nearly impenetrable barrier of branches along most of the stretch. The planted curtain ends at the large culvert located where the brook turns north toward the Panera Bread sandwich shop. Whether you prefer flies, spinners, or garden worms, always give the culvert pool a serious try before moving on.

The trash along the shopping center stretch, whether windblown or tossed from the windows of passing cars, is simply inexcusable, but every year a small platoon of volunteers gives the brook an Earth Day cleanup. Too bad that karma hasn't spread to the remaining segments of the stream. After the West Genesee street crossing, the brook flows north through a residential neighborhood, enters an overgrown meadow near Hart's Religious Shop, and then goes underground between Milton Avenue and Horan Road, a distance of several hundred yards. That once-fishable water bubbles down a steel tunnel that is buried under a four-lane highway ramp. It emerges from the culvert from just a few feet upstream from the bridge at Horan Road.

What follows is the fishiest water in Geddes Brook, but the landscape is daunting, the fish are wary, and the sport is challenging, at the very least.

During the first week or two of the season, until mid-April, the streamside cover below Horan Road is relatively sparse, consisting mainly of toppled tree limbs and snow-flattened shrubbery. There is also just about any kind of litter you can imagine, not counting Jimmy Hoffa's bones. But all this stuff is easy to see and, therefore, to safely get around. The same can't be said for the plant life that springs up from the muddy creekbanks from late April into late August or so. You can be certain that the usual hanging vines, multiflora roses, and stinging nettles will sprout up where they will be most inconvenient to anglers, but the dominant plants in the vicinity of Horan Road are the phragmites, whose towering stems crowd out more desirable vegetation and threaten to trip and drop headlong any angler who dares hurry from pool to pool.

If you find a straightforward route through this jungle, I'll be surprised, for I usually have to make my own path. In recent seasons, beavers have complicated the navigation process in Geddes Brook. Getting around their dams here can be a maddening task. My advice is to enter the stream corridor with permission of an adjacent landowner or business proprietor and carefully work your way upstream or down. Wear hip boots, not chest waders, so you won't be tempted to wade the silt-laden, treacherous fringes of the brook, where one misstep could take you into deep water. Live bait or streamer flies drifted through pools with the help of a small split shot or two will get you some fish—but the better browns, 12 to 15 inches long, won't come easily to your hook.

Geddes Brook was off limits to anglers from the end of Horan Road to its junction with Nine Mile Creek during 2013 and 2014, to keep fishermen safe while nearby industrial waste beds were being excavated. The work, decades in the planning, was part of a comprehensive agreement between government and industry for the cleanup of Onondaga Lake. Part of the task involved the redirection of the brook, through the creation of bend pools and other good habitat. Engineers overseeing the project anticipated that it would add up to much better trout habitat and improved fishing.

Meanwhile, if you wear blinders and are in sufficiently good condition to kick and slash your way from pool to pool, you will see Geddes Brook as an uncut gem, one that has lots of flash and sparkle but is in desperate need of a makeover.

SKANEATELES CREEK

RATING: ★★★★ (4 stars)
NOTEWORTHY: The longest no-kill section in New York, at 10.2 miles.
BEST TIME TO FISH: First week in May, when Hendricksons are hatching.

Talk about pollution! When I first began fishing, the outlet of Skaneateles Lake was as putrid as the lake itself was pristine. No fooling, the creek that runs clear today from the village of Skaneateles downstream to its confluence with the Seneca River at Jordan used to be one of the dirtiest, stinkiest streams in the state. Electrofishing expeditions and other studies conducted along Skaneateles Creek in the 1960s and early '70s showed the water was grossly polluted, and held no trout or any other species of game fish. The situation could not rightly be pinned on any one culprit, for the stream assays conducted by the DEC pinpointed discharge pipes that poured out daily doses of waste from local industries as well as residential sewage treatment facilities that were not up to modern standards.

But the creek was not dead, merely comatose. When industrial and municipal industries, sewage treatment facilities, and municipalities obtained state and federal grants to achieve better water quality, the creek quickly sprang to life. The Onondaga County hatchery in the town of Elbridge hastened the stream's progress by planting new populations of brown, rainbow, and brook trout in the pools from Skaneateles to Jordan.

That was in the 1970s, but by 1994 a local conservation and fishing club known as the Owaskantisco Anglers (the name standing for lakes

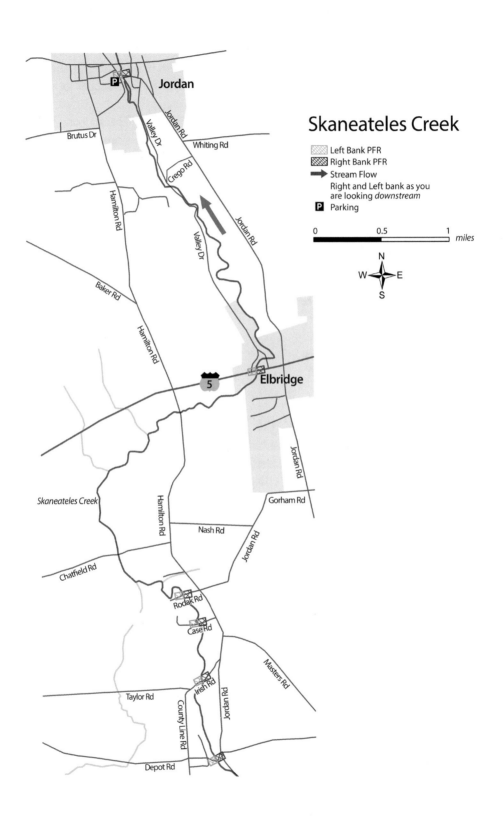

Skaneateles Creek

▨ Left Bank PFR
▨ Right Bank PFR
➤ Stream Flow
Right and Left bank as you
are looking *downstream*
🅿 Parking

0   0.5   1   *miles*

Jordan

P

Brutus Dr

Valley Dr

Jordan Rd

Whiting Rd

Crego Rd

Hamilton Rd

Valley Dr

Jordan Rd

Baker Rd

Hamilton Rd

5

Elbridge

Jordan Rd

Skaneateles Creek

Gorham Rd

Hamilton Rd

Nash Rd

Jordan Rd

Chatfield Rd

Rodak Rd

Case Rd

Masters Rd

Taylor Rd

Irish Rd

County Line Rd

Jordan Rd

Depot Rd

Owasco, Skaneateles, and Otisco in the eastern part of the Finger Lakes chain) convinced the DEC that most of Skaneateles Creek should be subject to special regulations. The proposal had a definite logic to it, for laboratory tests confirmed that trout captured in the creek had unacceptably high concentrations of polychlorinated biphenyls, or PCBs, in their flesh. Used as insulators in electrical power transformers, PCBs were strongly suspected of causing cancer, and state experts urged fishermen and others to avoid eating trout that were possibly contaminated with the stuff. After more than a year of patient lobbying, the Owaskantisco members convinced DEC officials that 10.2 miles of the creek, from the crossing at Old Seneca Turnpike in the village of Skaneateles north to the Route 31C bridge in the village of Jordan, should be put under no-kill regulations. Since then, wild trout have flourished and the Carpenter's Brook hatchery has continued to stock at the rate of roughly 4,000 browns and 'bows a year.

Oddly, the popularity of the creek began to wane almost immediately after the special regulations were adopted. Perhaps it was the stream's small size compared with other no-kill fisheries in the state, such as those in the roomy Beaverkill and Willowemoc in the Catskills. Or maybe the turnoff was the fact that some of the best fishing in Skaneateles Creek was in residential neighborhoods in Skaneateles Falls, Elbridge, and Jordan. Some anglers are simply not at ease wading past somebody's family picnic or excusing themselves when their passage causes a watchdog to start barking just before sunset.

All I know for sure is the people living along the stream tend to be friendly and inquisitive about friendly fly fishers, and I have enjoyed conversing with such folks. It is not backwoods angling, but the experience of fishing Skaneateles Creek has always been pleasurable for me. Grudgingly, I have learned to avoid some of the more rural sectors of the stream, where poachers are said to violate the no-kill law and spirit by using live bait and stuffing fish into their creels as long as nobody seems to be looking. Over the years I have heard plenty of excuses for this thoughtless behavior, including a laughable lament for "the poor kids" who supposedly can't afford to let their catch live to bite and fight another day. What bunk! If a youngster you know of seems disinclined to abide by catch-and-release rules, invite him or her to come along with you and show this angler-in-the-making how to cast and retrieve a Rooster Tail, Mepps, or other spinning lure. Pinch down the rear-end hook barbs to facilitate the task of letting them go, then praise the rookie generously when he or she gets it right.

Frankly, I don't think the kids would even think of breaking no-kill regulations if their fishing father or other adult mentor showed proper reverence and respect for the law.

One of Skaneateles Creek's attributes is its steady output of aquatic insect hatches in April, May, and June. If the water levels are conducive to fly fishing—and that's not a sure thing, given Central New York's unpredictable spring weather—I can anticipate decent surface fishing set off by hatches of size 18 or 20 blue-winged olive mayflies during the first week or two of the season. A smattering of early black stoneflies, no bigger than a size 16, light-wire hook, are also on the creek's menu by April 15, and a good hatch of Hendricksons starts up around April 28 or so. It lasts a week or more, and is just starting to taper off when the size 14 sulfurs, *Ephemerella invaria*, entice even the bigger Skaneateles browns to dine on top. Then come March browns, until June 10 or so. And did I mention that, during this whole period, an assortment of "stick caddis" larvae litters the back eddies of most pools?

Unfortunately, the creek's one shortcoming, as far as I can tell, is its summer temperature regime. The water climbs into the low 70s more days than not between mid-June and early September. Consequently, resident trout are stressed, uninterested in feeding, and forced to seek refuge in tiny tributaries and springs. If I have any doubts what my prospects will be in the tepid creek on a given day, I make a visit with a stream thermometer tucked in a convenient pocket. If the temperature is 70 degrees Fahrenheit or warmer, I do not bother to make a cast. This is the time to head for Nine Mile Creek or some other spot with colder flows.

This much-underrated stream is born on the north side of the U.S. Route 20 bridge in the village of Skaneateles, where the creek tumbles over the dam. Some folks will tell you the name of lake, stream, and village is hard to pronounce. But take it from a long-term resident of the area, there's nothing to it. I've heard the town, village, and creek sounded out as *Skinny-AT-till-eese* and *SKANNY-AT-liss*. Properly sounded, it's *SKAN-e-AT-lass*.

It's not all that hard to say, and it's not very difficult to wade or fish, either. Just keep at least one eye on the road as you follow the highway curves from Jordan Road in Skaneateles downstream to the Route 31C crossing in Jordan, where the no-kill area abruptly ends and all those poor urchins who can't mow enough lawns or scrub sufficient pots and pans to finance their own spinning lures can at least creel a couple of stockers.

CARPENTER'S BROOK

RATING: ★★ (2 stars)
NOTEWORTHY: The main water source for the Onondaga County
　Fish Hatchery.
BEST TIME TO FISH: Opening day, or soon after.

Ironically, the pulsing springs that fuel trout production at Onondaga County's very own hatchery don't offer much fishing, themselves. The fish factory straddling Carpenter's Brook in Elbridge is spring-fed and augmented by a deep well dug in the late 1960s, and as the stream exits the grounds it is swift, clear, and full of promise. It doesn't take long for the daydreaming angler to snap out of it. The POSTED signs spring up within casting distance of the hatchery gate, and variations on the "get out or else" theme are proclaimed on most of the brook from there to the Seneca River.

Heavy posting is a bummer anywhere, but it's not the only problem Carpenter's Brook poses to anglers. The silt load is heavy in most sections, and deposits from the spring runoff and midsummer showers throw smothering layers of muck on aquatic insects and trout fry, too. Then there is the thick brush and the innumerable deadfalls that make it virtually impossible to fish many of the little pools. Crashing through this stuff is difficult for young anglers, let alone their mentors. Finally, beaver dams are common in the meandering brook north of Route 5, and the private landowners so far have not been moved to hire trappers to deal with this infestation.

The stream is less than 15 feet across in most spots, and the narrow pools and runs are typically well guarded by overhanging limbs, but trout of 12 to 15 inches are not uncommon. The most dependable place to catch a large trout in Carpenter's Brook is in the pool adjacent to the hatchery entry road, off Route 321 in Elbridge, and I can tell you not only where but also when to give it a try. Just before the season opens, stocking crews drop a couple of dozen fish in the pool, on their way to more conventional trout-release sites. The season officially starts at one second after midnight on April Fools' Day, and you should be ready and waiting with a baited hook when the second hand on your watch or smart phone passes the 12. The seven or eight fishermen who ring the pool are targeting the several brood stock browns and rainbows left there by the county hatchery workers.

The hatchery outlet pool is seldom fished after the first weekend in April, but many pools produce nice browns all season long, despite thick bank cover and difficult wading and walking. Try the challenging water downstream of Route 5 in Elbridge. It's owned by a nature preservation group that allows angling on its property, and it fishes well after a heavy shower muddies the water a bit. The stream can be fished with flies, but with difficulty. Garden worms and salted minnows are more suitable, most of the time.

BUTTERNUT CREEK

RATING: ★★★★ (4 stars)

NOTEWORTHY: Picture miles of public fishing water that is barely
    bothered by fishermen most of the year.

BEST TIME TO FISH: May is prime but November can be great, too.

At first, the realization that a stream as beautiful as Butternut Creek is largely ignored by Syracuse-area anglers prompted me to marvel at the quality of sport in other regional waters. It must be wonderful, right? In point of fact, I can't believe that longtime fans of the creek that flows northward from the pleasant hill country around Apulia, LaFayette, and Jamesville would ever vacate this venue. Still, the evidence of a broken relationship is compelling—parking areas with few tire imprints, plus streambank footpaths that are disappearing in thickets of multiflora rose and other noxious plants that gung-ho trout fishers used to take pride in trampling. Fortunately, the water and its fish are as healthy and handsome as ever.

I fish Butternut mainly during the winter, when the creek is open to fishing (standard creel limits apply and bait, lure, and fly are all permitted) north of U.S. Route 20. With deep snow and ice shelves to slow my progress, and water temperatures seldom higher than 40 degrees, this is hardly prime-time fishing, but I have caught plenty of 10- to 14-inch Butternut browns between Christmas and April Fools' Day. My best-ever brown from the creek was just shy of 20 inches. Although the big boy took a night crawler on a frigid February afternoon, I've also landed some nice trout on nymphs and dry flies during spring and autumn trips in and around the village of Jamesville.

The Hendrickson hatch in early May provides some excellent sport from Route 20 north, but be forewarned: This section is stuffed with horned dace and other so-called trash fish. The little devils will pester bait or fly incessantly. One way to beat them is to fish spinning lures or swing large bucktails (on size 6 or 4 long-shank streamer hooks) across and down through the 15- to 25-foot-wide pools and runs. The smaller chubs try but can't get the hooks in their mouths.

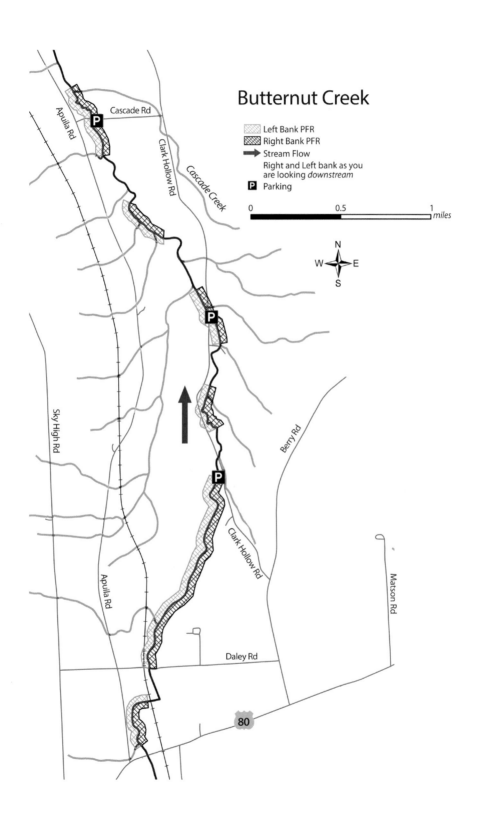

Butternut Creek

Left Bank PFR
Right Bank PFR
Stream Flow
Right and Left bank as you
are looking *downstream*
P Parking

0   0.5   1
miles

N
W E
S

Apuila Rd

Cascade Rd

Clark Hollow Rd

Cascade Creek

P

Sky High Rd

Berry Rd

Apuila Rd

Clark Hollow Rd

Matson Rd

P

P

Daley Rd

80

The DEC website's array of fishing maps includes a useful one on Butternut Creek. You can find plenty of fishy spots on your own by taking Route 20 east from LaFayette for about 2 miles to the crossing at Big Bend and working upstream or downstream from there.

If you are a dedicated worm fisherman, the water upstream of Route 20 will immediately strike you as being some of the best-looking habitat in the entire system. Open from April 1 through October 15, it is seldom fished at all. Explore it just after a spring or summer downpour gives the creek a murky tint. Focus on the thickets along Clark Hollow Road, located east of the Route 20 crossing, and park in one of the DEC fishing access areas along the way. Be prepared to do some serious brush-pounding, for you will have to fight your way to the better pools. You will earn each and every one of the plump browns you catch, but now and then the anglers who have stuck by Butternut will be rewarded with the unexpected *rat-tat-tat* strike of a pretty native brook trout.

LIMESTONE CREEK

RATING: ★★★ (3 stars)
NOTEWORTHY: Stocked heavily and holds big, wild browns, too.
BEST TIME TO FISH: Right after the Iroquois Chapter of Trout Unlimited
      does its float-stocking, usually early June.

Once upon a time but not all that long ago, Limestone Creek was widely considered one of the top three or four trout streams in Central New York, and possibly the best of all in Onondaga County. It was known, in particular, for its ability to produce whopper brown trout, fish of 4 to 7 pounds, even. Some of these fish, which were encountered more often than not in the first few weeks of the trout season, likely were brood stock, retired from the Carpenter's Brook hatchery and set free in the creek just before opening day. However, the creek was home to stream-born brownies, too, and I have not the slightest doubt that many of the hook-jawed specimens displayed in the Syracuse newspapers in the 1950s and '60s were as wild as they were huge.

Today, Limestone Creek is still a great spot to go trout fishing, but the fisherman who hooks an 18- or 20-incher once or twice a year is a superior angler, for certain. The creek may hide a genuine monster now and then, but the big boys are much less common than they were 30 or 40 years ago. Neither the county hatchery nor any of the fish farms in the state system have the extra money to turn those so-called retired breeders loose on a regular basis, for any extra carrying capacity they may have is jealously guarded—and skewed toward the output of the two-year-old browns that are wildly popular with most anglers. With rare exceptions—and the upper Genesee River near Wellsville immediately comes to mind—any 15-inch-plus browns caught in Limestone or other New York streams were hatched in a natural habitat and never banged their pectoral fins on the concrete walls of a hatchery holding tank.

While it is no longer the lair of lunkers, Limestone Creek remains a much-loved fishing stream. Today, it is the second most heavily stocked stream in Onondaga County, behind Nine Mile Creek. Because it winds and tumbles through a variety of terrains in the eastern towns of the county, it is the home water of hundreds of suburbanites who deeply appreciate what it has to offer.

One thing Limestone Creek does not appear to have a whole lot of is limestone rock formations such as those that help sustain Nine Mile's trout. As it wanders through the villages of Manlius and Fayetteville, Limestone now and then may break the trout temperature barrier. That is to say, the water can warm to 70 degrees Fahrenheit or more, especially during the day in July and early August. I would not fish under such conditions, but would try one of the creek's cooler tributaries, such as the West Branch of Limestone Creek, which runs through Pratt's Falls County Park. The West Branch, 10 to 15 feet wide in most places, heads north to meet the main stem of the creek in the village of Manlius.

Limestone has an excellent sulfur hatch from mid-May to late June, and is a great stream for nymphing, too. Pheasant-tail patterns, tied on size 14 and 16 hooks and ribbed with fine copper wire, are good imitations of the prevalent nymphs, while olive and olive-bodied caddis drys will usually draw a few browns in the choppy riffles and deep pools in Manlius and also Fayetteville, which is the next village downstream. Look for the many pull-offs along the creek, where most of the local anglers gain access to the suburban sectors of this still-popular stream.

FABIUS BROOK

RATING: ★★★ (3 stars)

NOTEWORTHY: Large brown trout and some of the better brook trout fishing in Onondaga County.

BEST TIME TO FISH: Late April, when the water has warmed enough to trigger hatches and stir the appetites of this stream's well-fed fish.

One of the fringe benefits of being the outdoors writer for a large metropolitan daily newspaper, as I was for 16 years, was the opportunity to review a nearly endless supply of big-fish photos. Anglers love to carry a photo or two of their biggest fish, and if said anglers happen to love trout, they are very likely to keep a snapshot of a dandy brown, brookie, or rainbow tucked safely amid prints of children, grandkids, and spouse—although not necessarily in that order.

While the Syracuse newspapers always had a fair number of "grip and grin" pictures waiting for review by the outdoors writer, thick stacks of stuff filled my mailbox after then–*Post-Standard* sports editor Dave Rahme suggested we begin a new Trophy of the Week feature. Before long we were running these captioned "hero shots" weekly, but readers were sending at least four or five a week. While I never asked readers to supply detailed directions to their favorite spots, many just couldn't help themselves and blurted out clues that sometimes pointed me to the piscatorial equivalent of Blackbeard's treasure. If I hadn't decided where to go fishing during a given week, I could always follow a reader's hot tip!

One of the most jaw-dropping leads I ever got from a reader, however, had nothing to do with Trophy of the Week and everything to do with Fabius Brook. At the time, the weekly column was just a gleam in an editor's eye, and the brook was a mystery to most Syracuse-area sportsmen because it flowed through one of the region's most lightly populated towns. You can imagine how I felt when I read about the capture of a 10-pound brown trout from a Fabius pool on a salted minnow. The brook was about 20 miles away but in those days it might as well have been in Alaska. The photo of the lunker that accompanied the Rod Hunter fishing and hunting column sure didn't look like a fake, but at that time I was in my early 20s and still thought a 10-incher was a nice fish. This was a 10-pounder, for Pete's sake. I told Rod's alter ego, Bob Peel, that I wanted to do a story on the Fabius water beast and its slayer, Tony Dennison of Cazenovia, for *Sports Afield*. Bob gave me a hero shot that one of the paper's staff photographers had taken of the angler and his prize. I tagged along with Tony, shot a few more photos of him standing by the pool where the big boy used to prowl, and wrote a long article, which *Sports Afield* ultimately rejected.

Even so, I learned a lot that day in the woods with Tony, and I fished Fabius Brook many times in the years that followed. If not the best brookie stream in Central New York, it is one of the best, for it harbors browns of 20 or more inches and natives that in my experience top out at around 13 or 14 inches. Foot-long browns and 10-inch brook trout are merely run-of-the-mill in Fabius Brook.

This 10- to 30-feet-wide stream, which crosses U.S. Route 80 just west of the village of Fabius and about midway between LaFayette and

New Woodstock, is tightly wrapped in layers of alders, cedars, and other ankle-snappers. You will work hard for every nice fish you catch in Fabius Brook, I promise. This stream, like many others I've encountered, fishes best after a heavy rain in June or July. The meandering channel downstream of Fabius Central School and continuing below Parker Road can be navigated by a determined brush-breaker, but even if you are one such, you will need to get permission from a landowner or two. Also worth a try after a downpour or any other time you are in the neighborhood is the stretch below Bardeen Road, where the DEC operations division installed a fishing access area in 2014. Finally, if you happen to be a skillful bait fisher or an ace with spinner or spoon, seek a landowner's okay to explore the west fork of Fabius Brook where it flows under the Herlihy Road and Bailey Road bridges; or the north branch, which flows parallel to Route 91 between Bryan Road and Route 80.

Although Fabius Brook has the usual Central New York assortment of aquatic insect hatches, some of the season's hottest action on the stream occurs in late August and September, when trout fatten up on grasshoppers and crickets. Wind or heavy rain will flush these terrestrial insects into the water, especially in the overgrown meadows south of the Bardeen Road–Toggenburg Road intersection. From this point downstream to Cuyler, Fabius Brook magically morphs into the West Branch of Tioughnioga Creek, thanks to the mapmakers who seem to delight in causing confusion among peripatetic anglers. Don't lose any sleep over your occasional wrong turns, as Fabius Brook and its branches all are worth a morning or afternoon of concentration.

ONONDAGA CREEK

RATING: ★★★ (3 stars)
NOTEWORTHY: The fishiest part of this still-polluted stream is in the heart of Syracuse.
BEST TIME TO FISH: Early October, provided the water is clear.

Many cities have trout streams flowing through their neighborhoods, but very few can lay claim to a spot like Onondaga Creek. Half a century ago, give or take a few years, the channelized stream that collects every kind of human refuse you can imagine—yes, even *that* kind—was almost but not quite dead. In those days, anyone who paused to study the water rushing beneath Jefferson Street or some other Syracuse boulevard that arched across the creek was more likely to see a floating corpse than a rising trout.

Then, as now, the creek's most persistent environmental shortcoming was the antiquated combined sewer system, which dealt with the annual spring runoff and other high-water episodes in Syracuse by allowing flows from storm sewers and municipal sewage systems to merge their currents when water levels ran much higher than usual. Even today, after decades of lawsuits and negotiations among corporate, civic, and government organizations over ways to clean up Onondaga Lake and its tributaries, city residents can only hold their noses after heavy summer rains. Making the situation even more embarrassing, in the view of ardent conservationists, is the channelization of the creek from the vicinity of Valley Drive at the city's south end to the gentrified Franklin Square commercial district not far from the creek mouth. The stream was straightened in an ill-conceived attempt to minimize flooding. Later, city officials caved in to lurid newspaper accounts of city residents—most of them children—who drowned in what the press referred to as "the Killer Creek." The measure of prevention did not completely eliminate the drowning problem, but did put the creek's various problems "out of sight and out of mind" as far as many residents were concerned.

Amazingly, trout not only survived such mismanagement but also enjoyed robust good health in some sections of Onondaga Creek. Where the creek first appears within casting distance of anglers, about 1 mile north of the intersection of Route 80 and Tully Farms Road, Onondaga County has established a small fisherman parking area. Watch for it on your left, just a bit farther down the hill after you pass Solvay Road. You can fish upstream or downstream from there, and bait and spinning experts should be able to hook wild browns and hatchery transplants, too, after any rain heavy enough to give the water a grayish tint.

There is a limited degree of public access from the Tully Farms parking area downstream into Syracuse. First the creek is colored with erosion from clay beds and silty mud boils as the water winds its way to U.S. Route 20 just west of the village of LaFayette and then proceeds through the Onondaga Nation reservation (no fishing allowed for non-Indians) before reaching the Valley neighborhood that straddles Syracuse's southern border. The fencing is impermeable by the standards of most anglers after Killer Creek slips under the bridge at Route 175, west of Salina Street. However, some of the best fishing available in this underdog of a stream is the mile or two of swift riffles and deep pools in or around Franklin Square.

In the last few weeks of the state's general trout season, from late September to October 15, brown trout up to 20 inches long hide in the darker, tree-shaded holes. I wouldn't eat these fish, but I am willing to answer the many questions asked when I fish my way past downtown office buildings and I don't mind wriggling through narrow fence openings to get a shot at a big brownie, either. I like tiny bluegill jigs with curly tails to hook such trout from Syracuse's premier trout stream.

More Onondaga County Trout Streams

New York counties that boast several outstanding trout streams frequently have at least as many waters that come close to qualifying for huzzahs and hallelujahs, themselves. The reasons they don't make the varsity generally have to do with stream size and ease of access. If they have good numbers of trout but are too small to tolerate much fishing pressure or are emphatically posted by somebody who is reluctant to share our natural resources, even with anglers who politely knock on their door, well, of how much value can they be to you or me?

The West Branch of Onondaga Creek is a fine example of a stream that has plenty of fish but very little fishing. Traceable to the joining of several small tributaries in the towns of Marcellus, Onondaga, and Otisco, it is a respectable 15 to 20 feet wide when it meets Onondaga Creek just east of the hamlet of South Onondaga. It has virtually no public fishing access, but local residents and property owners may grant permission to anglers who look for it along Cedarvale, Stevens, Tanner, and Nichols Roads. Brown trout are the targeted trout here.

If you like to get off the beaten path, try the seldom-visited **Spafford Creek**, which is the largest feeder of Otisco Lake. Posted for most of its length, it is open to fishing by courtesy of the landowner at the Sawmill Road bridge, about 2 miles south of the lake. The stretch is stocked with brown trout and holds some wild browns, too. Most run between 8 and 11 inches, but a 14-incher is possible. Be forewarned that beavers sometimes take a heavy toll on the habitat of this narrow creek, plugging it with dams that cover spawning grounds with silt and raising water temperatures to levels trout can't tolerate.

Another Otisco Lake tributary worthy of exploration early in the trout season, **Amber Brook**, enters the lake in the hamlet of Amber and flows along Amber and Fish Gulf Roads in the town of Otisco. It's a tiny stream, less than 10 feet wide in most spots, and access is by permission only, but wild brown and brook trout are present.

You really should be careful where you park your car and look out for suspicious characters, too, but with those caveats the inner-city neighborhoods in Syracuse have some surprisingly good trout fishing. Most of the action will be found in tributaries of Onondaga Creek. For wild brown

Kid Corbett on Spafford Creek.

trout, try fly or spin fishing early or late in the season in **Furnace Brook**, which tumbles through Elmwood Park, off South Avenue. Some brook trout are stocked upstream of the park near Corcoran High School. **Harbor Brook** is another Syracuse stream with wild brownies. It is primarily an early-season, bait and spinning type of stream, but there are more 8- to 11-inchers than you might think where it flows along Grand Avenue near Westhill High School and the Western Lights shopping plaza.

The suburbs of Onondaga County have a few overlooked trout waters, too. Among the better ones are **Pool's Brook**, which flows along Route 5 immediately east of Fayetteville in the town of Manlius; and **White Bottom Brook**, a tiny stream that bubbles along and under Fikes Road in the town of Elbridge. White Bottom is not stocked and is posted for most of its length, but the browns that live in the 6-foot-wide headwaters of the stream are as pretty as you will ever see. You have nothing to lose by asking for permission to give it a try. If nothing else is available, do a little culvert fishing on White Bottom. My son hauled a 15-incher from one of the brook's overlooked crossings, many years ago. It was his first sizable trout, and he has loved small streams ever since.

CAYUGA COUNTY

You wouldn't expect New York's top corn-growing county to be criss-crossed by trout waters, but Cayuga County is a sleeper. Between its towering rows of maize near Auburn and Moravia and the lush vineyards that overlook Cayuga Lake, anglers enjoy a variety of cold streams populated by browns, rainbows, and even a few native brook trout. The fishing isn't always easy, but the fish are there, especially in the creeks that veer away from angler parking spots and plunge into the thickets that make the average angler hesitant to follow. Some of the more foreboding streams are, arguably at least, four- or even five-star fisheries. On a fish-per-acre basis, a couple of Cayuga County's best streams are among New York's finest, too.

But I am a little biased, maybe more than a little. Aside from the first several days of the trout season, when my fellow fishermen follow each other from pool to pool like a bunch of creel-carrying lemmings in the hope of hooking a big rainbow during its annual spawning run, Cayuga County creeks suffer hardly any angler traffic. After mid-April, I am virtually guaranteed to have any stream in the county all to myself. If that's an exaggeration, it's a very slight one, for nobody was around to see the 28¼-inch rainbow I caught from a tributary of a tributary a few years back. Nor did anybody witness the 21-inch brown I caught just a couple of Mays ago, or the picture-perfect 14-inch native brookie that was waiting for my worm one day back in the shadows of a remote road culvert. If you fish long enough and well enough in Cayuga County, you won't be tempted to tell another angler anything but the truth. Honest!

OWASCO INLET

RATING: ★★★★ (4 stars)

NOTEWORTHY: Most anglers who fish for its spawning rainbows in April aren't aware the inlet holds nice brown trout year-round.

BEST TIME TO FISH: During the *Tricorythodes*, or Trico, mayfly hatch in July and August.

The most amazing thing about Cayuga County's best all-around trout stream is its great, good fortune to be overlooked by so many anglers. Owasco Inlet gets a fairly heavy turnout on April 1, the opening day of trout season, but the following two or three days usually see a mass exodus. By midday, old-timers are grumbling about the demise of their old favorite pools and itching to hit the highway, and the many dads who bow to family tradition by baiting hooks for sons and daughters often are apt

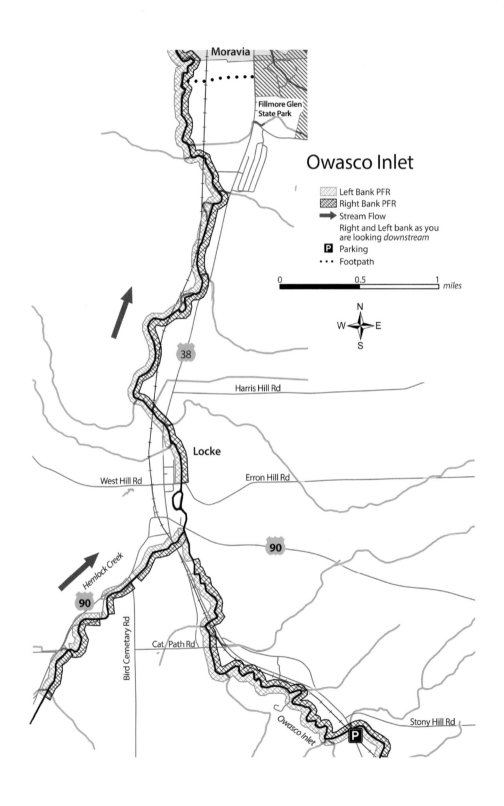

Moravia

Fillmore Glen
State Park

Owasco Inlet

Left Bank PFR
Right Bank PFR
Stream Flow
Right and Left bank as you
are looking *downstream*
P Parking
• • • Footpath

0 _____ 0.5 _____ 1
miles

N
W ✦ E
S

38

Harris Hill Rd

Locke

West Hill Rd

Erron Hill Rd

90

Hemlock Creek

90

Bird Cemetary Rd

Cat Path Rd

Owasco Inlet

Stony Hill Rd

P

to be homeward bound even before the climbing sun peeks over the low ridges. The following morning, some patient fishermen will be back for another try, but if that second effort doesn't pay off, they might not wade the stream again until the following spring.

I, on the other hand, always plan to come early and stay late at Owasco Inlet. The spawning rainbows that most of the inlet's regulars pursue on opening day may or may not wind up on my stringer, but I can usually hook a couple of nice browns, and a 14- to 18-inch brown is a heck of a consolation prize. Oh, you didn't know the inlet had good fishing for browns? Well, it is so good, in fact, that I am convinced most of the deep pools from Moravia upstream into Groton hold at least one brown measuring 15 inches or more. Each spring the DEC fans my optimism by stocking more than 3,000 browns, including 400 or so two-year-olds, but the majority of big fish I've caught had the arrow-shaped pectoral fins and brilliant colors of stream-born trout.

Paul McNeilley of Marcellus with a 16-inch brown trout, Owasco Inlet.

Among the dozens of Finger Lakes tributaries that have reputations for good rainbow fishing in the spring, only a few are home to substantial numbers of nonmigratory rainbows, browns, or brook trout throughout the season. Based on DEC data as well as my own experience fishing various tributaries, I'd include Springwater Creek (brookies), Naples Creek and its headwaters (browns and brookies), Keuka Lake Outlet (browns), Salmon Creek (browns), Dutch Hollow Brook (browns), Grout Brook (browns), Bear Swamp Creek (brookies), and Owasco Inlet and its feeders (mostly browns).

The inlet is by far the best of this bunch, in terms of season-long productivity. Whether the rainbow run is strong or weak in a given April, the brown trout fishing is dependably good from April 1 through December 31—in other words, for the entire length of the Finger Lakes tributary season—and the stream also harbors thousands of juvenile rainbows and unknown numbers of 'bows, up to 12 or 13 inches long, that vacate the creek a year or two later than the rest of their kind. The combination of trout provides plenty of action for bait and fly fishermen even during the heat of summer.

One of the most enticing aspects of the inlet is its easy access. Public fishing rights signs are posted along more than 13 miles of the stream, and even where one bank is marked NO TRESPASSING, the opposite side is probably open to hip boot traffic. Even better, almost all of the stream is closely paralleled by Route 38, which also overlooks the west shore of Owasco Lake, all the way north to Auburn. As you drive along the highway, you will see deep pools, along with flat, sandy- or gravel-bottomed runs that would cause many trout fishers to drool on their waders. However, the inlet frequently meanders slightly west or east of its existing channel, and in the process forms a seemingly endless string of undercuts and pockets capable of hiding some very large browns. Some of the most impressive holes can be found downstream from the bridge at the north end of the village of Locke, but the sinuous stretch across Route 38 from Stony Hill Road is one of my favorites. The angler parking lot there is opposite a towering statue of a Hereford steer, which my friends and I know as "the Brown Cow."

Besides its remarkable lengths of public fishing rights, Owasco Inlet is also appreciated for its robust and reliable mayfly and caddis hatches. The Hendrickson emergence that starts in late April and continues into mid-May often arrives while significant numbers of rainbows are still spawning. Those that have already finished their redds will often tarry in the stream for a few days to recover their strength. On their way downstream to Owasco Lake, these trout may feed greedily on Hendrickson nymphs or even sip their suppers from the surface, now and then. I will never forget the late-April 'bow that inhaled my Hendrickson nymph several hundred yards downstream from the bridge marking the northern boundary of the village of Locke. It was an even 25 inches long! A couple of years ago, I used the same fly pattern in the same pool and was rewarded with a 19-inch brown.

Hendricksons are fair-size mayflies, matched by artificials tied on size 12 or 14 hooks, and they are sizable snacks for big trout. Not as big but every bit as fun to try when the dog days have put many other streams on hold between cooling thunderstorms are the tiny Tricos. These tidbits, tied on size 24 hooks and fished on 6X leader tippets, hatch day after day for up to two full hours. The show usually starts around 8:30 or 9 AM, and dozens of trout will line up in some pools to get their share of the mayflies that swarm over every riffle and fall spent on the pools after mating. Most of the feeding fish are under 8 inches long, but now and then a lunker of 12 to 14 inches will take one of your delicate little drys.

Virtually every inch of Owasco Inlet, as well as its tributaries, will reward diligent anglers, and newcomers should not be discouraged by the grumbling of those who pine for half-true memories of the good old days.

DRESSERVILLE CREEK

RATING: ★★★★ (4 stars)
NOTEWORTHY: Home to a rare strain of nonmigratory rainbows.
BEST TIME TO FISH: Immediately after a spring shower.

I was seriously tempted to give Dresserville Creek a five-star rating, rather than the four-star rank you see above, but this 10- to 30-foot-wide stream's dearth of really large trout settled the issue. It's still a fine place to catch a bunch of fish, especially when it is high and slightly off-color on the heels of a heavy downpour. The presence of beautifully colored, wild browns and rainbows that have never seen a fish hatchery does nothing to diminish its appeal.

Dresserville Creek is a mapmaker's quandary. From its headwaters just east of Route 41A in the southeast corner of Cayuga County, it flows about 14 miles before it spills over a waterfall and merges with Decker Brook, another high-quality fishery that takes a sudden nosedive. Cartographers could have dubbed the combined currents below the steep falls as either Decker or Dresserville, take your pick. Instead, they rejected both of those perfectly reasonable names and opted to call the blended stream Mill

Creek, apparently after the old mill a few hundred feet downstream from the falls.

The nomenclature can be a little confusing, but Dresserville Creek's reputation rests solidly on the pools and runs upstream of the falls. The water below the falls is seasonal in nature, with modest rainbow runs occurring each April and very little else happening the rest of the year.

Dresserville has about 6 miles of public fishing rights on one or both banks. Some access points are well marked with the state's glorious green-on-yellow welcome signs but others, sadly, are not. The DEC obtains fishing access areas from individual owners, and the public ownership that results is in perpetuity, which means "forever." When the marked property changes hands, public fishing privileges are automatically retained by the state.

Some new owners either don't know or don't care what *perpetuity* means. They remove the public fishing signs or tack their own KEEP OUT or NO TRESPASSING signs on the same trees. In so doing they not only cause uncertainty among anglers but also violate the law. Fishermen who are faced with this problem on Dresserville Creek or any other stream should inquire about the situation by reporting it to a conservation officer.

The segments of Dresserville Creek available through public fishing rights (PFR) agreements are shown on a color map that's available via the DEC website. Download a copy and compare it with a Cayuga County Road map or simply plug in your TomTom or other navigational tool and follow the electronic directions. You will see that the creek flows mostly in a westerly direction, first through the hamlet of Dresserville, just north of Lake Como, then bumping and gliding through a curvy channel that occasionally is visible from Dresserville Road. The road dead-ends at the intersection with Route 38A, about half a mile north of the village of Moravia. The creek crosses 38A at the hamlet of Montville and plunges over the falls about 30 feet from the highway.

In my view, Dresserville Creek is suitable throughout its length for bait fishing but less appealing to spinning and fly-casting devotees. The best fly-rod sport is in the lower third or so of the stream.

If you're coming from the Auburn area, take Route 38A south, go past the intersection with Sayles Corners Road, and take your next left, Chestnut Ridge Road, which overlooks a shallow gorge that holds many 8- to 10-inch rainbows and now and then a 12- or 14-incher. Browns are also present here, but aren't as abundant as the 'bows.

The DEC says the rainbows in Dresserville Creek are a nonmigratory strain. That's very unusual in New York, where most rainbows spend the greater portion of their adulthood in deep, cold lakes—such as Owasco and several other Finger Lakes—but enter tributaries to spawn in late winter or early spring. Most of their progeny complete the rotation by hatching out of their eggs and then swimming down to their parents' home lakes when they are around 8 inches long. A few months or a year after that journey, the rapidly growing 'bows will be big enough to make their own spawning run.

In any case, watch your step as you explore the first mile or two of Dresserville Creek upstream from Route 38A. The bottom here is slick bedrock in many spots; you could take a serious spill if you aren't a cautious wader. Cleated wader soles are a big help, and I rely heavily on a wading staff, myself.

Many anglers skip the Chestnut Ridge Road section in favor of following Dresserville Road upstream from its Route 38A crossing. On your way toward the hamlet of Dresserville, check out any of the several bridges over the stream, and try the marked public fishing areas, too. Both rainbows and browns can be caught throughout the creek. Most are in the 8- to 12-inch range. My personal bests from Dresserville Creek are a 14-inch rainbow and 15-inch brown.

Good fly patterns for this stretch of the creek include Hendrickson and Light Cahill dry flies, Cased Caddis and Hare's Ear Nymphs, and Woolly Bugger streamers, among others. Hatches in this stream are varied but not overwhelming in terms of bug numbers, so the fish are not normally fussy about fly colors or even sizes. The farther upstream you travel, the tougher the fly fishing will be, and when I fish between bridges from the Morse Mill area to Dresserville, logic tells me to work those brushy little pools and riffles with worms or salted minnows.

The trout in Dresserville Creek are exceptionally beautiful, although rarely more than a foot long. All are wild, and DEC records indicate the stream has not been stocked for half a century. Rainbows caught here have myriad pepper-flake spots sprinkled over their rose-striped flanks. They bear very little resemblance to the trout with silver coats and relatively sparse patterns of black spots that live just a few miles away in the Finger Lakes.

DECKER BROOK

RATING: ★★★ (3 stars)
NOTEWORTHY: Good small stream, all wild fish.
BEST TIME TO FISH: Any day when runoff colors the water.

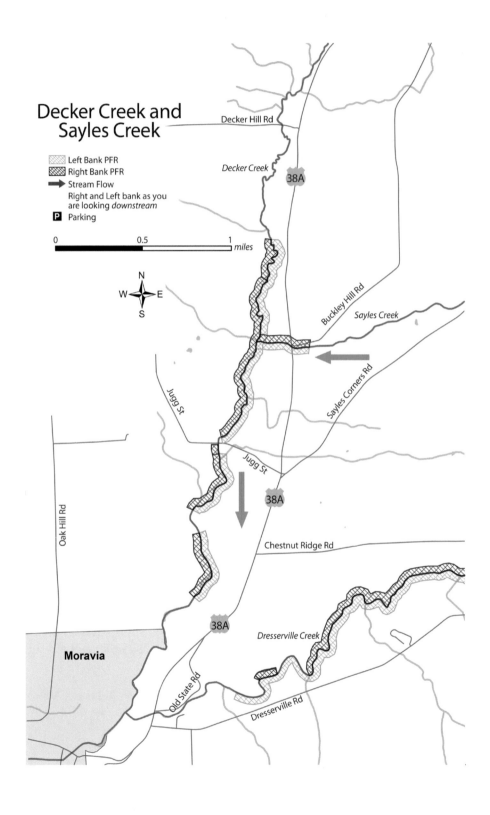

Decker Creek and Sayles Creek

Left Bank PFR

Right Bank PFR

→ Stream Flow

Right and Left bank as you are looking *downstream*

P Parking

0   0.5   1
miles

N
W—E
S

Decker Hill Rd

Decker Creek

38A

Buckley Hill Rd

Sayles Creek

Sayles Corners Rd

Jugg St

Jugg St

38A

Oak Hill Rd

Chestnut Ridge Rd

38A

Moravia

Dresserville Creek

Old State Rd

Dresserville Rd

If Dresserville Creek doesn't pan out or is already taken when you visit, drive 3 or 4 miles and wet a line in Decker Brook instead—or vice versa. The two streams both have excellent water quality, fish well all season long except during extended dry spells, and wind up merging within roll-casting distance of Route 38A, just north of Moravia in southern Cayuga County.

According to DEC Region 7 aquatic biologist Jeff Robins, Decker Brook has not been formally surveyed by state electrofishing crews since 1927. The reasons for the long time between visits are summarized in a familiar adage: "If it ain't broke, don't fix it." Robins and his colleagues rarely get any complaints about Decker Brook, which first comes into view in a boggy field near the intersection of Route 38A and Church Road, about 4 miles north of Moravia.

The brook is barely 5 feet across at that point, but it picks up the water from several small tributaries in the next 2 miles and then passes under a bridge on Jugg Road, just west of the hamlet of Wilson Corners. You can and should park near the culvert-style bridge, which has an 8-foot-deep plunge pool and is capable of holding some large trout. Upstream and down from this span, the state has public fishing rights on 2.9 miles of streambank. You can download a map of Decker Brook from the DEC website, and polite inquiries may get you additional opportunities on private property located along this stream.

While I have not closely analyzed the mayflies and other components of Decker Brook (or Dresserville), I have done enough posthumous stomach examinations and turned over enough rocks, mostly in April and early May, to feel confident in saying that in addition to night crawlers and black dace minnows, local trout relish cranefly larvae and assorted case-maker caddisflies. But I have taken some trout in Decker Brook that somehow managed to stuff three or four crayfish in their gullets simultaneously, and I've also done autopsies that revealed an obvious taste for large tadpoles and small frogs. These fish are opportunistic feeders. Decker Brook, above and below the Jugg Road crossing, has a churning mix of pools that changes significantly during extended runoff periods. When Mother Nature completes her annual stream makeover, the net effect can be anything from wanton destruction to sheer artistry—unless beavers are involved.

Old Chisel-Tooth's dams may give you a year or two of good fishing, but in the long run the stick-and-mud engineering projects add up to warming water, silt smothering of spawning beds, and other negatives. Fortunately trappers have done a good job of controlling beaver populations in Decker Brook.

My biggest trout from Decker was a 16-inch brown. I would not recommend this brook to anyone seeking a trophy, but it does hold good numbers of trout, including some native brookies in its headwaters.

DUTCH HOLLOW BROOK

RATING: ★★ (2 stars)
NOTEWORTHY: May be on the comeback trail.
BEST TIME TO FISH: April, during the rainbow run.

A good friend has been mourning the decline of his pet trout stream for at least 20 years. Fred's grief, although persistent, may be slightly premature, for the corpse of Dutch Hollow Brook appears to be reanimating.

The Hollow, a tributary of Owasco Lake, has a modest year-round population of brown trout plus a rainbow spawning run in the spring. It used to have a strong following among Auburn-area trout fishers, but in recent years only a few diehards have fished it.

The best fishing for spawning 'bows, such as it is, will be found between the creek mouth at Burtis Point (about 4 miles south of Auburn, on the east shore of the lake) upstream to the crossing at Rowe Road. Often as not, the bigger browns and rainbows will occupy the deep pools and riffles crossing the fairways of the Dutch Hollow Golf and Country Club, off North Road. Club members have cheerfully tolerated trout fishermen in the past, but few anglers have utilized that section of the stream lately. It just doesn't have the size or numbers of browns that it used to hold, and DEC biologists think they know why.

Dan Bishop, the natural resources supervisor at the DEC's Region 7 office, points to the walleyes that were stocked in Owasco for a decade, beginning in 1996. Like most mortals, Bishop likes to eat walleyes, but he is keenly aware that walleyes also like to eat fish—and do so at every opportunity. In Owasco Lake, one of the most dependable smorgasbords available to adult walleyes is the blended school of yellow perch, alewives, and juvenile rainbow trout that roams the shore near rain-swollen tributaries. Bishop was concerned about the decline in Owasco's rainbow trout population following the walleye plantings.

"We can have a good trout fishery or a good fishery for walleyes but Owasco Lake won't support both," Bishop said. While the walleye fans in the Auburn area were devoted to the tasty game fish, Bishop believed the majority of anglers fishing the lake preferred trout over walleyes, but just to make sure he commissioned a scientific survey. The people who responded to the DEC questionnaire on the issue favored trout over walleyes by a margin of approximately two to one, and Bishop and his Bureau of Fisheries colleagues took the vote as an affirmation of their decision to cease walleye stocking in the lake until further notice.

Time will tell whether the pro-trout stand has a major impact on Dutch Hollow, but other issues are also in play. The brook's upper reaches, located along the winding Route 38 in the town of Niles, are subject to intermittent colonization by beavers and occasional leaching of agricultural fertilizers from nearby crop fields. None of these things is kind to the 8- to 10-inch wild browns that are commonly encountered by fishermen, but the considerably larger brownies that live in or near the golf course stretch are probably more threatened by the recurring dry spells that have reduced the brook to a bony trickle during recent summers. Despite these ongoing issues, DEC biologists remain confident that reduced predation by walleyes will substantially increase the number of rainbows and browns in the watershed. Better fishing is bound to follow, they say.

If the experts are right, perhaps my friend Fred will soon be doing less complaining and more fishing on his favorite Cayuga County stream.

Meanwhile, trout lovers recently got good news about Dutch Hollow as the result of two ongoing DEC initiatives, namely, trout stocking quotas and the acquisition of public fishing rights on selected streams.

First, state officials told members of the Region 7 Conservation League that they had approved, until further notice, increased stocking quotas for the Dutch Hollow watershed. Starting in 2015, the stream will be seeded annually with at least 10,000 juvenile rainbows, DEC representatives announced. To get that expanded stocking effort off to a fast start, state fisheries workers beat the quota by releasing more than 13,500 surplus rainbows in Dutch Hollow.

BEAR SWAMP CREEK

RATING: ★★ (2 stars)
NOTEWORTHY: Elusive native brookies.
BEST TIME TO FISH: Immediately after a good gully-washer.

It has been said that if wishes were horses, beggars would ride. Oh, how often I have wished for better access to Bear Swamp Creek! This meandering stream, which begins near Iowa Road in the town of Sempronius, flows north through a boggy gauntlet of beaver dams, muck, and alders before taking a spectacular series of cliff dives and finally gliding into Skaneateles Lake at Carpenter's Point.

Bear Swamp Creek has a population of native brook trout—some of them more than 12 inches long. The knowledge of those pretty fish has caused me and many others before me to spend long, lonely nights poring over aerial photos and topographic maps in search of Bear Swamp's secrets. Virtually all of those tortured efforts were a complete waste of time.

As far as I have been able to deduce, the 3,600-acre state forest that nearly surrounds the creek corridor has no secret trails to connect parking spots to flowing water. There may be a pathway from a state trailhead or from private lands, but I have never found a shortcut of any value, despite plenty of searching. The vegetation along the creek is so thick that it is likely many Bear Swamp brookies live out their lives without ever seeing a baited hook.

These fish do encounter plenty of nonhuman predators, however. Conspicuous among them are great blue herons, mink, and river otters. All three species eat trout at every opportunity, but they can't hold the proverbial candle to Brother Beaver in the trout-killing department. In the short term, beavers build dams that block trout movement. Long term, that impounded water warms up and fills with sediment that suffocates aquatic insects and juvenile trout even before they can hatch. It's a lose–lose situation for trout and trout fishermen alike.

Beavers have prospered in Bear Swamp for decades, but fur trappers lately have done their best to turn that situation around. The next time you see a trapper, thank him or her for their service to our country.

The natives in Bear Swamp Creek are seldom very active unless the water is muddied by heavy rain. Even on those rare occasions, you can count on catching 15 or 20 chubs for every brook trout that takes your worm or other bait. It is a humbling experience.

One possible way to get more fish for your trouble is to launch a canoe or a personal pontoon boat at the crossing at Hartnett Road, which is behind the Colonial Lodge restaurant, on Route 41A between Iowa Road and Curtain Road. Be extremely careful, as this is an unimproved and unofficial launch site. Once in the water, you can paddle south for 100 yards or so to a large beaver dam. The area near the dam is about 8 to 10 feet deep and is reputed to hold some nice natives.

NORTH BROOK

RATING: ★★ (2 stars)
NOTEWORTHY: Light pressure on holdover browns.
BEST TIME TO FISH: Late April and May.

If someone you know swears that North Brook holds some large brown trout, he's not telling "fish stories." The Auburn-area stream gives up more 15-inchers than the average Central New York fishing holes. However, such trout are runts compared with some of the whoppers that used to call North Brook home.

Mike DeTomaso of Camillus, who runs the White River fly-fishing shop in Auburn's Bass Pro store, lowers his voice just a bit when he talks about the old days on the stream.

"You know, North Brook has a reputation for big browns, but when I was a kid, a big one there was really big," he said. "I'm talking about browns that weighed up to 5 pounds or so. You don't hear about browns like that anymore but just the fact the stream once had fish so large tells me North Brook has a lot of potential."

On the other hand, maybe this creek—which flows between Auburn and Weedsport—still holds a few trophy-size browns. The DEC hasn't conducted a serious sampling of the stream since 1992, and heavy posting limits opportunities for wandering anglers to explore the brook. DeTomaso noted the creek has only a couple of short stretches that have public fishing signs along the banks. The dense woods that keep much of the brook in the shade can be discouraging to fly fishers, too.

"It doesn't have much in the way of fly hatches, either, but there are enough caddis to get the trout feeding on the surface sometimes," DeTomaso concluded.

North Brook is 10 to 20 feet across at most locations, but it is a tiny stream at its beginnings near Soule Cemetery, which is on Old Seneca Turnpike just east of Auburn. It gets gradually larger as it slips under Route 34 and flows northwest through the hamlet of Throop. The brook runs within sight of Centerport Road, and cuts through the Meadow Brook golf course near Weedsport. Some of the deep holes on the course look very promising to me, but I have not yet sought permission to fish that stretch.

The creek joins with the Seneca River just outside of North Weedsport.

Public fishing rights are secured along a small section of Mills Road, which is about 2 miles south of the golf course; and Potter Road, located just west of the hamlet of Throop. Although it's very brushy, DeTomaso also likes a quarter-mile piece of the brook that's posted BY PERMISSION ONLY. It's off High Bridge Road, which links Route 34 and Centerport Road about a mile south of Mill Road.

More Cayuga County Trout Streams

In addition to aforementioned waters, Cayuga County has several other streams that have limited numbers of trout or marginal habitat but are still capable of producing some nice catches now and then. I'd include **Salmon Creek**—or part of it, anyway—in this motley grouping. I'm writing here about the section of the creek above the scenic waterfall in Ludlowville. The pool at the base of that beautiful cataract probably gets as much fishing pressure in April as the rest of the creek during the entire fishing season. That discrepancy is not owing to poor fishing above the falls, but rather to the poor access. Only a fraction of a mile in the upper part of the creek and its two branches is labeled public fishing. Whether you get your chance or not depends on your diplomatic skills as you knock on farmhouse doors.

Many of the rural property owners living along the main stream and east and west branches do give polite strangers the go-ahead to fish on their land, but it behooves anglers to get busy early in the season. After mid-May, some stretches of the creek that looked good on opening day will have dried up between pools. However, if those pools are deep and shaded, their residents may hold over from one year to the next. State stockings amount to only 2,000 or so trout over more than 30 miles of water, but some of those trout grow old without seeing their first streamer fly or stickbait.

From the hamlet of Genoa north to Scipio, Big Salmon Creek (aka the east fork) is crossed by six bridges, and these would be good spots to test your ability to win friends and influence people. The Little Salmon is crossed by seven bridges between Route 90 east of King Ferry and Poplar Ridge Road, where the creek is small enough to step over in some places.

Another well-known stream is **Hemlock Creek**, a tributary of Owasco Inlet that is a spawning ground for some Owasco Lake rainbows. It is the very spot where I caught my biggest Central New York trout, a mammoth rainbow that weighed 10½ pounds and measured 28¼ inches from the tip of its snout to the point of its tail.

Hemlock flows into Owasco Inlet in the village of Locke. While it seldom produces the giant rainbows of yesteryear, it remains a good opening-day spot. Although many fishermen flock to the 10- to 15-foot-wide creek early in the trout season, it is basically deserted by May 1. Few anglers seem to know that Hemlock Creek, like the inlet, has a decent population of wild browns, including some in the 15- to 18-inch range.

Pine Hollow Brook is a tributary of Hemlock Creek off Route 90 that provides some nice spawning sites for the rainbows that migrate upstream in the spring. Although the DEC lists it as a trout stream, it is heavily posted and gets virtually no fishing pressure except perhaps from local property owners.

Ed Dunn of Marcellus fishes in Hemlock Creek, Cayuga County.

Another stream which has very limited access and an air of mystery about it is **Cold Spring Brook**, the major tributary of North Brook. The DEC's Jeff Robins says Cold Spring is reputed to hold wild brook trout, but verifying its fishiness depends mainly on word-of-mouth testimony, because the stream has no public access. You will need permission to check out this small, spring-fed brook, which takes a course slightly westward of the one carved by North Brook. The two streams link up in Weedsport.

Weedsport has one other trout water, although the DEC does not list it as such: **Putnam Brook**, a 10- to 20-foot-wide, swift-running stream that crosses under Route 31 just south of the Weedsport High School campus. In years when spring rains are heavy, Putnam is capable of producing some nice wild browns and rainbows, ranging up to 16 or 17 inches long.

MADISON COUNTY

I like *our* Madison County better than the one inhabited by Meryl Streep and Clint Eastwood in a certain oldie-but-goodie chick flick because our county has more trout than theirs. And don't bother to tell me about all those made-for-Hollywood bridges, unless you know which ones, if any, were the hiding places of big brown trout. As I remember the movie, it paid more attention to bathtubs than bridges. Eastwood's character liked to photograph bridges, but not as much as he enjoyed consoling lonely housewives. I'd be willing to bet that the majority of fishermen who were dragged along to the movie by their wives or girlfriends spent more time checking their watches and getting popcorn at the concession stand than gawking at rural bridges.

Central New York's genuine Madison County has some fine bridges of its own, but they are better at getting cars and trucks safely across swollen streams than posing for photo spreads on sunny summer days. For example, make yourself an appointment to personally inspect the dozen or so bridges that span Chittenango Creek between the villages of Cazenovia and Chittenango. Don't forget your fishing rod!

Milt Franson of Pompey explores a tiny Madison County trout stream.

CHITTENANGO CREEK

RATING: ★★★★★ (5 stars)

NOTEWORTHY: Name your favorite water type—pools, pockets, riffles, runs—and this stream has it in abundance.

BEST TIME TO FISH: First week of May if you don't mind crowds, or the last week of January if you are a rugged individualist.

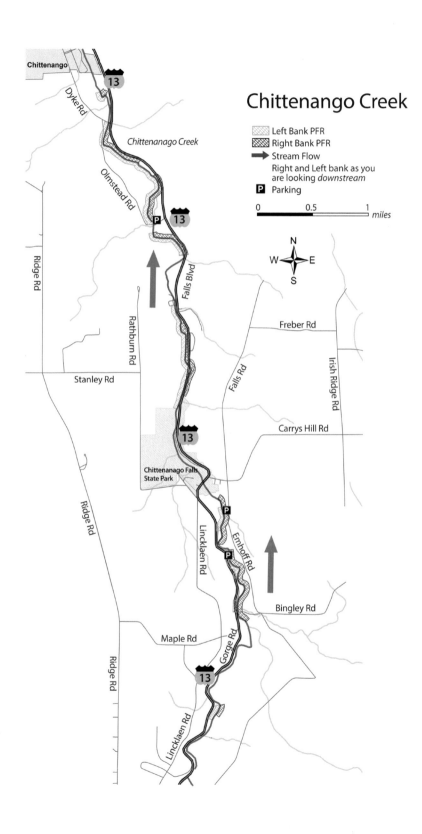

Chittenango Creek

- ▦ Left Bank PFR
- ▨ Right Bank PFR
- ➡ Stream Flow
- Right and Left bank as you are looking *downstream*
- 🅿 Parking

0   0.5   1 *miles*

N W E S

Chittenango

Dyke Rd

13

Chittenanago Creek

Olmstead Rd

🅿 13

Ridge Rd

Rathburn Rd

Falls Blvd

Freber Rd

Falls Rd

Irish Ridge Rd

Stanley Rd

Carrys Hill Rd

13

Chittenango Falls State Park

🅿

Lincklaen Rd

Emhoff Rd

🅿

Bingley Rd

Ridge Rd

Maple Rd

Gorge Rd

13

Lincklaen Rd

Just how good is Chittenango Creek? For starters, the DEC is so sanguine about its robust health and long-term prospects that it governs the stream with some of the most liberal regulations in the state. From U.S. Route 20 in the swanky Madison County village of Cazenovia north to the Conrail track in the Onondaga County town of Manlius, the creek is open to fishing all year, with a daily limit of five trout. Two of the five can be longer than 12 inches, and you may use bait, lure, or fly to catch them. Anglers must watch for one major exception to these warm and fuzzy rules. Namely, from a conspicuous sign near the intersection of Route 13 and Olmstead Road downstream (north) to another special-regulations marker at the south end of the village of Chittenango, the stream is ruled by catch-and-release apostles, all year. Only flies and artificial lures are allowed there. However, DEC biologists say there does not seem to be much of a difference in trout biomass or other scientific measurements between the no-kill area and other prime sections of the creek. Generous stockings by state hatchery crews—about 15,000 browns annually, with around 2,000 chunky two-year-olds included—help keep the creek's reputation nice and shiny. Simply put, the entire stream is loaded.

Chittenango gets its start as a converging bunch of brooks, just south of Route 20. One by one these boggy, heavily vegetated streams go with the flow until the main stem has attained an average width of about 25

Jake DeCapio of Marcellus fishes for winter trout in Chittenango Creek.

feet. Some of the larger pools in this stretch are between 3 and 5 feet deep. And by the time the creek glides into the village of Chittenango it will be at least half again as wide and average about 6 to 12 inches deeper than it was in the vicinity of Route 20. Some pools in the last mile or so between "Caz" and Chittenango are 5 or 6 feet deep.

Thanks to the influx of refreshing spring seeps and the occasional summer storm, the pampered trout in this creek enjoy some of the best all-round cold-water habitat in the entire central region of the state. Temperatures are extremely trout-friendly, with midsummer readings rarely topping the 70-degree barrier that, once broken, leaves trout lethargic and even gasping for oxygen.

Trout in Chittenango Creek are quite wary when the water gets low, but the survival of resident or stocked trout has never been seriously threatened by summer temperatures or oxygen levels. Like Nine Mile Creek in Onondaga County and Oriskany Creek in Madison and Oneida Counties, Chittenango Creek has superb water quality year-round. Brown trout dominate in this stream, as they do in most other eastern waters, but some sections of Chittenango are home to brook trout. Among the few haunts that harbor wild natives, probably the most productive location is in the Nelson Swamp, a mile or two southeast of Cazenovia. Should you hit the state-owned swamp with a can of crawlers immediately after a drenching rain, you might catch a couple of brookies in the 9- or 10-inch range, along with the sleek, butter-colored brown trout that share space with natives in this rugged place. Just consider this helpful hint before you give it a try: Do your stretching exercises. If you weren't troubled by a sore back before entering the Nelson Swamp, you are bound to have a knot between your shoulder blades when you finally emerge, stiff and bone-tired. The aches and pains are the result of walking bent over, and occasionally stumbling through some nearly impenetrable cover. Unless you are short enough to squeeze beneath cedar limbs and other natural obstacles that most adults behold with shivers of fear, you will have to take an awful thrashing from the streamside alders.

Fortunately for fogies like me, the Nelson Swamp is far from the only place in Chittenango Creek to wet a line. Most of the creekbank is fairly easy to prowl, and the stream itself is not at all daunting to wade, presuming it is flowing at normal levels. Although the mostly slow-moving currents south of Route 20 can be very enjoyable to fish, the real jewels of the creek are found in the bouncy pocket water that begins just downstream from the Cazenovia sewage treatment facility. This area can be subdivided, for the reader's sake, into "the fast water above the falls" and "the fast water below the falls." Brown trout weighing from ½ to 1½ pounds, and measuring 12 to 15 inches, are quite common in both pocket-water stretches. Many of these muscular trout were stocked as hatchery two-year-olds, but Chittenango Creek is quite capable of producing and sheltering wild browns of that size, too. The slick bottom in the gorge below the state park falls makes it easy for anglers to lose their balance in midstream.

Frequent fishers of these swift currents rely on hip boots or waders with boot feet and soles of old-fashioned felt or screw-in metal spikes. Invariably, they also lean hard on a metal or wooden wading stick whether they are crossing the stream or simply shifting their position in the current.

I have had much good fortune drifting Cased Caddis and Beadhead Nymphs in assorted colors above and below the falls, and you, too, should fish the pocket water diligently. The prettiest pool on the entire creek, however, is the one at the base of the state park cataract, so it figures that a small critter that clings to survival in that very spot is big enough in environmental protection circles to keep us anglers several double hauls away from it. The beast I refer to is the amber ovate snail, which seems bound for extinction. Many researchers have concluded that the snail is in this place and nowhere else. Hence it is protected, and we anglers can merely guess at the proportions of the trout that swim in the foam beneath the falls.

Except for the off-limits "Snail Hole," most of Chittenango Creek is well worth fishing, anytime. It is particularly enticing during the spring hatches—Hendricksons, sulfurs, green drakes, and others—and again in September when the slate drakes (*Isonychia bicolor*) emerge throughout the stream. Its trout are surprisingly active in the winter months. Thanks to the relatively easy regulations mentioned earlier, a period of mild weather in January or February can turn the trout on. I will never forget, among other Chittenango trout, the matched set of 17-inch browns I caught and released one winter afternoon near the "Stinking Springs." That's what I call the sulfurous little ditch located about halfway between the state park and the village of Chittenango. Those two fish happened to be the largest browns I have ever taken while fishing the creek.

There are many more holes that support 2- to 4-pound trout in Chittenango Creek, but don't expect anything over 20 or 21 inches, no matter how skilled or lucky you happen to be. Chittenango Creek has some hog trout, and its ecosystem seems to pump out one healthy year-class of trout after another, and the end result is a fishery full of fish—one-, two-, three-, four-, and five-year-olds that typically measure about 6, 9, 12, 14, and 16 inches or thereabouts. What's wrong with that? Nothing, in my opinion.

Be sure to take note of special regulations such as these on Chittenango Creek.

Fine trout fishing is available in Chittenango Creek from its head-waters north almost to Bridgeport, where it empties into Oneida Lake. The last couple of miles are closed to angling until the season for walleyes opens on the first Saturday in May. Fishermen who are dying to take a crack at post-spawn walleyes can get the fix they're looking for by simply walking the banks and peering through sunglasses with polarized lenses into the lower end of Scriba Creek. The creek runs through the Constantia hatchery, and the walleyes you see there in late March and April will be stripped of their eggs, if females; the males can count on being forced to contribute their milt to the reproductive process. While Chittenango Creek is not nearly as critical to the state walleye program as is Scriba Creek, it has better fishing, and every so often some unsuspecting trout lover is shocked when a nice walleye somehow becomes attached to his monofilament line or leader.

Such was the case a few years back when a heavy fish inhaled my buck-tail as I swung it through a riffle upstream of Chittenango. The lunker pattern was a dace imitation, weighted with a few wraps of lead wire and sporting a Muddler-like deer-hair head and a trailing strip of white rabbit fur. The walleye it attracted measured 19 inches, and made a delicious supper the following evening.

You ought not forget the winter season on Chittenango. It can be surprisingly pleasant and productive, provided the weather in the Syracuse area has been benign for a day or two.

Kid Corbett fishes for late winter trout in Chittenago Creek.

CHENANGO CANAL

RATING: ★★★ (3 stars)
NOTEWORTHY: The canal's degree of difficulty is legendary.
BEST TIME TO FISH: Dusk in early June, when the *varia* drakes emerge.

There was a time when I must have been a glutton for punishment. That's a self-analysis I conducted one summer, and I have not sought the assistance of a professional shrink in this matter. Rather, I came to this conclusion on my own one day when I was waist-deep in the Chenango Canal and trying to remember the last time I had actually caught a fish there. I wanted desperately to take a big, fat brown in the canal, and, worse, to accomplish that goal with a dry fly on my tippet. As usual, the trout didn't seem to give a damn about my yearnings. At that point, I was in my early 30s and had been trying to make it happen for 10 years. The obstacles to my success were the same as always. First, the resident browns finned lazily on the edges of conflicting currents, where drag-free presentations were to die for. Second, it was almost impossible to sneak along the steep, vegetation-covered old towpath adjacent to the canal without spooking the fish, one or two at a time; and, finally, if you were to hook a trout, how could you ever hope to land it?

My rate of failure, as far back as I could remember, was just about perfect.

Finally, when my rod time on the 15- to 25-feet-wide stream was down to one or two quick stops a year, the solution came to me. I sat quietly in the thick grass along the bank until several fish were rising. Then I quietly waded out to midstream, well above the feeding stations chosen by my targeted trout. After selecting a fly pattern that looked about right, I just stood there for a good 20 minutes. Just as I had thought, the trout resumed their suppers, one by one. I picked out a decent fish that was sipping at the surface and facing toward me. Knowing I was out of that brown's field of vision, I cast to a spot on the water about 10 feet short of my nemesis. Then I pulled a few yards of fly line from the reel and shook the rod from side to side, forming drag-resistant S-curves on the water. As the loose line approached the trout, my fly disappeared in a subtle dimple. It was not even necessary to set the hook, for the trout, which turned out to be a 12-incher, virtually inhaled the cream-colored little floater.

You can hardly imagine how good that ordinary trout made me feel, for like most of the browns in the Chenango Canal, this one was wary of danger and inclined to burrow deep into thick weeds at the slightest indication that anything might be going wrong in its little patch of water.

Oddly, I had used a slight variation of that trick on other streams for many years but never tried it on the canal because I assumed its trout were just too wise.

Well, trout fishers should never make assumptions, especially about beguiling tricky waterways such as the Chenango Canal.

A 19th-century construction project designed to get extra water to the much larger Erie Canal, the Chenango Canal these days looks like a weedy, straight-as-a-string ditch. No, it doesn't just *look* like a ditch, it *is* a ditch, as any angler it fools is bound to declare.

For anyone who flexes a fly rod now and then ought to be able to haul a fish from a 20-foot-wide ditch, right? I always thought so until I made my first visit to the canal. A fishing pal mentioned the place to me back in the early 1970s and, after getting some background from Les Wedge, who was the top trout biologist on the DEC's Region 7 staff in those days, I confidently set off for the canal one Saturday. Upon arrival, I could not believe my eyes. Trout, many of them in the 2-pound category, were everywhere. Some small mayflies were hatching, and I remember the stylish swirls the big browns made when they grabbed those floating insects. I trembled as I selected a fly and began to fish my way along Canal Road between Bouckville and Solsville. My first cast, delivered from the sloping, brush-covered south bank, put the target fish down, instantly. It burrowed beneath the clumps of aquatic vegetation and stayed there for at least 10 minutes, when I reluctantly moved upstream. I spotted another trout, a good 16 inches, which treated me as rudely as the first one had. The third one went through the same drill, and so did fish number four. This was a humiliating experience, believe me, but most of the members of our angling fellowship need a dose of humiliation now and then.

The canal begins, these days, about 5 miles east of Morrisville. It is the outlet of lower Leland Pond, which is connected to upper Leland by a short channel under Route 26. The canal makes a gradual turn north and then flows slowly through Bouckville, the Madison County village that hosts a huge antiques show every summer. The canal spills over a low dam into Oriskany Creek, about 2 miles from Bouckville and ¼ mile from Solsville. In between those two crossroads, along Canal Road, is an unusual stream that holds the wariest trout I have ever encountered in New York.

Whether you manage to catch any of the canal residents, you will at least enjoy trying to match the sometimes heavy hatches of mayflies that are part of the local charm. The most dependable of those emergences include the Hendricksons in early May, the yellow drakes (*Ephemera varia*) in early June, and the swarming little Tricos that appear daily, often in midmorning, in July and August.

Fine leaders and accurate casting will be a step in the right direction on the canal, but don't forget to bring your sense of humor when you tackle this fascinating stream.

ORISKANY CREEK

RATING: ★★★★★ (5 stars)
NOTEWORTHY: Madison County's share of this creek needs no stocking.
BEST TIME TO FISH: After a summer rain muddies the water just a bit.

My list of Central New York streams to fish following a heavy summer rain—as opposed to a storm of the same volume in April, May, or June—is a short one, consisting of Mill Creek in Steuben County, Factory Brook in Cortland County, Nine Mile Creek in Onondaga County, and Chittenango Creek and Oriskany Creek, which are both partly in Madison County.

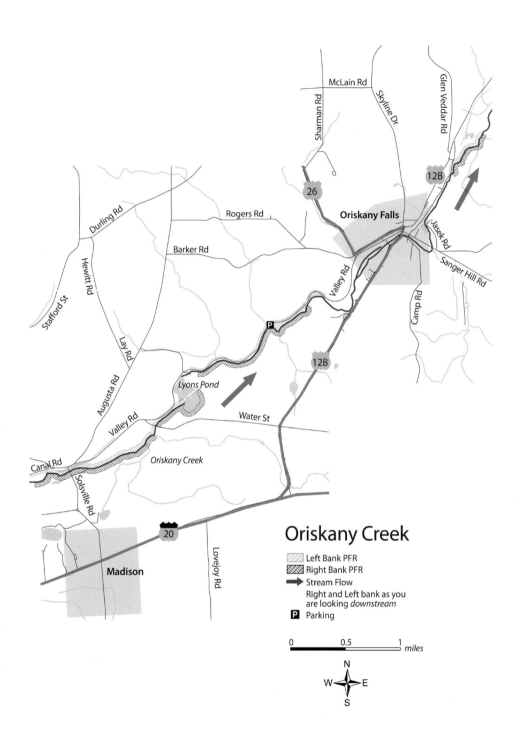

McLain Rd

Sharman Rd

Skyline Dr

Glen Veddar Rd

Rogers Rd

26

Oriskany Falls

12B

Jasek Rd

Durling Rd

Barker Rd

Sanger Hill Rd

Hewitt Rd

Stafford St

Valley Rd

Lay Rd

Camp Rd

P

Augusta Rd

12B

Lyons Pond

Water St

Valley Rd

Canal Rd

Oriskany Creek

Solsville Rd

20

Lovejoy Rd

Madison

Oriskany Creek

Left Bank PFR

Right Bank PFR

Stream Flow

Right and Left bank as you are looking *downstream*

P Parking

0   0.5   1 miles

N
W — E
S

These five waters stand out from the pack because of their dependably cold summer water temperatures. Many fine streams get an invigorating jolt of cold water when a spring gully-washer stirs their currents, but the creeks mentioned here have just what the fish doctor ordered, pretty much year-round. Tuck a stream thermometer in your shirt pocket the next time you fish one of these waters during the summer months and you likely will notice that the water temperature is in the comfortable 60s. Trout survival rates in such streams are much better than the norm, and the wild browns that live in Oriskany Creek usually grow up to be healthy, wealthy, and wise. They have a diet rich in mayflies and crayfish, among other aquatic organisms, and in the summer that main plate is supplemented with frequent snacks—grasshoppers, ants, and other terrestrial insects—that fall onto the water when gusty winds shake nearby tree limbs.

Only about 2 miles of Oriskany Creek lie within Madison County. That stretch includes the mouth of the Chenango Canal and extends to the Oneida County border, which is just south of Oriskany Falls. None of this water is stocked and none of it needs to be. It is simply crammed with gorgeous browns. Most are 6 to 10 inches long but skilled nymph and dry-fly fishers will catch fish that are a bit bigger than that, say, up to 14 inches or so. My favorite hatch in this area, by far, is the late-May and early-June emergence of the *Ephemerella dorothea*, commonly called

Paul McNeilly, fishing in the Solsville Dam pool on Oriskany Creek.

the pale evening dun. These size 16 or 18 duns, with gray wings and plump, pale-yellow abdomens, come off the water in impressive numbers just before sunset. Their imitations, if fished with little or no drag, draw eager strikes.

Downstream from Oriskany Falls (where a handicapped-accessible fishing platform offers those who use wheelchairs or walkers an unusually good chance of hooking a wild brown or two), the creek gradually widens from an average of 15 feet to as much as 40 feet across. Several bridges offer access between Oriskany Falls and Clinton, but watch out for NO TRESPASSING signs. The water with the most enticing public fishing opportunities will be found upstream and down from the DEC parking area off Route 12B, on the outskirts of Clinton. Pay special heed to the deep runs and pools upstream from the bridge, but allow plenty of time get back to your car, as you may cross the stream several times.

Although the trout population is not as dense below Clinton as it is upstream, the odds of getting a really nice brown on your line increase as Oriskany Creek flows northeast through Kirkland, Clark Mills, and Coleman Mills before winding up in the Mohawk River.

EAST BRANCH TIOUGHNIOGA CREEK

RATING: ★★ (2 stars)
NOTEWORTHY: Sometimes it pays to ask.
BEST TIME TO FISH: Rainy days or Sundays.

If you wanted to drive in circles, up and down steep and dusty roads, past barnyards festooned with POSTED signs and houses patrolled by big, barking dogs, you could vow to fish only public water or even give up on trout fishing altogether. On the other hand, you could stop the car, take a deep breath, and knock on the closest door.

You never know what friendly face might say yes to your request to wet a line on that pretty stream you just eyeballed from the bridge. Take southern Madison County, for instance. I had that feeling of déjà vu as I drove slowly down a busy road south from New Woodstock and then east out of DeRuyter. The name on the mailbox clinched it. I won't repeat it here; suffice to say I remembered this fellow as a frequent source for story material back in the day when I covered the agribusiness beat for the *Syracuse Herald-Journal*. I had visited his farm only once before, but I remembered his easygoing temperament and, just as clearly, the swift stream that slipped under a bridge 100 yards or so from his milking parlor. Luckily he remembered me, too, and in a positive way, at that. After two or three minutes of small talk, he was showing me where to park and apologizing for not having the time to join me on the water.

In a short while I confirmed my first impression that the East Branch of Tioughnioga Creek was a pretty good trout stream, and it fished well over the next couple of hours even though its bed was half dry after a long heat wave. A small brook trout and two nice browns came to net that morning, and I have become acquainted with a few more trout during subsequent trips to the stream, which joins its sister branch a mile or so north of Cuyler.

The East Branch is a spate stream that can rise and fall dramatically depending on major storm systems and seasonal runoff. Scouring of the gravel and sand bottom can change pool contours from one year to the next and also has an adverse impact on mayfly populations. Its trout are therefore opportunistic feeders, and consistent action depends on your ability to move stealthily and present a bait or lure in a natural manner more than on any knack for hatch-matching. Of course, this is typical of small streams, and the lessons learned on the 10-foot-wide East Branch have universal value.

To find the East Branch, drive south on Route 13 from Cazenovia through New Woodstock and take the same road to De Ruyter. In that hamlet, take a left onto County Route 58. As you head east, you will see stream crossings at Wood Road, Dublin Road, and finally on Route 58 itself, just before its intersection with Carpenter Road.

CHENANGO RIVER

RATING: ★★ (2 stars)
NOTEWORTHY: Mainly put-and-take but capable of big surprises.
BEST TIME TO FISH: Before the dog days of summer.

I think of the Chenango River as more of a walleye, pike, and bass fishery than one tailor-made for serious trout anglers. It's almost two streams in one. The upper part of the river, from Morrisville south to Eaton and Randallsville, is generously stocked by the DEC hatchery system. The fish dispersals include about 3,900 brown trout, among them 350 or so two-year-old browns. Along with the stockers, area anglers can target wild browns in the section of the river between Route 20 and Eaton. Tributaries that join the river on its southeasterly journey are also worth serious investigation during an April shower or a spring mayfly hatch. The upper river has a pretty good Hendrickson mayfly hatch starting about May 1.

The bottom half of the Chenango, in contrast, really is not much of a trout stream. It is, however, a place where a lucky sportsman—or a very wily angler, take your pick—might be able to catch a monster brown, if he sticks to it. Before drawing the conclusion that we blankety-blank outdoors writers can't make up our minds about anything, let me briefly explain the nature of the Chenango River and wide, valley streams like it. The Chenango, the Tioughnioga River near Cortland, and the last few miles of the Otselic River before it flows into the Whitney Point Reservoir seldom have the habitat and water temperatures to which wild trout are accustomed. Yet a few trout that swim into these surroundings not only survive, but thrive.

The browns that make a good living in the lower Chenango do so by settling in water that is marginally cool enough to support trout in the summer. Suitable spots do not accommodate many trout but may harbor one or several whoppers. The key is having just enough cover for small browns to grow into big browns before they can be ambushed or chased down by pike or other predators. Such spots are reasonably common in the Norwich-area section of the Chenango. On a couple of occasions, friends of mine have landed 4- to 5-pound browns in this stretch, near the local high school off Hale Street. These fellows were wading and bank fishing with live bait, but I suspect they could catch the big boys on a fairly frequent basis if they chucked minnow-mimicking stickbaits into river pools from a canoe. The old Rogers Nature Center, off Route 12 in Sherburne, is a convenient place to start a float, and any of several pull-offs between there and Norwich will serve as a takeout.

If you're not much of a float-tripper, hunt for big browns in the deep pools between Randallsville and Sherburne. What lures? A diving or suspending Rapala with a black-and-silver finish will work anywhere, providing your "anywhere" is shrouded by clouds or a crescent moon. Big browns feed mainly at night, but they often throw caution to the winds when rising water sends them a fresh food supply.

OTSELIC RIVER

RATING: ★★★ (3 stars)
NOTEWORTHY: A state fish hatchery sits on the banks of the Otselic.
BEST TIME TO FISH: Before the summer heat.

I confess, I haven't fished the Otselic River nearly as much as I should have over the years. That is mostly because so much other good trout water flows between Point A and Point B—my home and that relatively distant river. If you think that's a pretty lame excuse, I challenge you to simply make a list of the many intriguing spots I must hurry past to make an early fishing date in rural Madison, Chenango, Cortland, or Broome County, which all have a share of the Otselic. Before I get anywhere near the Otselic, I must resolve to sneak past streams like my home water, Nine Mile Creek; Chittenango Creek; Fabius Brook; and many others that beckon to wandering anglers.

Late summer on the Otselic River.

Sometimes the journey will be well worth the effort. The Otselic, more than 30 miles long and fed by dozens of small tributaries, tends to become very roily after a drenching rain and does not clear quickly, either. In the worst-case scenario—a bank-gouging flood—Otselic pools may be wiped out or reconstructed by the unpredictable flows.

What the Otselic sportsman hopes for is rain of happy medium magnitude. Such a storm will leave the river up an inch or two and tinted gray rather a muddy brown. It will also clear up within a day or so, which means that long round trip to the Otselic and home must not be postponed when conditions are right.

The first time I fished the Otselic, after a long ride in Jake DeCapio's cramped sports car, I unlimbered by catching just two trout, but they were

Fishing the marginal trout water, or transition zones, can pay off with good early-season catches (Otselic River).

definitely quality fish. One was a brown of 17 inches and the other a native brook trout exactly 12 inches on my measuring tape. Who would ever consider an outing that resulted in the capture of two such fish to be "slow" or "disappointing"?

DeCapio has caught 20-inch browns in the Otselic, mainly between Georgetown and Cincinnatus, along Route 26. This part of the river flows through the southeast corner of Cortland County, and is accessible via numerous road crossings. Yet it is seldom fished after mid-May, which means it holds plenty of trout waiting for those few anglers willing to make a long drive through some of New York's most hilly farm country.

Jake DeCapio with a nice Otselic River brown.

While the Otselic holds plenty of wild browns and brook trout upstream from the hatchery and at spring-infused runs and riffles through most of its length, state hatcheries augment those fish with plantings of about 10,900 browns in the Cortland County section of the river and 3,500 more browns in the Chenango County part. Of the more than 14,400 stockers, approximately 1,600 were two-year-olds that measured about 13 inches each when they were turned loose.

SANGERFIELD RIVER

RATING: ★★ (2 stars)
NOTEWORTHY: Mainly stockers but big pools hide holdovers, too.
BEST TIME TO FISH: April and early May.

Some anglers look down their noses at put-and-take trout streams, and suggest it is a waste of money and effort for state hatcheries to stock such waters. On the surface, these naysayers have a point, for the currents in put-and-take streams are too warm or too something else to support many trout after mid-June. Critics of put-and-take waters would like to scratch them off the stocking schedule. If they got their way, state hatchery crews would be rerouted from put-and-takes to streams capable of supporting trout, wild or domestic, year-round.

These earnest folks have forgotten a couple of things. First, shutting off the free flow of hatchery trout to streams like the Sangerfield River in eastern Madison County would force more anglers to crowd fewer pools. Second, put-and-take trout fare better in some streams than others. Our neighbors to the south, in the Pennsylvania Commonwealth, have learned this through many years of experimenting with "Delayed Harvest" regulations. Stretches of rivers designated for Delayed Harvest are stocked fairly heavily, in most cases. Once stocked, they may not be creeled until mid-June. At that point, trout in Delayed Harvest waters are subject to general state trout regulations. The midseason switch gives anglers maximum bang for their bucks A trout stocked in Delayed Harvest waters can be caught and released multiple times, providing fun and excitement for more than one fisherman during the spring mayfly hatches. Then, once the Delayed Harvest period is over, and trout start to be stressed by warming water or other natural factors, anglers who wish to do so can remove a few fish for the frying pan.

The Sangerfield River, which winds through a seemingly endless series of sharp bends between the hamlet of Sangerfield in southeastern Oneida County and the village of Earlville in southern Madison County, would be a good candidate for a New York Delayed Harvest program. It is stocked with about 2,330 brown trout in April and early May, and about 200 of those browns are two-year-olds. Most of the stockers are removed by local anglers but, no matter what you've heard elsewhere, some last into June and there are always a few that hold over from one year to the next by finding safe hideouts in tributaries or spring holes. Some of the bigger ones likely hang out in the Ninemile Swamp, which is a stone's throw from Route 12 near the border between Madison and Oneida Counties.

More Madison County Trout Streams

Whether you like the convenience of well-stocked streams that flow within sight of busy highways or don't mind poring over topographic maps and knocking on doors to locate and gain access to remote creeks, Madison County has the kind of trout waters you crave. Besides the streams just reviewed, you might want to check out the following.

Beaver Creek, in the town of Brookfield, is aptly named after the furbearing animal whose well-placed dams keep much of the stream inundated. Between ponds it offers fair fishing for stocked and holdover brown trout. Route 99, also known as Beaver Creek Road, follows the creek from South Brookfield to the Oneida County border, a distance of about 5 miles through blocks of state forests and privately owned land.

A nice stream that has somewhat limited access is **Canaseraga Creek**, which crosses Routes 5 and 13 about 2 miles east of Chittenango. Like Chittenango Creek, Canaseraga eventually winds its way to Oneida Lake, near Lakeport. From its headwaters north almost to the lake, it has a healthy population of wild browns, some of which measure 14 inches or better. With no public fishing rights along its entire length, Canaseraga Creek is best explored by parking at obvious pull-offs that are not marked with NO TRESPASSING signs or, better yet, asking permission while wearing your friendliest smile. That Route 5 crossing east of Chitttenango is a good place to start.

East of Canaseraga are a couple of productive brown trout waters, **Canastota Creek** and **Clockville Creek**. Both streams flow under Cottons Road in the town of Lincoln. Canastota Creek, stocked with about 2,000 browns annually, processes slowly northward to the village of Canastota and a few miles later loses its identity in a complicated maze of irrigation ditches. Clockville Creek flows east from its namesake crossroads to join yet another brown trout stream, **Cowaselon Creek**, just east of Wampsville. Cowaselon is stocked with about 1,000 browns annually and has some wild brownies, too. Clockville, which is very brushy and less than 15 feet wide in most places, is not stocked but harbors wild browns and brookies.

The waters of Madison County also include **Munger Creek**, a tributary of Chittenango Creek, which merges with the larger stream north of Cazenovia at the intersection of Route 13 and Bingley Road; and **Blue Creek**, a small brown trout stream in the towns of Eaton and Stockbridge between Pratts Hollow and Munnsville. Finally, although they are generally difficult to access, **Bradley Brook** and **Kingsley Brook** in the town of Lebanon, and **Tallette Creek** in the town of Brookfield, are all brown trout streams of merit.

CORTLAND COUNTY

It was my good fortune—or my bad luck, depending on when I am reflecting upon the event—to plan and execute the New York State Outdoor Writers Association's annual Spring Safari in May 2012. The safari, in contrast with NYSOWA's fall conference, is basically a glorified fishing and hunting trip. Little or no official business is conducted during the spring outing, and the dozen or so writers and photographers who take part do their best to catch or kill whatever sort of fish and game for which our host county is famous. The 2012 conference was held in Cortland County, and most of us were after trout or turkeys. Now, if you have ever taken a fishing or hunting trip yourself, you know that, however meticulously we plan said junket, there is one thing we can't control. Yep, you guessed it—the weather.

Our spring and fall meetings always start with participants checking in at a hotel or cabin or whatever lodging has been made available, proceed with two full days of outdoor pursuits, and end with a Sunday-morning breakfast. When we finished our Thursday supper, the skies were an ominous gray. And when we clambered out of bed Friday morning, Cortland County was soaking wet. The turkey hunters simply dressed in rainproof camo and carried seat cushions to help them keep themselves warm and dry.

Those of us scheduled to do a little trout fishing had to make more significant adjustments. The streams that were skinny little trickles on Thursday were the color of hot chocolate with extra cream come Friday morning. We took one look at the creeks and rivers we had planned to fish and headed upstream until we found tributaries that were high but fishable. The fellows in my group didn't exactly slam the trout, but each of us caught one or more native brookies by focusing on plunge pools and culverts where fish might lie in ambush for the tidbits washed from the banks by pounding rains.

Equally important as those occasional rod-bends, my buddies and I were still in good spirits, and when the Cortland-area streams began to drop and clear that afternoon we were looking forward to Round Two.

Grinnel Road culvert pool, Cortland County.

The Saturday safari results were astounding. Instead of the spidery feeder brooks miles away from our hotel, we opted to fish nearby waters, which were still muddy but low enough to make clear the outlines of pools that were hard to distinguish a day earlier. Trout were hitting, hard, as if making up for the slim pickings associated with a dry spell. To my amazement, I caught and released a 22-inch brown trout, my largest ever in a Cortland County stream. A couple of hours later, Fulton writer Leon Archer netted another beauty. His 19-incher sideswiped a spinner no more than 50 yards upstream from the spot my fish called home. That evening, over steak dinners, several other writers fairly overflowed with praise for the local fishing.

It is pretty good, at that, which is why NYSOWA scheduled a return trip to Cortland County in October 2014, and why many other ardent anglers will want to explore it on their own.

FACTORY BROOK

RATING: ★★★★ (4 stars)
NOTEWORTHY: Big fish in a small stream.
BEST TIME TO FISH: During the sulfur mayfly hatch in early June or after any spring shower muddies the currents.

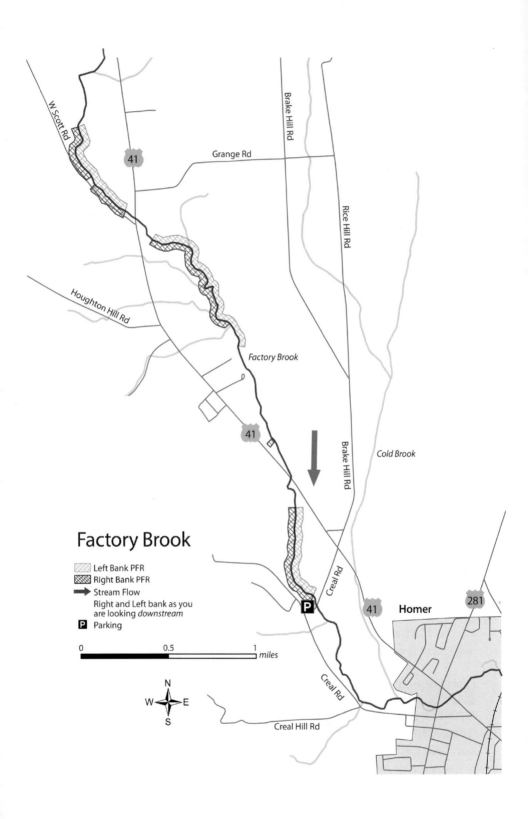

Factory Brook

- Left Bank PFR
- Right Bank PFR
- → Stream Flow
- Right and Left bank as you are looking *downstream*
- P Parking

0   0.5   1
▬▬▬▬▬▬▬▬▬ miles

W N E S

W Scott Rd

41

Brake Hill Rd

Grange Rd

Rice Hill Rd

Houghton Hill Rd

Factory Brook

41

Brake Hill Rd

Cold Brook

Creal Rd

P

41   Homer   281

Creal Rd

Creal Hill Rd

All right, if you aren't wondering where I caught the 22-inch brown mentioned just a couple of paragraphs ago, you must not have been reading very carefully. Go back and re-read it, if you must. The place was Factory Brook, Cortland County's premier trout stream, and one of the best in the state, at that.

Before you scold me for parting so easily with that information, know that I have fished Factory Brook dozens of times in the last several years, and mentioned its attributes in many newspaper and magazine articles. I have not seen the slightest increase in angler traffic on the stream as a result. Not even the locals appear to pay it much attention. Yet Factory Brook is so full of wild trout, both browns and brookies, that the DEC does not bother stocking it, and instead leaves its fate to the whims of nature.

Besides that 22-inch male, which hit a night crawler, I have caught a 21-incher and several other Factory Brook browns that measured between 17 and 19 inches in recent years. My best brook trout from the stream was a 14-inch male in full spawning colors. Natives up to 11 inches or so are fairly common, the more so as you fish farther upstream. However, such fish don't come easily, and that may be why this gem of a brook doesn't tempt more anglers.

Factory Brook sprouts from ice-cold springs along West Scott Road, which meets Route 41 about 4 miles south of the hamlet of Scott. The stream cuts under the same road about a mile and a half farther south, after curling behind the Emerald Estates housing development, then is crossed by Route 41 for the last time about 100 yards after 41 intersects with Route 281.

There are two stretches of public fishing rights on Factory Brook, north of Homer. The first one starts near the formative springs adjacent to West Scott Road. It's a good bait-fishing spot but most anglers find it extremely difficult owing to its rugged ground cover, which consists mainly of alders, both standing and toppled. This part of the brook has a few devoted followers, who must love wild brook trout above all creatures to inject so much sweat and determination into their sport.

You can find intermittent public access from the West Scott section down to Emerald Estates, and there are some nice pools behind that housing development, too. My friend Les Wedge, a retired DEC regional fisheries manager, has caught browns more than 20 inches long there, using small Rapalas and other spinning lures, and some years ago I used size 16 dry flies to fool a couple of dozen trout, both brookies and browns, which were taking *Ephemerella dorothea* mayflies one June evening.

Paul McNeilley lets a little one go at culvert pool on Factory Brook.

My favorite public water on the brook, however, is the stretch from the second crossing of Route 41 downstream to Creal Road, a blind intersection fitted with a conspicuous blinking light. Coming from the north, I make a right turn at the light and drive about 500 yards to the brook and an adjacent fisherman parking area. If the fish are hitting, and my legs are up to the trek through dense patches of orchard grass, goldenrod, and other vegetation, I like to fish upstream all the way to Route 41, then turn around and hike back to the car, stopping along the way to try pools that failed to produce the first time through. This is not an easy area to fish, but it offers the opportunity to tangle with wild trout of a nice average size.

When I say these trout are difficult to catch, I suspect many readers will conclude that I am attempting to discourage fellow anglers' ambitions to fish Factory Brook. No wonder the place is seldom fished, the discontented few might say. Kelly, that sly dog, has been bad-mouthing this stream for years. Well, I encourage anyone to give it a go. I will be waiting to hear what they have to say about the spooky trout that bury themselves in the silt when a human shadow falls upon them, and the boggy ground, just upstream from the Creal Road bridge, which is knee-deep on a rainy day. How about those leg cramps the night after your Factory Brook expedition? Believe me when I say a stream is not easy to fish. I am not kidding about that, but I am not about to leave Cortland County's best trout holes to other anglers, either.

While Factory Brook is no cinch to wade or fish (did I mention it is less than 10 feet wide in most sections?), some parts are easier than others. When I am bone-weary from crashing through alders and feeling the mud sucking hard on my hip boots, I park in the village of Homer, in the long, narrow parking lot that lies across Route 281 from an A-frame professional building. One of the most dependable pools in the brook is behind the A-frame, and there's another dandy hole just upstream. Don't you dare dunk a lure or bait in the straightaway run that contains the streambank just across the bridge from your parked car, however. You will see a NO FISHING sign there, courtesy of the local government and the municipal waterworks. On the opposite side of the brook, no more than 20 feet from the NO FISHING warning, there stands a historical marker acclaiming one of the best-known trout fishermen in history. Leon Chandler, the deceased vice president of the Cortland Line Co., lived and worked in the Homer area and was widely credited with popularizing fly fishing in Japan and Poland, among other places. Leon was a patient, easygoing gentleman, but I have no doubt he is up yonder asking St. Peter if he can't do something about that sign situation.

WEST BRANCH TIOUGHNIOGA RIVER

RATING: ★★★ (3 stars)
NOTEWORTHY: Wild brook trout near headwaters, stocked browns farther down.
BEST TIME TO FISH: During the *varia* hatch in early June or the Trico hatch in July and August.

The CDI Fly Fishers, a club consisting mostly of sportsmen living in the Cortland, Ithaca, and Syracuse area, enjoyed some of the best brook trout fishing in Central New York from the 1970s through the 2000s. Their home water, leased and posted, was the West Branch of the Tioughnioga River, upstream from Goodale Lake. It was a beautiful stream and still is, although the club suffered a discouraging loss in 2012, when one of the four farms involved in the lease was sold. The new owner withdrew his property from the less-than-ironclad agreement, and the remaining parcels were not as full of fish or as pretty to look at. The old beat, perhaps a quarter mile long, looked like an English chalk stream, with a weedy bottom and fish rising everywhere when the evening hatch was on.

I became a member the year before the key parcel was withdrawn from the club's control, but before that I had the honor, occasionally, to accompany CDI member Rod Cochran as his guest. Ever the gentleman, Rod always insisted that I fish well ahead of him, especially when we drew near the Trout Pool in the last hour of the day. Invariably I found at least a dozen trout rising, all brookies. Most were 5 to 8 inches long, but every such evening at least one 10- or 11-inch native would grab my floating fly pattern. The most remarkable events during those trips, however, were the sounds and sights of large brown trout jumping up and over a low wooden dam at the foot of the Trout Pool. I watched one of those fish jump six times one evening before it found the right spot to wriggle through the currents spilling over the dam. Those browns were, like all of their kind, born fish-eaters, and whenever they were able to haul their heavy bodies over the dam they were looking for a couple of tasty brook trout.

No wonder the club's no-kill rule was amended, to permit the capture and removal of large browns. I saw one member land a 23-incher late on a June evening, but there were bigger ones, still, in the digger pool at the tail end of the Trout Pool.

I suppose that's enough reminiscing about the lost club water, but there's much more to say about the remainder of the West Branch, from its swampy origins in the town of Preble to the stream's junction with the East Branch of the Tioughnioga beneath the elevated Interstate 81, on the outskirts of the city of Cortland.

Look at a Cortland County map—available on the computer or from the county's Convention and Visitors Bureau or via a snail-mail request sent to the same outfit. Run your eyes over the town of Preble until you see Tully Lake and the small outlet at its southern tip. Just to the right, you'll notice another tiny stream, called Dry Creek, that closely approaches and then goes under Route 281. These flows enter a mile-long by mile-wide swamp, then emerge into a slightly less boggy area that the CDI has been proud to call its own for more than four decades. All of these waters still hold brookies, but few fishermen are physically able or sufficiently bold in spirit to tackle all the sinkholes and water snakes that guard the streambanks.

After passing through Goodale Lake, a shallow and weedy 45-acre pond with big bass and virtually no public access, the West Branch flows into the village of Homer, picking up the currents of Factory Brook as it passes. A couple of miles beyond Homer, it joins the East Branch to form the main stem of the Tioughnioga River.

For wary rising trout in June, approach from upstream and feed slack line to keep your fly floating drag-free. West Branch, Tioughnioga River.

Wild brook trout are occasionally caught in the lower reaches of the West Branch, but the farther downstream from the mouth of Factory Brook you travel, the greater the odds are against hookups with some of the natives. Most of the stocking done by state hatcheries in the West Branch takes place in or below Homer. While there are no designated angler parking areas in this stretch, the sharp-eyed angler can find many pull-offs and even empty commercial parking lots within easy walking distance of the river. Some pools in the Homer–Cortland part of the river are quite deep, and chest waders are recommended.

One unusual spot to fish the West Branch is in the shopping plaza just north of Interstate 81's exit 11 in Cortland. (It's the one identified by the large signs advertising the Wendy's, McDonald's, and Arby's fast-food franchises.) If you're coming from the north, turn right at the end of the exit ramp, then take your next right into the plaza. Look for a place to park upstream from the Mickey Dee's. Ignore the litter that has been deposited along the river bank and focus on the water, instead. Most of the time you will be able to spot a fair number of trout sipping mayflies or caddis in the long, weedy flat that parallels the pavement. The wags in the DEC's Region 7 office, which is only a couple of miles away as the crow flies, long ago dubbed this unsightly but fishy spot on the West Branch "the Shopping Cart Pool."

About that litter—when I suggested you ignore it, I meant only until you're done fishing. On your way to your car, grab a plastic bag and pick up some of that trash before you head for home.

The West Branch of the Tioughnioga River is stocked with approximately 3,700 brown trout, including about 500 of the state's hatchery-reared two-year-olds. Most of the fish are stocked in mid- or late April, but several hundred yearlings are held back until May.

EAST BRANCH TIOUGHNIOGA RIVER

RATING: ★★★ (3 stars)
NOTEWORTHY: Full of surprises.
BEST TIME TO FISH: Late May.

Do you pursue the same species of fish year-round, or do you like a fishy smorgasbord now and then? If you are in favor of a little variety, the East Branch of the Tioughnioga River could be just the stream you are looking for. The DEC stocks it at the rate of approximately 5,400 brown trout a year. That total takes in about 700 two-year-olds. Wild browns, while not really common, can be targeted with success anywhere upstream from Truxton, and the majority of the tributaries that enter the river from that point on up to the Madison County border have healthy populations of wild brook trout. I will leave it to you to find the rumored 12-inch natives; but a 10-incher definitely would win the daily lunker prize in most of these creeks.

The East Branch, which is approximately 20 miles long and averages about 4 feet deep and 50 feet across, stands out from the typical Central New York trout stream because of its abundant warmwater species. Walleyes and northern pike both thrive in the river between Truxton and East Homer, and once you locate a few, you stand an excellent chance of landing one or two nice ones. Happily, while there are no formal public fishing sites in the Truxton–East Homer stretch, most farmers in the area at least tolerate fishermen who know enough to take home any trash they generate and to walk carefully along the edges of crop fields they must navigate to reach a favorite pool.

Most of the East Branch is within short walking distance of Route 13, from its mouth in Cortland upstream to Truxton, Craine Mills, and Cuyler, which is where the East Branch of Tioughnioga Creek becomes the East Branch of the Tioughnioga River.

In the parts of this rural stream that are apt to give up a pike or two, trout fishers might think it worth their while to carry two rods, one of them rigged with a fine-diameter wire leader and a suspending stickbait

5 or 6 inches long. As for a lure finish, I'd suggest either a black-and-silver Rapala, which does a fair imitation of a small sucker, or a perch pattern intended to resemble a food source that's common in the slow pools and eddies of the East Branch.

TROUT BROOK

RATING: ★★ (2 stars)

NOTEWORTHY: What this stream could be, but probably won't.

BEST TIME TO FISH: After a May shower.

My first acquaintance with Trout Brook was like a dream. More recent encounters were closer to nightmares. The ups and downs of this potentially grand stream are instructive to anyone who has seen trout water in a period of decline.

Way back in 1981, I opened the new trout season on April Fools' Day by first catching five fat browns in my home water of Nine Mile Creek. Since it was only 6 AM at that point, I decided to stretch my outing a bit by making a long drive to a stream I had never seen before: Trout Brook, which flows from Solon to McGraw in Cortland County. How I happened to pick that particular stream, I am not quite sure, but I think a DEC fisheries biologist must have given it a rather glowing endorsement. In any case, when I got there late that morning, I found a swift, gravel-bottomed stream perhaps 15 feet wide on average, and crammed full of my favorite trout—native brookies. Using fat garden worms, I caught 13 natives, 4 of which measured between 11 and 15 inches. To this day, the biggest of that bunch remains the largest wild brook trout I have ever caught in a stream.

Naturally, I returned to Trout Brook more than a couple of times in later years, but I never did nearly as well. Several factors played roles in the long fade that followed, including destructive floods and erosion, and the beaver invasions that plague most Oswego County streams sooner or later. Suffice to say Trout Brook has never quite measured up to the promise it showed me on that long-ago opening day. What a shame that is, for this frigid, gin-clear brook has the basic ingredients of a great trout stream. It fairly begs for a helping hand from the DEC or Trout Unlimited.

If it were up to me, the reclamation of Trout Brook would begin with the state's acquisition of some public fishing rights upstream from McGraw. No PFR exists along the entire length of the brook now. I'd follow that purchase up with the removal of as many beavers and beaver dams as possible and then install a few current deflectors, digger pools, and other stream improvement structures. Finally, although my big catch so many years ago was made with live bait, I would prohibit the use of bait and require anglers to return all brook trout they caught in this intriguing stream.

Meanwhile, anglers who wish to check out the stream for themselves must gain permission from landowners first. Given the go-ahead, you can expect very rugged terrain, including dense vegetation along the brook; in some places there is no choice but to wear chest waders and walk in-stream for long distances.

Natives dominate the upper end of Trout Brook, but the fish from McGraw downstream to the mouth of the creek at Polkville are mostly browns.

GROUT BROOK

RATING: ★★★★ (4 stars)
NOTEWORTHY: Overlooked brown trout fishery.
BEST TIME TO FISH: May and June.

The various Finger Lakes, combined, have dozens of tributaries that are known for attracting spring runs of spawning rainbow trout, but do not offer much fishing the rest of the year. To keep this book down to a manageable size, the only "tribs" I've included are those that have at least some season-long opportunities to catch resident, brooks, browns, or 'bows. Grout Brook easily qualities for inclusion, for its abundant wild browns are almost completely overlooked by area anglers.

A 23-inch brown from Grout Brook.

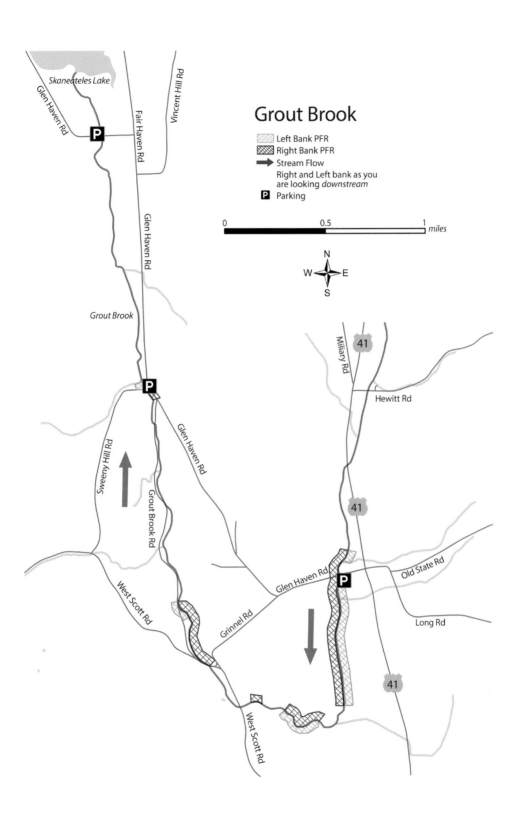

Grout Brook

Left Bank PFR
Right Bank PFR
→ Stream Flow
Right and Left bank as you
are looking *downstream*
P Parking

0   0.5   1 miles

N
W ✦ E
S

Skaneateles Lake

Glen Haven Rd

Fair Haven Rd

Vincent Hill Rd

Glen Haven Rd

Grout Brook

Sweeny Hill Rd

Grout Brook Rd

Glen Haven Rd

West Scott Rd

Grinnel Rd

Glen Haven Rd

West Scott Rd

Miliary Rd

Hewitt Rd

41

41

41

Old State Rd

Long Rd

I am one of the regulars during Grout Brook's spring rainbow run, and have caught April spawners there up to 25 inches long. When the run is heavy, I share the brook with many other rainbow-chasers, but on those warm days in early June when I think twice about donning my usual long-sleeved shirt, I seldom run into another fisherman on Grout Brook. I do, however, find an encouraging number of trout.

While a late-running rainbow is always possible, my June catch typically consists of all browns. After a spring rain—one of my favorite times to fish regardless of place—I often catch a dozen or more. Every one of them is wild and most range from 8 to 15 inches long, but I have caught quite a few larger than that. Eighteen-inchers are not at all rare in this 10- to 15-foot-wide stream, and my two best browns from it were 23 inches apiece.

It may seem, at this point, that Grout is an easy stream to fish, but I assure you it can be extremely challenging at any time during the spring and summer months because of the local browns' extreme wariness and the need for anglers like you and me to approach its small pools through dense, shirt-grabbing vegetation. In particular, Japanese knotweed and multiflora rose seem to occupy every available space along the bank by late June. Fly casting is impossible in much of the brook, but a black Woolly Bugger or a Little Rainbow Trout streamer can be fished effectively in the larger pools after a heavy rain has discolored the water. The secret is to approach likely pools from upstream. Enter the water as quietly as you can, wait a few minutes for things to settle down, then cast down and across.

Let the fly swing in and out of the main current, then tease it back upstream, one hand-twist or short strip at a time. This tactic works quite well, but only in the more open sectors of the stream and only when the water is off-color.

Dead-drifting a fat night crawler, on the other hand, is almost always effective.

Grout Brook is the major tributary of Skaneateles Lake. It is a trickle barely 4 or 5 feet across where it first appears on the map, at the bridge on Ripley Hill Road in the southwest corner of the town of Spafford, but it roughly doubles in volume by the time it goes under Hewitt Road and then beneath Route 41 at Scott. In that hamlet, the brook takes a mile-long run south before sliding under a bridge on West Grout Brook Road and taking a major U-turn and heading due north to the lake. Most of the Scott section of the stream is marked with yellow, green-lettered public fishing rights signs, but the water downstream has limited access. POSTED signs are common all the way to the Homer Rod and Gun Club. From

Paul McNeilley fishes the bridge pool on Grout Brook, Cortland County.

there to lower Glen Haven Road, residents have been welcoming to this angler, but it would be a good idea if all anglers checked for permission before trespassing.

From the Glen Haven bridge to the lake, fishing rights belong to the public, but the action for summer browns is slower there than what's available a bit farther upstream.

Because it is a tributary of a Finger Lake, Grout Brook is subject to special regulations. The daily limit is three trout or salmon (a strain of landlocked Atlantics is stocked annually and has a pretty solid foothold in Skaneateles Lake) and the minimum creel length is 9 inches for browns and rainbows and 15 inches for salmon. Other rules are spelled out clearly in the Finger Lakes section in the state's *Freshwater Fishing* guide, which is issued at no cost to anyone who purchases a fishing license.

More Cortland County Trout Streams

Along with the waters discussed above, Cortland County takes in many more trout streams. Most are on the small side, but are capable of holding some very nice fish. For example, **Cold Brook**, which runs under Route 281 about 2½ miles north of Homer en route to its junction with the West Branch of the Tioughnioga River, is so tightly posted that most anglers don't bother seeking permission to fish. It is also discouraging to see how low and tepid the stream gets in the summer months. Yet this stream can very productive. When I obtained permission to fish one short section of Cold Brook a few years ago, I resolved to try my luck only in the cool early season, when the water was barely into the 40- to 50-degree range. The strategy paid off on several occasions, usually following a spring rain. Once in early April I caught two nice browns on consecutive casts—16 and 18 inches long! This stream holds many wild brook trout, too.

Another good one is **Merrill Creek**, a tributary of the Otselic River that's about 10 miles long. It runs through the towns of Marathon and Freetown in southern Cortland County before emptying into the Otselic in the northern Broome County town of Triangle. Look for it along Merrill Creek Road, which intersects Route 221 between Marathon and Cincinnatus. It is populated by stocked brown trout (about 550 released annually) and wild brookies. Be forewarned, this creek is brushy, narrow, and very difficult to fly fish.

Kid Corbett brings in a brown on Gridley Creek.

The town of Virgil, known mainly as the location of the Greek Peak Ski Center and Lake Hope Lodge these days, has even more going for it, including two trout streams that at least one DEC biologist considers to be among the most productive fishing holes in the region. **Gridley Creek**, which flows through the Greek Peak property on Route 392, has no formal public fishing rights along its banks, but some landowners from the ski center downstream do not post their properties against fishing. The creek is less than 10 feet wide in most places but is big enough to shelter brookies and browns. It runs into the Tioughnioga River just south of the Route 392 crossing. If you add this creek to your bucket list, be sure to take note of its fast drop in elevation, slippery bedrock, and stark clarity. Be extra careful when you wade. Most fly-fishable pools are downstream of the ski center.

Virgil Creek is one of the more overlooked trout streams in Central New York. Its rural location, relatively small size, and tendency to run off-color for days after any substantial rain are all factors that tend to suppress angler traffic. The creek also has a moderate to heavy degree of POSTED and PATROLLED signs, and that, too, does nothing to boost fishing pressure. So why bother, you wonder, with so many other productive streams just a few miles—or at most hours—away? One reason Virgil Creek might be worth a little extra effort is its reputation for outsize trout. State fisheries managers and field biologists who assayed the creek with electrofishing

Brown trout, Gridley Creek.

gear knew it for the number of hefty brown trout they found, examined, and released. Some of those browns weighed more than 5 pounds and took up 24 inches on the researchers' measuring boards. That's why we bother. Depending on the attitude of nearby property owners, you should try your luck around West Meeting House Road, which is in the southwest corner of the town of Virgil. If you find this stretch to be on the dark and dingy side after some substantial rain, try a dark-colored fly, such as a black Woolly Bugger with a few strands of reflective tinsel added to the tail, or a nymph that looks like one of the cased caddis larvae plentiful in this creek.

Cortland County also takes in at least a dozen small brook trout waters, all of which are great places to hit with worms or wet flies in April and May, when the natives are taking advantage of rain, rising water, and their own kicked-up appetites. The better-known ones include **Morgan Hill Brook**, **Labrador Creek**, **Haight Gulf**, **Albright Creek**, and more. These are all feeders of the East Branch of the Tioughnioga River, and all enter the river from its north bank. You can check them off your to-do list, one by one, by driving east on Route 13 to Truxton and a bit beyond. As you might expect, there are also plenty of brook trout waters entering the East Branch of the Tioughnioga along Route 41. Look for **Maybury Brook** near Solon, which is a tiny but fish-filled tributary of the aforementioned Trout Brook. However, looking is all you will get to do at Maybury and most other streams in rural Cortland County unless you gain permission to fish from the landowners. There are few public fishing areas on these brooks except for those areas where the targeted waters flow through state reforestation plots.

Since half the fun of catching native brook trout is finding remote or overlooked hot spots you can call your own, I'll simply say that the tributaries to the tributaries are worth a shot, as is any stream that causes a fishing buddy to lose his voice or memory.

OSWEGO COUNTY

It's a safe bet that the thousands of fishermen who spend between $40 million and $50 million a year fishing in Oswego County don't cast much of that cash in the vicinity of wild brook trout. To the contrary, the fish that prompts anglers from all over the eastern United States, Canada, and elsewhere to whip out their credit card or checkbook at Fat Nancy's in Pulaski or Malinda's in Altmar are big enough to use 8-inch brookies as appetizers. Nobody is complaining about that state of affairs, either, for the salmon and steelhead fishery that the state DEC launched with

FLIES FOR CENTRAL NEW YORK TROUT STREAMS

Diamond Braid Egg Sac

Elk Hair Caddis (dry fly)

Griffith's Gnat

Foam Beetle

Haystack (dry fly)

Rusty Spinner (note yellow egg
sac at end of abdomen)

Queen of Waters (one of the
author's favorite wet flies)

Red Fox Squirrel Hair (RFSH)
Nymph

Nine Mile Scud, a popular nymph on Nine Mile Creek and other Syracuse-area streams

Cased Caddis Nymph

Snowshoe Emerger Nymph

Isonychia Nymph, sometimes called a Dun Variant

Little Brook Trout

Black-nosed Dace

Badger Streamer

Woolly Bugger

Hendrickson Nymph, one of the top trout-catchers of all time

fingers-crossed stockings in the late 1960s has grown into a multibillion-dollar economy.

Money talks—and I've made a few bucks on Lake Ontario salmon and steelhead myself over the years, by writing about where New Yorkers can catch them, and how. So I hope readers won't think me too strange if I say something nice about the fish that used to be Oswego County's finest. After all, *Salvelinus fontinalis* had a lot going for it then, and still does today. Aside from its drop-dead gorgeous good looks, which I certainly will allude to somewhere else in this book, our state's native trout is a scrappy battler on a hook and one of the tastiest fish in fresh water. But the best thing a wild brookie has going for it is the neighborhoods where it hangs out. Oswego County's backcountry is a prototype of brook trout habitat, and at least a couple of my fellow outdoor writers have declared that virtually any small creek, brook, or rill an angler can drive across or jump across in the county harbors a population of brookies.

I don't know if I should take that assessment as the honest truth or anything close to it. Seekers of brook trout are even bolder than muskellunge maniacs, when it comes to exaggerating the day's catch. Yet I can understand why the captor of a 6-inch native might be tempted to yank a brother angler's chain a little when he sees just how puny his pretty fish looks when it is in repose next to one of the humongous fish that populate the lower Salmon River and other Lake Ontario tributaries these days. Even so, I was very pleased to find out how thick the natives still are in their historic haunts in the mosquito- and blackfly-patrolled Tug Hill Plateau.

Because brook trout are such a fragile resource, more threatened than most of their relatives by deforestation, pollution, or even climate change, this chapter won't be quite as informative as some others. Mum's the word, as Huck Finn once put it. Sharing the location of a good brown trout creek is one thing, but dishing the details about a brookie redoubt is quite another. While our precious natives still thrive in dozens, maybe hundreds of Tug Hill–region streams, some Oswego County brook trout waters are now in perilous proximity to salmon and steelhead that excavate gravel and cobble-rock spawning nests the size of a Hollywood Hills bathtub. Because the kings and cohos need lots of room to propagate, they either chase away any resident trout or ignore their presence and build their own nests anywhere they wish—often on top of the redds trout have already constructed.

Fortunately, many of the most important brook trout waters in Oswego County, though not all, are located upstream of dams or waterfalls or other natural or man-made barriers that block the upstream migrations of Pacific salmon and steelhead.

NORTH BRANCH SALMON RIVER

RATING: ★★★ (3 stars)

NOTEWORTHY: If it's solitude you want, you're headed in the right direction.

BEST TIME TO FISH: May or early June, but bring lots of bug dope.

Face it, the North Branch of the Salmon River isn't what it used to be. But let's not write the river off, just yet. We don't want to be like those old cranks who hang out at rural taverns and spend their free time tricking angler-tourists into buying them a beer or two instead of swinging a cast of wet flies or maybe a big bucktail through a promising pool. The main problem I have with these gloomy types is that they don't really know the subject of the day's lecture. Oh, they were pretty good at taking the pulse of the North Branch or any other river they might have called home many years ago, but the chronic grumblers who hold court in barrooms and diners would be more knowledgeable if they actually went fishing now and then. Rivers change from year to year, and fishermen either keep pace or fall behind, and we are better off trading a few flies with the local high school student who grabs a spinning rod off the front porch and pedals his bicycle to the river than absorbing the negative prospects offered by the bards of the barroom.

Of course the North Branch has changed, some for the good and some not. For one thing, its brook trout, whether wild or hatchery-born, aren't as plentiful as they once were. The river has taken some major hits from Mother Nature in recent years, mostly from drenching rain and runoff. If you want to know what I mean, walk along the river's edge downstream from the mouth of Mill Stream, which is one of several nice-looking tributaries that keep the North Branch flowing in good shape more years than not. When my friend Kid Corbett and I hiked downriver from the Mill Stream junction in the summer of 2014, the rocks kept rolling beneath our feet, and we could see that the floods had tossed grapefruit-size cobbles well up on the sloping banks. The weather that spring had dug some deep holes, too, and I caught and released a couple of nice natives while working through them. One of the fish was 11 inches, which is a decent brookie in any New York river.

After an hour or so of pool-hopping, Kid told me he was going to leave a couple of spots to me in order to get the first crack at a wide, deep hole within sight of the spot where the North and East Branches mingled in the Salmon River Reservoir near Redfield. I stuck with the spot I had chosen, and was rewarded with another nice brook trout and a couple of 12- to 14-inch smallmouth bass. I was drowning night crawlers that afternoon, out of sheer laziness more than any other reason, but I have gotten pretty good at safely hooking and handling fish over the years, and managed to release everything I caught. I was starting to wonder how Kid's day was going. As he was a good 300 yards distant, I did not holler but instead slogged on downstream to a spot where I could wade across the river for a look-see. Kid's rod was bent over double, and it stayed that way for about another hour. My partner's floating Rapala was good for at least a dozen dandy bass, and I added four to the unofficial total. Two of mine were 16-inchers, impressive bronzebacks according to anybody's tally sheet, but for every smallmouth I caught, Kid hooked two or three.

There were at least 100 chunky bass in that pool. Presumably, they were still spawning, or dropping back toward the reservoir after finishing their propagation duties. I will let my fellow trout sobs and bass assassins argue among themselves whether all those bass are good for what used to be a brook trout gathering place.

From my vantage point, the East Branch was almost always a happy place, but never quite as good as it looked. The overall quality of its sport was sufficient to draw a visit out of me once every two or three years, but the river was also a good 90 minutes from home, and that distance was just long enough to keep it out of my regular rotation of streams.

Along with brook trout, of which a majority are stocked rather than wild, the 30- to 60-foot-wide river holds brown and rainbow trout. Most of the browns and 'bows have never met one of their hatchery-reared cousins.

The North Branch is worthy of a full day of your time, or better yet a couple of days if you don't mind short runs back and forth between the river and one of the motels, private campgrounds, or other lodging alternatives that cater to salmon and steelhead on the main stem of the Salmon River.

To get to the North Branch, take Interstate 81 to the Pulaski exit, and instead of following Route 13 along the south bank of the big river, take the Richland road (Route 2) all the way through Orwell and Little America to a T-intersection with County Route 17. A right turn there will point you to Redfield, about half a mile away. At Redfield, turn left and proceed north on Harvester Mill Road, which first crosses the North Branch and then parallels it for about 2 miles before going over a second bridge. That's just the start of what usually proves to be an interesting trip.

Access along the North Branch of the Salmon River is not easy, despite the several bridges just mentioned. There are eight formal angler parking sites along the stream and its tertiary tributaries, and these lead to roughly 9 miles of riverbanks that are open to the public, including one at Harvester Mill Road. However, the majority of these sites are merely trailheads, with long hikes between your parking spot and productive water.

If you decide to visit the North Branch, or for that matter any of the brush-country rivers, creeks, and brooks in the Redfield area, be sure to bring some navigational tools and let a friend or family member know where you'll be fishing and when you expect to return. More than a few anglers have had to spend an anxious night in Oswego County's alder jungles after making a wrong turn and losing track of time.

Don't forget to pack an assortment of bushy dry flies, either. The North Branch and its riverine neighbors are known for their hatches of big mayflies in May and June. March browns are a good bet to emerge in numbers, and if the river bottom hasn't been too seriously altered by the latest runoff, you should see an assortment of caddis and even a few giant stone flies, as well.

EAST BRANCH SALMON RIVER

RATING: ★★★ (3 stars)
NOTEWORTHY: A reputation for big trout.
BEST TIME TO FISH: After a summer shower.

If you ask me, there is no contest as to which of the Salmon River's branches is the better stream. The East Branch has a richer variety of habitat, and is more likely to reward a diligent angler with a trophy-size fish. It's also easier to find, considering the long walks in and out of the woods that are typical of the North Branch. Too bad it has only about 2 miles of water in Oswego County! The rest of it flows through Lewis County, which is beyond the scope of this book. (Hey, we had to draw the line somewhere, right?)

Aside from all that, the East Branch is a fine stream, and the Oswego County segment can be covered fairly well in a day if you're a confident wader and decent caster. I am a bit skeptical when I hear whispered reports about 6- or 8-pound brown trout hiding under its logjams, undercut banks, and other shady cover within a few hundred yards of its junction with the North Branch, but I have little doubt that those same pools lend shelter to brownies that stretch the tape measure to the 20-inch mark or beyond. Four-pounders, real 4-pounders, do not require embellishment or exaggeration in the slightest degree, and many honest anglers can recall doing battle with browns of such a size while fishing the Oswego County part of the East Branch. And why not, since the river has all the ingredients for such a recipe?

The lunkers are mainly wild browns, although the river is stocked annually with about 1,050 yearling brookies and 1,150 yearling rainbows. State fish farm crews used to stock browns, but the species became entrenched via natural reproduction. No matter where browns are introduced, they seem to do quite well as long as their basic habitat requirements are met, and in the East Branch all the pieces of the puzzle are there. For example, water temperatures are within the browns' preferred range of about 55 to 70 degrees throughout the April 1–October 15 fishing season, except for a short period during and after the spring runoff or when the river is shriveled by drought. In both cases, most resident trout can survive for weeks simply by moving into holding positions near springheads or tributary mouths. Such cold-water locations, known to biologists as thermal refuges, are heavily utilized during extended hot spells in rivers throughout the United States. In some of these places, such as the mouth of Horton Brook on the north bank of the Beaverkill in Delaware County, anglers are prohibited from fishing at specified times of the year. The idea behind these special regulations is to assure that heat-stressed trout will not be pestered by sportsmen until water conditions are better suited to the fishes' survival.

While trout living in the East Branch of the Salmon River are rarely subject to conditions so dire as I have just described, the fishing in the stream can be quite challenging during the dog days. If you can only try it once or twice a year, I recommend you do so in May or June, when neighborhood hatches of tan caddis and various other aquatic insects almost outnumber the swarms of biting and stinging bugs.

To get to the East Branch, follow directions to the North Branch given above, from Pulaski to Redfield. Instead of turning left on Otto Mills Road, take County Route 17 across the east end of the Salmon River Reservoir. Then make an immediate left onto Waterbury Road, where you will start to see some deep pools in a 30- to 40-foot-wide, gravel-bottomed stream and telltale signs with the DEC's green-and-yellow public fishing message. About a mile and a half of the banks on one or both sides of the East Branch are available to anglers. Fly, bait, and lure experts are all invited.

ORWELL BROOK

RATING: ★★ (2 stars)

NOTEWORTHY: Brook trout compete with introduced rainbows.

BEST TIME TO FISH: Mid-May, right after the steelhead run is over.

In my youth, Orwell Brook would have merited three stars, perhaps even four. It was a brook trout stream of very high quality, although anybody who crouched as long as required to get through a few hundred yards of its alders and gloomy groves of reforested pine earned every strike or nibble. You worked hard, yes, but usually you had it to yourself, and the pleasant weight in your creel at the end of the day always put a smile on your face.

That was pre-coho and chinook, and pre-steelhead, also. Once the DEC began stocking those amazingly large and prolific West Coast–strain salmon and trout in Lake Ontario streams with an abundance of spawning gravel, the native brookies were in deep trouble. The last time I checked the data, Lake Ontario had been seeded with non-native salmon and trout for more than 40 years. The overall fishing is just as challenging and rewarding as ever, but the catching of wild brookies is a whole lot harder than it was back in the day. Brook trout still live in many of the Oswego County creeks that serve as both boudoir and nursery to the salmon, but their lives are harder than they used to be. Many are pushed off favorite spawning sites by the much larger salmon; others are simply eaten by famished steelhead, which feed ravenously upon finishing their own mating assignments.

Even a 10-pound steelie would have needed two big bites to swallow my first Orwell Brook native. It was 12 inches long, a dandy by the standards of anglers who ply their craft on New York streams. Nobody I know catches many natives that measure more than a foot, whether they focus their efforts on the streams of the Adirondacks, the Catskills, or the Tug Hill Plateau. The beauty I caught in Orwell actually bit on a mesh spawn sack I was drifting through some deep pools in search of spawning coho salmon. Talk about spawning colors; that fish had more glitter than Liberace!

As you might have guessed, I have never again taken a brookie as large—or as flashy—from Orwell Brook.

Several anglers I have conversed with along the stream have told me they still catch a lunker native from the brook every so often. The likeliest time to catch Orwell brookies of any size, they declare, is during or after a substantial downpour that happens to occur in the second half of May or the first week of June. Steelhead have cleared out of the brook by that time, and resident trout have a shot at a good meal in their absence.

Other than pounding the lower sections of the stream with worms or streamer fly patterns when the rain is drumming on the car roof, they recommend exploring the isolated, knee-deep, and mile-long riffles that rush through the forests along Route 2 and side roads located east of the hamlet of Orwell. Some of this water slices through state lands and some is on private property. I'll leave it to you to tell one from the other and, of course, ask permission where necessary.

TROUT BROOK

RATING: ★★ (2 stars)

NOTEWORTHY: Wild brookies compete with stocked rainbows.

BEST TIME TO FISH: Late May, early June.

This tributary of the Salmon River should not be confused with any other Trout Brook in Central New York, such as the one in Cortland County. It does harbor a decent population of natives, however, and is well worth exploring if your outdoor wanderings take you through the towns of Richland and Orwell. Just be advised that this Trout Brook does not shelter nearly as many brookies today as it did 10 or 20 years ago, most likely because steelhead are more numerous than in the past. It boils down to the dominance of the larger species. Natives that seldom attain a length of 10 inches can't be expected to hold their own against fish that often weigh 10 pounds, can they?

Even so, anglers who tiptoe upstream along this 10- to 15-foot-wide brook starting where it slips under County Route 2 east of the hamlet of Richland stand a good chance of hooking a few natives. In the process, they might even pull off an unusual triple play, by hooking a brookie, a brown, and a rainbow—all in the same brook.

If you find yourself drawn to Trout Brook, save an hour or two to check out one of the stream's feeder creeks, called **John O'Hara Brook**. It is pretty much a carbon copy of Trout Brook, only smaller. Both streams flow through a mix of state forests and privately owned land, and can be counted on to produce at least a few native trout when you visit them.

MAD RIVER

RATING: ★★★ (3 stars)

NOTEWORTHY: You will need your walking shoes to get the best out of the Mad.

BEST TIME TO FISH: After the blackflies but before the mosquitoes.

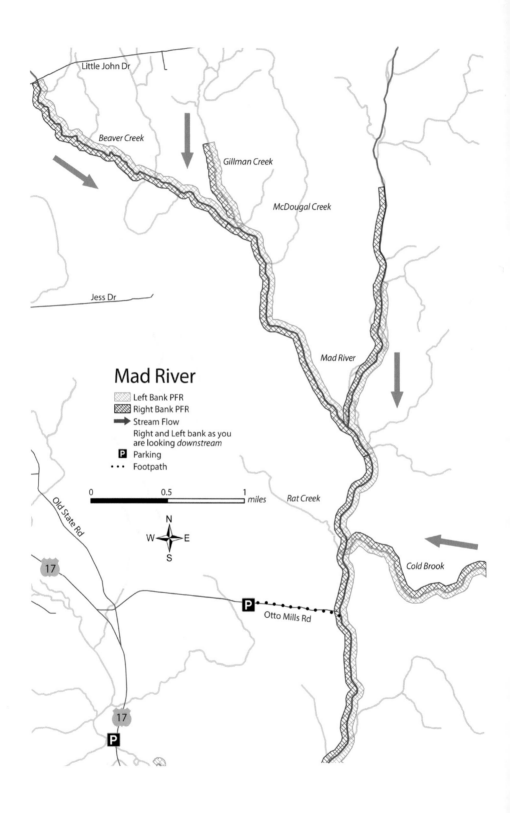

Mad River

	Left Bank PFR
	Right Bank PFR
➤	Stream Flow
	Right and Left bank as you are looking *downstream*
P	Parking
• • •	Footpath

0   0.5   1 miles

W—⊹—E
N
S

Little John Dr

Beaver Creek

Gillman Creek

McDougal Creek

Jess Dr

Mad River

Old State Rd

17

17

P

P • • • • • • • • •
Otto Mills Rd

Rat Creek

Cold Brook

In my grandfather's day, before the Great Depression, trout fishermen thought nothing of walking a mile or more to get to a favorite fishing spot, but the thick greenery that sprouts on and over the roads and paths along the Mad River in eastern Oswego County attests to the laziness of modern anglers. This Mad, which frequently is confused with the one in Oneida County, is owned in large part by a private hunting club that enforces its POSTED signs with vigor. Although the state's public fishing rights signs sprout from trees and fence posts along 6.7 miles of the river, access trails in some places traverse a mile or more of boggy rails and road shoulders. Whether public or private, these trails eventually lead to deep ledge pools, toppled pines, and other in-stream cover that shelters many gorgeous brook trout, along with an occasional brown. The browns, though few in number, are often of exceptional size, perhaps between 15 and 20 inches long.

How those browns got there is a bit of a mystery, because the DEC has not stocked browns in the Mad for several decades, at least. The most logical explanations include illegal introductions, either by well-intended club members or by other anglers who might have introduced browns by stocking them upstream or down from the club water.

The main problem with the Mad, from the perspective of today's convenience-oriented angler, is how to get there, quickly. As a former honorary member (by dint of being the outdoors writer for the region's most popular morning newspaper), I can tell you the answer isn't to join the Mad River Club and thereby get member privileges. They are a nice bunch of hunters and anglers, but the last I heard, the club had a long waiting list and that doesn't seem likely to change.

I think the best you can do, if you've never fished the Mad, is to get connected with somebody who has been there and done that. You may not be able to join the Mad River Club, but who would stop you from joining one of the Central New York chapters of Trout Unlimited—such as the Iroquois Chapter, which meets monthly at Barbagallo's restaurant in East Syracuse. Somebody in attendance will either be a Mad River veteran, himself, or know somebody else who has the same attribute.

Short of that, call the DEC Region 7 office in Cortland (607-753-3095) and grill the biologist who is currently overseeing Oswego County trout waters. Ask him or her about the current access situation. If the biologist merely advises you to hike in from the parking areas at Otto Mills Road or Harvester Mill Road—both of which are accessible by taking Route 17 north out of Redfield—ask for specific distances, trail markers, and so forth. Get every detail you can and read it aloud for verification.

Your final and probably most important step prior to a Mad River junket is to acquire a set of topographic maps that cover the Redfield–Osceola sections of Oswego and Lewis Counties. Whether the maps are on paper or digital doesn't really matter, just so you can figure out how to navigate the woods off Otto Mills Road and Harvester Mill Road. The critical skills include the ability to use both a compass and a GPS unit well enough to avoid getting lost or arrested for trespassing.

One more thing—if you aren't absolutely sure of yourself in a situation such as I've been hinting about, bring a trusted fishing companion along and don't leave each other's sight.

More Oswego County Trout Streams

You never know, before taking a few temperature readings, whether a good-looking stream in a remote setting is likely to hold wild brook trout. Natives that have never wasted a day hustling for Trout Chow in a hatchery environment depend on cold, well-oxygenated water for sustenance, especially during the stifling heat that typifies the last two weeks of July and the first two weeks of August. If you find a stream that, in whole or in part, maintains temperatures below 60 degrees Fahrenheit, you are probably in possession of a "secret" brook trout spot. Oswego County has many such streams within its boundaries, but not all of them are easy to get to and many wander their way through private lands that are jealously guarded by their owners. Ironically, most of these isolated streams are posted NO TRESPASSING with hunters, rather than anglers, in mind. In any event, it doesn't take long to politely inquire about the possibility of fishing on a previously unfamiliar section of a stream. The worst thing that can happen is being turned down, and if that happens you can ask somebody else about a different spot.

Kid Corbett and I have asked permission often and been turned down occasionally, too. It doesn't hurt all that much and once you get permission to drop your bait into a culvert pool on one road, the next driver that comes by may welcome you to try the brook that flows through his camp, too. That scenario unfolded last June on a road crisscrossing the border between Oswego and Lewis Counties. The stream we were invited to fish turned out to be full of wild brookies.

Many Oswego County streams, besides the ones mentioned in detail a while back, are well worth exploration. The county's northeast corner, especially, is a prosperous place for those who like to check out culverts and other structure that's not far from the gravel road. One such stream is

Cottrell Brook, which flows through the Little John Wildlife Management Area, and is crossed by County Route 17 just north of that road's intersection with County Route 15. In the same vicinity, keep a sharp eye out for **Little Sandy Creek**. Little Sandy is a good spot for both brookies and browns, especially in the vicinity of Boylston Center.

East of the village of Mexico, in the Happy Valley WMA, the tiny outlets of several small bass-fishing lakes are good places to catch a traditional "mess" of wild brook trout. **Whitney Pond**, **St. Mary's Pond** and several others south of Route 104 are worth prospecting. Get a good topo map of Oswego County and make yourself a checklist. Some of the brookie streams in or near Happy Valley are state-owned and therefore do not require landowner permission. Bring along a pal as a navigator, because the local roads are often short and twisting. Look closely for the telltale roadside pull-offs, and travel light, for you will be required to beat some brush if you hope to get into the better pools.

Also worthy of some exploring is the **West Branch of Fish Creek** between Kasoag Lake and Williamstown. It is a popular stream on the opening day of trout season, depending on the weather of course, especially in its more remote sections, such as the Lover's Lane Road access north of Williamstown. Brook trout of 6 to 10 inches are the rule, but every once in a blue moon one of the deep pools on the West Branch produces a 3- or 4-pound brown.

The streams in the vicinity of Central Square and the north shore of Oneida Lake are rather intensively posted, but the DEC has just enough public access along these waters to make them of significant interest to anglers.

Most of the north shore creeks have surprisingly good fishing for brown trout, and a few hold wild brookies, as well.

Write yourself a memo about the possibilities offered by **Big Bay Creek** and its major tributary, **Dykeman Creek**. Both have browns and brookies, of wild ancestry. Better, the two streams have more than 6 miles of PFR marked on their borders.

Scriba Creek, the one on Route 49 in Constantia that has the state walleye hatchery on is banks, is seldom thought of as a trout stream, but it is. I vividly recall having a barber next door when I was a kid. Joe Malcom was his name, and he and his fish-loving wife, Dorothy, brought many nice walleyes home on Sunday afternoons. My house was occupied by trout fishermen who now and then accepted Joe's proffered packets of firm walleye fillets.

Dykeman Creek, Oswego County.

Scriba flows through Constantia, along County Routes 23 and 25A. The DEC has purchased public fishing rights on approximately seven-tenths of a mile of this gravel-bottomed stream, but it is not particularly productive. Wild browns and brookies are the normal fare—good colors, decent size, but not really numerous.

CHAPTER THREE

Trout Waters
of the Southern Tier

STEUBEN, CHEMUNG, SCHUYLER, TOMPKINS, TIOGA, BROOME, and CHENANGO COUNTIES

Growing up in the Syracuse area, I was quite envious of people who lived in the Southern Tier region along the New York–Pennsylvania border, and especially those with Steuben County addresses, because they enjoyed fabulous deer hunting. At that time, during the early and mid-1960s, most hunters in Onondaga County concentrated their autumn efforts on small game, chiefly ring-necked pheasants and cottontail rabbits. A few really dedicated sportsmen in my town hunted deer in earnest, but I do not remember any folks in the village of Marcellus who filled their freezers with venison each November, as so many do in this era. Local deer were relatively scarce, and if I had known then what I know now about the trout fishing in a part of the state that was a mere 50 or 60 miles from my hometown, I believe I would have grabbed my gear, told Mom and Dad what was up, and hitched a ride out of town before anybody could stop me.

Great deer hunting has pretty much been taken for granted in the Southern Tier region since the 1960s, if not longer. You could look it up in one of those annual reports that the DEC files after each deer season. The booklets feature row after row of statistics, but the most important pages, in my mind, are the ones that summarize the county-by-county deer kills. Almost annually, Steuben County tops all others in numbers of bucks and total deer (bucks, does, and fawns) slain by hunters. There were a couple of seasons when Delaware County tiptoed into the top spot, but those were statistical anomalies—flukes, really—and everybody knew that Steuben County was the real deal for deer hunters.

For much of my life-to-date I have clung to the conviction that Nine Mile Creek, my home water, is to trout as Steuben County is to deer hunting—meaning, it is in a class by itself, on the top rung of the ladder and still climbing, or just plain primo.

But in the course of researching this book, I forced myself to reevaluate some of my core beliefs about trout-fishing places—and deer densities and such, as well. I reminded myself that Steuben County is not one of those "one-trick ponies" we are always hearing about. When I scanned the roster of New York trout waters, I discovered that Nine Mile Creek and its Syracuse-area trout stream neighbors are as good as advertised. I also affirmed that some of their strongest competition comes from the Southern Tier in general and one county in particular. And yes, I'm talking about the one with all the antlers.

STEUBEN COUNTY

Along with fantastic deer hunting, Steuben County residents should feel free to whoop and holler now and then about their trout fishing. To sum it up, you visiting anglers who drop a line or two in Mill Creek, the Cohocton River, or several other underrated waters in "the tier" stand a great chance of making your piscatorial dreams come true. Bottom line, this region contains several of the top-ranked trout streams in the entire Empire State.

I must admit to being a slow learner in this instance. In my newspaper job and also when I first began writing magazine articles that suggested "10 great June trout streams" or "great trout waters close to *your* home," I was inclined to be cautious, and perhaps overly so. I simply had no desire to ruin anybody's favorite stream, and I took care not to exaggerate how good—or bad—the fishing was in some places. However, as I became more comfortable with these assignments, I took a look around and discovered that some of New York's more famous waters were a bit overrated, while certain other spots easily lived up to their reputations, or even exceeded them.

Many times, the creeks and rivers that had been flowing under my personal radar for years turned out to be some of the most interesting waters in the state. Those streams of the Southern Tier have been on my A-list for years now, and I expect they will stay there in the foreseeable future.

COHOCTON RIVER

RATING: ★★★★★ (5 stars)
NOTEWORTHY: Forty miles of great fishing for brown and brook trout.
BEST TIME TO FISH: A huge Hendrickson mayfly hatch begins in late April, and can run into mid-May.

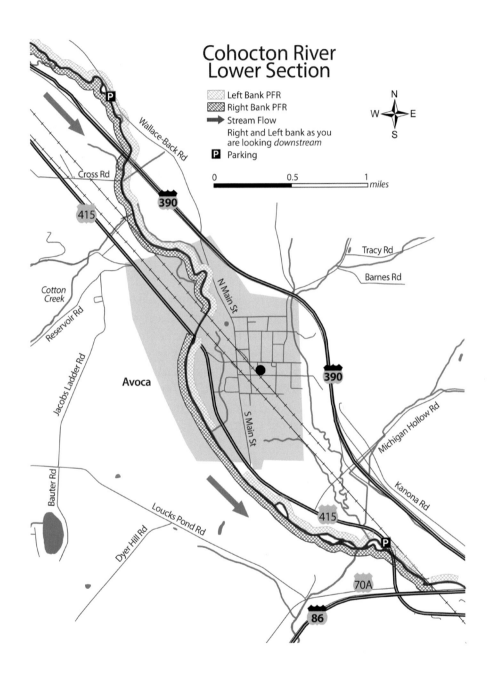

Cohocton River
Lower Section

Left Bank PFR
Right Bank PFR
→ Stream Flow
Right and Left bank as you
are looking *downstream*
P Parking

N
W   E
S

0   0.5   1
miles

P

Wallace-Back Rd

Cross Rd

415

390

Tracy Rd

Barnes Rd

Cotton
Creek

Reservoir Rd

Jacobs Ladder Rd

N Main St

Avoca

390

S Main St

Michigan Hollow Rd

Bauter Rd

Loucks Pond Rd

Dyer Hill Rd

415

Kanona Rd

P

70A

86

If you intend to fish the Cohocton River often, you need to be aware of the decades-old debate that swirls around its currents. Is it the *CO-hocton* or the *CON-hocton*? The maps all go for the former, but many trout fishermen in the Bath area insist on pronouncing it *CON-hocton* because (according to them) that's what the native Iroquois called it. An old-timer once told me the name means "logs in the water," which doesn't seem all that controversial—except for the punch line of this fellow's story, which alleged that the painter who hung the original WELCOME TO CONHOCTON sign was drinking on the job when he left out a letter. For the duration of this book, at least, I will stick with the extant Cohocton River spelling and just hope no readers blow their corks over the issue.

No matter how you spell it, the Cohocton is a blue-ribbon trout stream. With more than half of its 40-plus miles being open to public fishing and a season-long progression of mayfly and caddis hatches to fill the bellies of local brown and brook trout and challenge anglers to be at the top of their games, what's not to like?

The river takes form in the very southeast corner of Livingston County but courses mainly through Steuben County. As it starts its journey southward, it slowly gathers the currents of one tributary after another. Many of these feeder streams are good fishing spots themselves, with the caveat that "you have to know somebody." Access is difficult on some Cohocton tributaries, more often than not. But even a posted-up brook with a history of stingy access serves anglers in the long run, by providing spawning grounds and seasonal sanctuaries during a long, hot Southern Tier summer.

If you can take a little rejection now and then, don't be afraid to wake the farmer's dog when you pull into a country driveway near the Cohocton River. That woofing lets the powers that be know you are in the neighborhood. On the other hand, *do* respect the beast, for he may be earning his meals by keeping strangers like you at bay.

Should it prove to be a tough day for angler–landowner conciliation, and you get one or two "nays" with nothing positive to show for it, remember that the main branch of the Cohocton has 20 miles of streambanks that are already available to you. That is a nice consolation prize by most standards. The Cohocton is rarely crowded, although some of the larger flats that sprawl between the banks do seem to fill up quickly when the summer-morning hatches of Trico mayflies have begun.

The Cohocton is brook trout water in Livingston County, but heading south from its crossing of the county border near Atlanta it quickly becomes suitable for brown trout, too. Big browns, at that. Twenty-inchers

Cohocton River, in the Village of Cohocton.

live in many of the deeper pools from Atlanta to the village of Cohocton, and there are two great opportunities for tangling with one of these butter-bellied beauties every year. One, get out early in the season and arm yourself with the fattest, wiggliest night crawlers you can find. Run your baits under root-balls, cut banks, and other shadowy snags. Hang on tight.

The second effective method for luring one of the big boys to net is reserved for fly fishers only. It requires the practitioner to schedule three or four evenings in a row on the stretch between Cohocton and Avoca during the Hendrickson hatch. It's not all that unusual to find 3-pounders shoving smaller browns aside when this fly-fishing main event is about to peak. So go get 'em, tiger! Just make sure you have a dozen or so of your favorite Hendrickson nymphs, emergers, duns, and spinner patterns when the hatching commences. (Look up chapter 9 for a few suggestions.) And once you have located a few surface-feeding browns of impressive proportions, don't say good night until it is getting so dark you need a headlamp to find your way back to the car. Hendrickson spinner falls frequently start between 5 and 6 PM, but it is not unusual for trout to be feeding on the spent egg-layers well past sunset.

The Cohocton River is not a huge stream, but it has some holes that are much too deep to wade. You'll find these mysterious yet very fishy-looking spots most readily on the outskirts of Bath and in downtown Avoca, but there are some deep, dark hiding places in the Atlanta stretch of the river, also. Chest waders are necessary if you want to give every spot a thorough try. You needn't be a fly-fishing school graduate to execute all the necessary casts, as the stream is less than 50 feet wide in most sections. Quite a bit of it, in fact, is from 15 to 25 feet across. Those are not imposing dimensions, by any means. They put a premium on fast, accurate casting and mending, and the less line you pay out via false casts, the more trout you are likely to catch on the Cohocton. On this stream, like most others I have fished, I prefer a long fly rod, say, 8½ or 9 feet, for the simple reason that it is easier to maintain control of a slightly longish rod than it is to cope with extra lengths of line. If that sounds to you like a radical or foreign concept, get a few friends to put their short fly, bait, or spinning rods to the test. Give those buddies of yours some instruction on the virtues of long rods, then turn them loose—one at a time, of course—and let them enjoy half an hour or so using your pet fly, lure, and bait sticks. After a clumsy first four or five minutes, they'll get the hang of a long rod and I guarantee most will be curious regarding the cost of the tool you just demonstrated.

From the Rochester area, the Cohocton is easily reached by taking the Genesee Parkway, also known as Route 390, to the village of Cohocton exit. From the exit ramp, you can follow highway directional signs to Route 415, which is connected to the river by a series of local roads. There are numerous access points for anglers, including state-supplied yellow-and-green public fishing signs and many unofficial roadside pull-offs.

A few of the more popular locations to access the river are the railroad museum parking lot on Maple Avenue in the village of Cohocton, the Owens Road access about 1 mile south of Avoca off Route 415, and a dead end at Cross Road, which is about ½ mile north of the Owens Road access.

The Cross Road access is located within one of the two special-regulations areas on the Cohocton. Each area is open to fishing year-round, but only artificial lures or flies may be used. Anglers may creel two trout per day; however, each fish kept must be at least 12 inches long. One special-regulations area extends from the north property boundary at the U.S. Veterans Administration Hospital in Bath upstream to the Route 415 bridge crossing; a second lies between the north boundary of Avoca village and the mouth of Neil Creek.

DEC hatcheries supply the Cohocton River with more than 10,000 brown trout a year. The total stockings include about 2,000 two-year-old browns, which measure about 13 or 14 inches, on average, when they are turned loose. While these quotas attest to the high quality of the Cohocton's fishing, the more impressive information, by far, is the prevalence of wild trout in the watershed. Gorgeous stream-bred browns thrive in at least a dozen tributaries; native brook trout continue to multiply in the headwaters of the river in the vicinity of Atlanta, and also do well in spring-chilled feeder streams. These natural resources are not apt to be wasted in the near future. One of the most pleasing aspects of the Cohocton is its sheer toughness, for it is well known among fishermen and New York's trout biologists, too, that the system has withstood floods and droughts alike in recent years.

The best way for most anglers to help the Cohocton River withstand familiar or as-yet-unknown scenarios for natural disasters is to fish it as often as possible and please, tell your friends and neighbors all about it.

Besides the Hendrickson series of wet and dry patterns, most Cohocton River regulars keep March Browns (sizes 10 and 12), assorted Sulfurs (sizes 14 through 18), and tiny Tricos (sizes 20 through 26) to cover the majority of important spring and summer mayfly hatches. A variety of Elk-Hair Caddis imitations are very useful between hatches, and just about any generic aquatic nymph or larval imitations (such as the Gold-Ribbed Hare's Ear or a Cased Caddis pattern) will collect you a fish when nothing much else seems to be working.

Add a couple of beetles or black ants for late-summer prospecting and a black-and-olive or black-on-black Woolly Bugger to mimic minnows or crayfish and you should be good to go on the Cohocton for the rest of the trout season.

MILL CREEK

RATING: ★★★★ (4 stars)

NOTEWORTHY: One of the most dense trout populations in New York can be found in this short but productive stream.

BEST TIME TO FISH: Late April, when spring showers give the crystal-clear creek just a hint of color.

Upon hearing or reading the story of Mill Creek, a certain friend of mine would ask, "What's wrong with this picture?" After all, there has to be a reason, and a darned good one, why the average trout fisher seems to ignore this fish-rich stream in the northwest corner of Steuben County. With so many things going for it, you would assume Mill Creek takes a year-round thumping from Rochester-area sportsmen, and it's not hard to picture more anglers from Syracuse and Binghamton test-driving the stream, either.

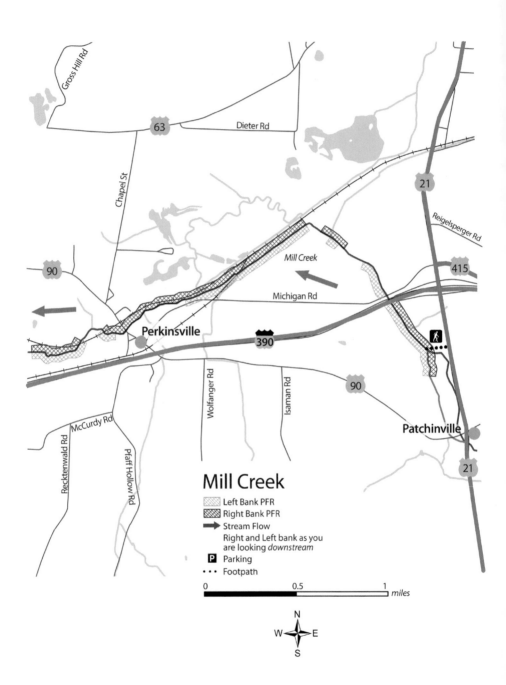

Gross Hill Rd

63   Dieter Rd

Chapel St

21

Reigelsperger Rd

90   Mill Creek   415

Michigan Rd

Perkinsville

390

Wolfanger Rd   Isaman Rd

90

McCurdy Rd

Recktenwald Rd   Pfaff Hollow Rd

Patchinville

21

Mill Creek

Left Bank PFR
Right Bank PFR
Stream Flow
Right and Left bank as you
are looking *downstream*
P Parking
••• Footpath

0   0.5   1
                              miles

N
W   E
S

Spider Rybaak fishes Mill Creek, Steuben County.

On its behalf, Spring Creek has plenty to offer. It is so thick with wild browns and brookies that the DEC has not bothered to stock it for many years. With the stream already at its biological carrying capacity, adding more trout to the mix would be like mashing another scoopful of mint chocolate chip ice cream on top of a king-size cone that just broke in your hand. DEC Region 8 fisheries crew member Pete Austerman recently told me that the last time state workers used electrofishing gear to study Mill Creek, the team collected an average of 1,050 adult trout per mile, or, to put it another way, 140 pounds of trout per acre. Those stats suggest that Mill Creek, which is narrow enough in some places for an aged high-school-athlete-turned-Outdoor-Channel-couch-potato to clear with a running jump, has one of New York's thickest trout populations. One reason for this abundance is its frigid temperatures, which persist even during the dog days of summer. Another is its abundance of freshwater scuds, sow bugs, and other food sources associated with streams that have high pH levels and low temperatures. Add to these assets the convenience of having a trout stream that literally flows beneath a major highway entrance ramp and you would think Mill Creek had it all.

In fact, it has everything a trout stream could ever need, except, perhaps, a cadre of fly-fishing groupies to guard against pollution, unwanted development, and other potential threats to its ecological perfection. So when you are trying hard to crack the Mill Creek code, you notice nobody else is in sight and begin to wonder: Where are all the other fishermen?

My personal opinion is that they have thrown up their hands and are simply fishing elsewhere. Mill Creek is too clear and its trout are too wary for most fishermen to handle, most of the time. Instead of visiting the creek when it has been muddied by runoff, as I would suggest on most tough creeks, you might instead want to try it on a bright, sunny afternoon when it has gone two or three weeks without rain. Walk along its banks as quietly as you can, but you are still bound to set off chain reactions of fleeing trout. Startle one and it will startle two more, and so on until the creek itself is rocking and rolling. Don't be overly concerned, for if you wait for things to settle down, some nice trout will resume feeding.

Although the typical Mill Creek brown is between 7 and 10 inches long, the stream shelters many bigger specimens, too. Fish of 14 to 16 inches are present in some of the deeper pools, and once in a while you might stumble into an 18-incher. Wild trout of Mill Creek parentage are fat but firm, brilliantly spotted, and inclined to go airborne once or twice when hooked. Unfortunately, there are days when these fish simply refuse to be caught, and that high degree of difficulty probably accounts for the low fishing pressure on the stream.

Mill Creek is a little hard to find if you rely solely on road maps, but the following directions will get you to the headwaters. From Canandaigua on U.S. Route 20, drive south on Route 21 (overlooking the west shore of Canandaigua Lake) to Naples. Continue on 21 from there to Wayland. Look for the Gunlocke office furniture factory on your left, and after passing it, keep a sharp eye out for Michigan Road. It's a right turn, just before the Route 390 on-ramp. A crossing over Mill Creek is just a couple of hundred yards ahead.

At that point, you're in the hamlet of Patchenville. Upstream from the bridge at Michigan Road the creek is narrow, averaging about 8 to 10 feet across, and the browns share space with some very pretty brook trout. Access is intermittent. Some pools can be fished without problems, but a few properties are labeled with NO TRESPASSING or KEEP OUT signs. Downstream from Michigan Road, a long, mostly straight channel is a bit wider than the stretch just above and has some 3- to 5-foot-deep pools with chunky browns in residence.

Of the few anglers who give Mill Creek the attention it deserves, most prefer the quicker flows and shaded pools a mile or two downstream from the Michigan Road crossing, in the village of Perkinsville. Turn right into this quaint community and park just beyond the bridge. Upstream, step carefully to avoid a small property guarded by electric fencing, then walk along the old railbed and clamber down it to fish the spots that strike you as most interesting. Be forewarned, this is not an easy place to fish with flies, lures, or bait, because it is thickly bordered by alders and other vegetation. The rewards can be considerable, however, especially after a warm-weather downpour reinvigorates local fish.

Alternatively, pick your way up, down, and over the gullies and rocky runs downstream from the Perkinsville crossing. Browns of 12 to 14 inches are fairly routine in this water.

Don't worry about what other anglers might do to complicate your Mill Creek visit. I've enjoyed the stream on numerous occasions and have never bumped into more than one or two other trout fishers, and of course, that was fine with me in all instances.

About 2 miles of Mill Creek is marked with public fishing rights signs.

CANISTEO CREEK

RATING: ★★ (2 stars)
NOTEWORTHY: Watch out for the canoe hatch!
BEST TIME TO FISH: Late April.

One place that beckons to sportsmen frustrated by their Mill Creek experiences is Canisteo Creek. Aside from the fact that both hold trout, Canisteo and Mill are different in virtually every way. Each spring, Canisteo Creek is stocked with approximately 3,780 brown trout, few of which will hold over through the ensuing summer and winter. Mill Creek is not stocked at all, but is inhabited by some of the largest and healthiest wild browns found anywhere in New York. Brook trout do well here, too, although they are not nearly as plentiful as the browns. Especially comforting to many beginners, Canisteo Creek is not window-glass clear, and visiting anglers do not need to crouch and crawl constantly in order to catch a trout or two.

The trouty section of Canisteo is located in the town of Hornellsville, and mainly upstream of the city of Hornell. Most other stretches of the creek are occupied by warmwater species, such as smallmouth bass, walleyes, and assorted panfish.

About 5 miles of the Canisteo, between Hornell and Arkport, is managed for trout. This part of the stream is about 30 to 40 feet wide, on average, and very suitable for either fly fishing or using spinning gear. It is also good bait-fishing water, especially following any significant rain. The creek bottom is mostly made up of gravel and rocky rubble, and hip boots are adequate in most spots.

Beginning trout anglers should do quite well by working the deeper pools in the creek throughout the month of April and into May. After that, temperatures are tolerable but no longer inviting to stocked trout, although you can expect some stockies to survive their first year in the wild by schooling around tributary mouths and well-oxygenated riffles. Even the occasional native brook trout can be caught in the same places. Most likely, these fish left the tributary streams where they were born because the water got to be either too high or too shallow.

Canisteo Creek can be shadowed by driving your car along Canisteo Creek Road (County Route 119) between Addison and Hornell.

BENNETTS CREEK

RATING: ★★★ (3 stars)

NOTEWORTHY: Here's a tributary that often fishes better than the stream it flows into, especially during warm weather.

BEST TIME TO FISH: Debatable, but I'd pick mid-May, when the hatchery truck drivers have done their duty and assorted mayfly hatches have barely gotten started.

Bennetts Creek flows north for about 14 miles from its headwaters in the town of West Union to Canisteo, but only the first 4 to 5 miles, between Rexville and Greenwood, can be recommended as real trout water, and even that is mostly of a put-and-take nature. The creek is stocked with about 800 brown trout in the spring, and just about all of them are your standard-issue stockies, measuring 8 to 9 inches. As a rule, the DEC does not schedule releases of hatchery two-year-olds in trout waters that are marginal, temperature-wise, or that don't easily support the older, larger browns.

The creek is accessible at several points along Route 248, and property owners are not averse to sharing information with those who seek it without being impolite. Pete Austerman, of the DEC's Region 8 fisheries crew, tells me anglers who are willing to access road culvert pools or manage to get permission to fish are very apt to be rewarded with strikes from 5- to 8-inch-long native brook trout, which thrive in the uppermost parts of Bennetts Creek.

LITTLE MILL CREEK

RATING: ★★★ (3 stars)

NOTEWORTHY: Brook trout throughout!

BEST TIME TO FISH: Early morning, as a rule, because that's a great time to get first-cast hookups from resident brookies and browns.

The scaled-down tributaries of bigger, more famous trout streams are typically like the star football player's youngest brother—a bit disappointing. That's not the story with Little Mill Creek, however. Let's just say this swift-running feeder stream has been proven worthy to bear the family name.

Little Mill Creek blends with the waters of Mill Creek about 3 miles before the latter stream joins Canaseraga Creek near Dansville. Most of Little Mill is in Livingston County, but it cuts across the northwestern corner of Steuben County to conclude its merger with Mill Creek.

Little Mill has approximately equal numbers of brown and brook trout. Unlike Mill Creek, which has brook trout only in its upper reaches above Michigan Road near Patchenville, Little Mill has good numbers of brook trout, plus plenty of wild browns, throughout its length.

Unfortunately, public access is difficult on Little Mill, due to posting and the stream's tendency to meander a good distance from the local roads. A newcomer's best bet would be to drive to crossings at County Line Road or Mendoleine Road and start looking for landowners who might happen to be in a generous mood.

NEIL CREEK

RATING: ★★★ (3 stars)

NOTEWORTHY: More than 5 miles of public fishing rights on this Cohocton River tributary.

BEST TIME TO FISH: Early July can be great, because dropping, warming water impels many Cohocton River browns to migrate into tributaries in search of the cold bubbly.

How refreshing it is to find a productive, readily accessible tributary of the Cohocton River! More than 5 miles of Neil Creek are marked with friendly, familiar green-on-yellow signs. Better, this not barren water or a meandering stream that flip-flopped and spilled its gravel on steep banks after a ferocious storm. It's the good stuff, with a nice pool, riffle, pool sequence promising worthwhile fishing for wild browns that sometimes grow to be 15 inches or better.

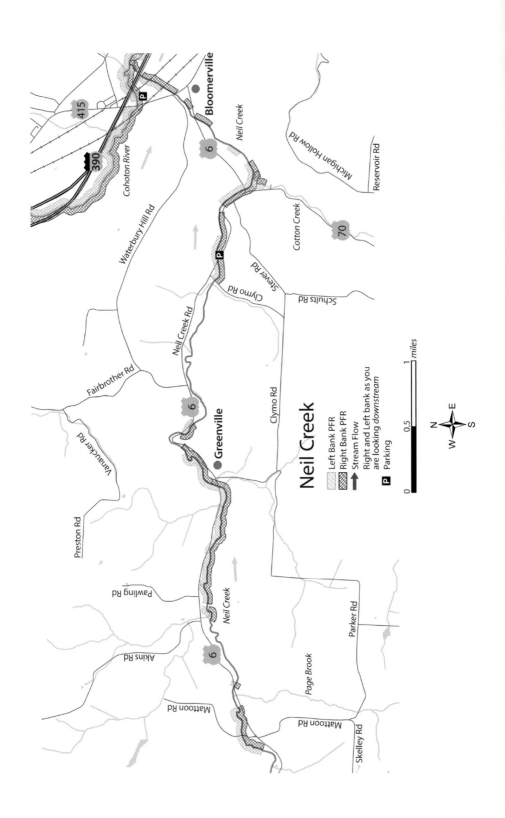

Neil Creek

Left Bank PFR
Right Bank PFR
Stream Flow
Right and Left bank as you
are looking downstream
P Parking

0   0.5   1
miles

N
W   E
S

"It has some real nice pools," said DEC worker Pete Austerman. "I'd guess the deepest might be 5 or 6 feet deep."

Neil Creek has a handsome tributary of its own, called Castle Creek, which Austerman touts as a reliable place to catch wild browns and brookies, especially after a thunderstorm has roiled the currents a bit.

To locate Neil Creek on a map, put your index finger tip on Wallace, a small community roughly midway between Cohocton and Avoca. Notice County Road 6, which joins the Cohocton at Wallace. As you follow that road to the west on your map, you will see that you are heading upstream on Neil Creek. A bit farther to the south of County Road 6 is County Road 70, which runs from west to east along Castle Creek for approximately 4 miles. Between Route 6, where you will see an angler parking area, and the mileage along County Road 70, readers who might be worried about dealing with unexpected low-water conditions should find enough cold, shaded water to keep themselves busy on a warm summer afternoon. The junction pool where Roads 6 and 70 join is within earshot of the other junction, where Castle Creek and Neil Creek link together.

Remember, large tributaries of a popular river invariably harbor much the same assortments of mayflies, caddis, stone flies, and terrestrial insects as are commonly seen on the big water. As the spring hatches start to wane, you should come prepared for fly fishing, and keep landing your buggy-looking dry flies on current edges and other good feeding stations.

GOFF CREEK

RATING: ★★★ (3 stars)

NOTEWORTHY: This stream has limited access but loads of trout. It begs for more anglers, but permission of the landowners is crucial.

BEST TIME TO FISH: Late April is when trout start to feeling frisky again, because that's also when afternoon water temperatures become tolerable to fish and fishermen alike.

Because it is barely 10 feet wide in most places, the reported presence of big brown trout in Goff Creek raises eyebrows. However, DEC Region 8 stream-survey data confirm that the creek holds good numbers of 12- to 14-inch browns, plus a few neighborhood bullies that stretch out to 17 or 18 inches. On top of that, Goff Creek's upper sections are occupied by some wild brook trout, too. The question is, how are you going to get near these places, unless you first get the owners' blessing?

Goff Creek flows from west to east in the towns of Howard and Avoca before joining the Cohocton River a couple of miles south of Avoca village.

The local road, Route 70A, runs alongside the creek. Fishermen get some long looks at this creek as they proceed upstream.

More Steuben County Trout Streams

The large majority of trout rivers, creeks, and brooks in Steuben County are quite remote and in some cases hard to find, but anglers who sit down at a brightly lit kitchen table with a *DeLorme New York State Atlas & Gazetteer* and study the hair-width blue lines and their proximity to federal, state, county, and local roads will be astounded at how many fishing holes they can find.

There are literally dozens of small to medium-size trout streams in Steuben County, and I haven't enough space to give all of them their proper due. I can, however, mention some that merit inspection, protection, and, of course, expanded access opportunities for the public. In addition to those covered a bit earlier in this book, consider checking out the following spots when chance puts you and the streams close together.

One place you ought to find to your liking is **Campbell Creek**, another tributary of the Cohocton River that flows east from near the crossroad called Buena Vista in the town of Howard. The interesting thing about Campbell Creek is that it has only a small number of trout, but many of its tributaries, according to DEC biologists, are home to wild brookies. Some of the feeders you should try include **Sinclair Creek**, **Chamberlain Creek**, **Maxwell Brook**, and **Buck Settlement Creek**. All are in the towns of Howard or Bath, and each has at least one bridge crossing it. If I were to visit them (or any other cluster of small, rural streams), I would schedule my visit for mid- or late April. On my way, I would simply buy or dig a few trout worms, which can't be beat for some old-fashioned culvert fishing.

Most Steuben County streams don't get mentioned in outdoor magazines or books like this one. Generally the deterrent is the lack of formal public access. This does not have to be a discouraging factor, however. Most fishermen who make it a habit to seek permission from landowners get it, now and then. My own rule on this issue is, it never hurts to ask. If you want to help your chances, get in the habit of picking up a bag full of litter when you are fishing back-road creeks. Make sure the landowner sees you in the act first, and then go knocking at his door.

Among many wonderful streams that have only very limited access for anglers, I think of **Carrington Creek**, which is a 15-foot-wide tributary of the Canisteo River. It winds through the towns of Dansville, Freemont, and Hornellsville, and its cold currents have a reputation for growing some nice brook trout, up to 10 inches or so. You might benefit by calling the DEC Region 8 office (585-226-2466) in Avon, to get specific directions to unposted sections above the Hornell Reservoir.

Now and then a good stream actually flows through public lands, and that's the case with **Stony Brook** and **Sugar Creek**. Part of Stony Brook runs through the state park of that name, which is in the town of Dansville, off Route 36. It is a tributary of Canaseraga Creek, which is mainly a put-and take fishery for stocked trout, but Stony Brook trout (both browns and brookies) are all wild.

Cryder Creek, which runs through the town of West Union, is another nice brown trout stream, with about 1.9 miles of public fishing rights in Steuben County.

Also worth visiting, **Dyke Creek** in the town of Greenwood has fair fishing for wild brook trout, but there's no PFR, which means you should obtain permission before trying your luck.

CHEMUNG COUNTY

You would have to do the math to be positive, but I don't think I'd be too far off the mark if I said it would take the average angler at least a couple of months to make a half-serious stab at fishing every trout stream in Steuben County. I am thinking about allotting half a day per stream, and estimating there are approximately 50 streams, of all sizes, that are likely to shelter at least a few trout. Volunteers, anyone? In contrast, it shouldn't take more than a day or two to test the waters in Chemung County, which is Steuben's next-door neighbor. I don't mean to disparage Chemung County's fishing, which is not bad. Instead, I'm demonstrating the diversity of angling opportunities that await readers in the Southern Tier and, for that matter, Central New York as a whole. It is remarkable to consider how widespread trout streams are in some counties, and how scarce they are in other parts of the region. One fishing hole that is shared by three counties, Cayuta Creek, is a standout where it currently lives, but it is so long and so widely admired that I decided to assign its address to Chemung County and then let the chips fly where they may.

CAYUTA CREEK (SHEPHERD'S)

RATING: ★★★★ (4 stars)

NOTEWORTHY: Shared by three counties and fishing is good throughout.

BEST TIME TO FISH: Early to midsummer when terrestrial insects fall on the water daily.

When I asked the somewhat seasoned senior sportsman (translation: old guy in fishing clothes) where he had caught the pair of 18-inch-long trout that hung from his belt on a rope stringer, I got two answers for the price of one.

"The rainbow came from that deep pool up around the bend," he said, waving his hand toward the trailer park that sat along my favorite stretch of Cayuga Inlet. "And the brown I caught over to Shepherd's."

That second part surprised me, because until that moment I had never heard of "Shepherd's." My puzzlement must have been obvious, for I am always anxious to find a new stream, so the somewhat older gentleman elaborated.

"Shepherd's Creek," he said. "It's over the hill a little way."

Actually, is was a fairly long way, in another county, even. Gradually I came to realize that Shepherd's was officially referred to as Cayuta Creek. It originated in Cayuta Lake, an easy-to-miss but productive little fishing hole for bass and walleye about 6 miles east of Watkins Glen in Schuyler County. As the crow flies, I'd guess it was around 15 miles away from me and my new friend with the shiny fish draped about him.

In the intervening years, of which there were many, I've learned much more about Cayuta Creek, and passed some of it on to fellow Central New York anglers. Some of that knowledge I forwarded with some reluctance, because Cayuta Creek—aka Shepherd's—has that effect. In an area of the state where many streams that look to be fishable in April are nearly dried up in June, Cayuta Creek is a reliable source of trout action right through the hot summer. From its source in Schuyler County it flows in a south-easterly direction along Routes 34 and 224 through Chemung County and then hustles due south through Tioga County, where it joins the Chemung River at Waverly.

Trout fishermen need not clutter their notebooks or their minds with information about the last few miles of Cayuta Creek. From the hamlet of Reniff down to the Pennsylvania border part of the Chemung, the stream is too warm for trout, with the possible exception of the first two or three weeks of the season. You might, and I emphasize the word *might*, luck into a holdover brown at that time by working big spinners or stickbaits in the deeper pools. If it happens, the trout will be a lunker that is looking for a few big chubs to chew on before it migrates, upstream or down, to colder water.

Upstream from Reniff, the creek varies in width from about 20 to 50 feet, and water temperatures are tolerable to trout virtually year-round. The DEC manages Cayuta Creek as a put-and-take proposition for the most part, with one notable exception. From the Wyncoop Creek Road bridge in Chemung County upstream to the Route 223 bridge, anglers are prohibited from using bait and must stick to artificial flies or lures only. Also, the daily creel limit in this special-regulations stretch is two trout over 12 inches per angler. This section, open year-round, is very popular with fly-fishers, who enjoy the usual succession of mayfly and caddis hatches in April, May, and June, followed by the splashdowns of ants, beetles, and other tasty tidbits along the creek's grassy and wooded banks.

DEC Region 8 fisheries biologist Brad Hammers reminded me that the entirety of Cayuta Creek is open to fishing year-round, to increase the range of opportunities available to area anglers. The creek is heavily stocked, with approximately 15,000 browns ticketed for the 20-mile section from Reniff, which is in Tioga County, upstream to the mouth of Jackson Creek in Schuyler County. Hammers thinks an angler who knows how to work the water in the special-regulations area has a shot at catching a brown trout of 16 inches or better almost any time of year.

NEWTOWN CREEK

RATING: ★★★ (3 stars)
NOTEWORTHY: Wild trout upstream, stockers downstream.
BEST TIME TO FISH: Early May, when caddis hatches combine with seasonal
   showers to trigger feeding.

Elmira-area fishermen get heavily involved with the spring rainbow spawning run in Catharine Creek, but most save a few days for the local brown trout streams, too. Among the favorites, Newtown Creek stands out for its 2⅓ miles of stocked water. DEC policy in Region 8 does *not* allow for dumping hatchery trout where angler access is denied, so you can count on getting landowner permission here. Note, however, that angling pressure is fairly high on Newtown Creek. It was stocked with 1,075 browns, including 75 two-year-olds, in 2014. The creek has a modest population of wild browns, mainly toward its upper end, south of Park Station Lake, but depends mainly on stocked trout as it flows west along Route 223 and then slides along Route 17 on Elmira's east side.

One thing Newtown Creek has in its favor is a width of 20 to 25 feet in most spots. That's comfortable for bait-, spin-, and fly-fishing specialists.

McCORN CREEK

RATING: ★★ (2 stars)
NOTEWORTHY: A secluded tributary of Cayuta Creek, known for small but
   wild brown trout.

BEST TIME TO FISH: Most years, you want to visit these small creeks in mid- to late April.

Access to McCorn Creek is a bit tricky because the stream flows through a very remote part of Chemung and Tompkins Counties. Posting is not a huge problem, because the state owns public fishing rights on approximately 9/10 mile of this creek. However, you may have a hard time locating the stream or even mistake it for one of the other brooks in the vicinity. Look for the intersection of Route 224 and County Road 13 about midway between the hamlets of Cayuta and (to Cayuta's south) Van Ettan. That will get you in the ballpark.

POST CREEK

RATING: ★★ (2 stars)
NOTEWORTHY: Heavy angler traffic on this one.
BEST TIME TO FISH: Given all that fishing pressure, get to your spot early. Sunrise is not too soon, even during the cold weather in April.

This is a shared stream, one that runs through Schuyler, Chemung, and Steuben Counties, but for the sake of convenience we will consider the creek as a whole, here and now.

Since most of the state stocking quota is deposited in the 3 miles of water between Chambers and the Steuben County border, that's where fishermen like to get dropped off, too.

Post Creek joins the Chemung River in the city of Corning, but in its upper reaches it is capable of showing anglers some dandy brown trout. Locals consider it to be primarily a bait-fishing stream, due to its narrow span (around 15 feet across on average) and heavy bank cover. A definite plus, on the other hand, is its gravel bottom, which makes for easy wading.

This modest but popular stream stocked with about 1,650 hatchery browns in Chemung County, including about 250 two-year-olds. Another 1,260 browns, including an average of 200 two-year-olds, are ticketed for the Steuben County part of Post Creek.

SING SING CREEK

RATING: ★★ (2 stars)
NOTEWORTHY: Bring a stream thermometer to locate cold springs that prolong the good fishing for weeks in some sectors of Sing Sing Creek.
BEST TIME TO FISH: Mid-April is as good as any.

Although it is not one of the Southern Tier's better trout waters, Sing Sing is stocked with about 1,300 brown trout each April and also hides a wild brown or two.

This stream is a short drive from Millport, a community that straddles the upper part of Catharine Creek. Catharine, of course, is renowned as the principal spawning ground of Seneca Lake rainbows, and some anglers who live in the Elmira area like to fish Sing Sing Creek when the Finger Lakes rainbow action is slow; and vice versa.

Sing Sing is invigorated by cold water erupting from spring ponds in the vicinity of the Route 17/U.S. Route 86 bridge. For that reason, fishing just downstream from the span is better than it looks, and anglers often catch a mix of wild and stocked browns in the creek. It's about 15 feet across, on average, and has good bank cover to provide shade and minimize erosion.

You can find Sing Sing Creek easily by driving west on Route 17 out of Big Flats and looking for the sign directing motorists to the Elmira–Corning airport. Just past the airport is Sing Sing Road, which crosses

A 19-inch rainbow, early spring on Catharine Creek.

the stream. Stocking takes place along 3 miles of the creek, from County Roads 64 and 352 just outside Big Flats, while the wild browns are most plentiful east and north of the airport.

WYNKOOP CREEK

RATING: ★★ (2 stars)
NOTEWORTHY: One to hit on your way back home from another spot.
BEST TIME TO FISH: When you happen to be in the vicinity.

It is by no means what you'd call an angling destination, but Wyncoop Creek might save the day for you after a disappointing trip to some other stream in Chemung County. The water quality is pretty good, overall, and the modest stocking quota of about 400 yearling browns suggests that biologists think Wyncoop Creek should fish better than it does. Given the small number of hatchery transplants, it is likely that most of the nicer trout caught here are going to be wild fish, and there's nothing wrong with that.

Wyncoop Creek Road more or less follows the stream from just west of the crossroad at Beantown south to its confluence with the Chemung River, in the southeast corner of the county.

SCHUYLER COUNTY

When I agreed to write this book, I had just written another—*Fishing the Finger Lakes*—which gave detailed advice about the 11 bodies of water in that chain. It also offered tips on fishing the tributaries of the various lakes for spawning rainbow trout. To avoid pitting one book against the other, I decided that *Trout Streams of Central New York* should focus on rivers, creeks, and brooks that are occupied by wild or stocked trout year-round. Rainbow spawning streams like Owasco Inlet that, even in July, had the cold water temperatures and other necessities of life for rainbow, brown, or brook trout made the cut. In contrast, waters unable to provide for any significant number of trout other than spawning rainbows, such as Cayuga Inlet, were left out.

Dividing trout streams in this manner enabled me to logically group these natural resources, county by county. While this methodology would make it relatively easy to list and locate individual creeks for reference purposes, I knew it would also result in some confusion, too, most likely when a stream wandered back and forth across county boundaries.

The main drawback to grouping streams by county is that some chapters will inevitably be much longer than others. As a reader, I like that occasional change of pace. Once in a while, I need to catch my breath for a few minutes before diving back into a particularly engrossing chapter.

Schuyler is one of the state's smaller counties, at 342 square miles. It's about one-fourth as large as neighboring Steuben County (1,404 square miles) and not surprisingly does not have anywhere near as many trout streams to claim as its own. A couple of the waters that do flow are sort of secondhand. Cayuta Creek, for example, is one good stream that is shared by Schuyler, Chemung, and Tioga Counties. I cover it in the Chemung County section of this book. Still, the county does have a couple of creeks for traveling anglers to explore.

Before you flip another page, this might be the right time to do that breath-catching thing.

CAITLIN MILL CREEK

RATING: ★★ (2 stars)

NOTEWORTHY: An impassable falls blocks the spring rainbow run, but brown trout are present from there upstream.

BEST TIME TO FISH: During deer season in late November and into December, rainbows will run this Catharine Creek tributary, but if it hasn't happened yet when you show up, look for browns upstream.

In early April, hundreds of anxious anglers will charge en masse to get a crack at the part of Caitlin Mill Creek that lies below the impassable waterfall, but few of those folks will try for brown trout upstream from that cataract. That's a shame, for the fishing upstream can be fairly good, if you're among those who like catching browns that are pretty but on the small side.

Caitlin Mill Creek, which is connected to the L'Hommedieu Flood Diversion Channel, can be reached by driving south on Route 14 out of Watkins Glen and turning left onto Route 224 in Montour Falls. You will see the creek on your right. A hiking trail of about a quarter mile ends up below the falls, but if you want to try for the browns, continue driving up Route 224 toward Odessa. As you approach the village you will notice a small tributary, Cranberry Creek. It's also a brown trout stream.

This creek is not stocked. Anything you hook will be wild.

HECTOR FALLS CREEK

RATING: ★★ (2 stars)

NOTEWORTHY: A very small stream, about 10 feet wide on average.

BEST TIME TO FISH: Check this one out if you happen to be fishing
Catharine Creek on or shortly after opening day.

Forget about trying for the big rainbows that wiggle and worm their way
out of Seneca Lake and into the pool at the base of Hector Falls, which
is heavily posted. Instead, take a ride on Route 79 and fish the creek
upstream from the falls. This scenic creek starts near Reynoldsville, on
the eastern fringes of the Finger Lakes National Forest, and flows west
along 79 through Bennettsburg and Burdett, for about 8 miles, before
approaching the falls. Several side roads cross the creek.

Although the DEC has not acquired public fishing rights on Hector
Falls Creek, you should be able gain permission from landowners adjacent
to the stream.

TAUGHANNOCK FALLS CREEK

RATING: ★★ (2 stars)
NOTEWORTHY: A long stream with no public fishing rights, this creek is
underfished and some of its wild brown trout are decent-size.
BEST TIME TO FISH: As is the case with most small streams, go when a
shower has raised and colored the water.

Taughannock Falls Creek is born within a mile or so of Caitlin Mill Creek,
but quickly heads in the opposite direction. Caitlin Mill heads toward
Catharine Creek, while Taughannock flows north along Route 228 from
South Valley and then crosses Route 79 at Mecklenburg.

Best known for its wild browns, Taughannock Falls Creek likely hosts
a few wild brook trout live in its uppermost part, too. That's because the
DEC hears of natives being caught in tributaries of this creek, near South
Valley and Reynoldsville.

Taughannock Falls Creek crosses the border into Tompkins County
near Podunk and takes a couple of spectacular plunges in the state park
that bears its name before gliding into Cayuga Lake. Fishing for brown
trout is not as good near the park as it is above Mecklenberg, due mainly
to warming water temperatures in the wider, downstream sectors.

SHEQUAGA CREEK

RATING: ★★ (2 stars)
NOTEWORTHY: Eight miles of trout water most fishermen have never
heard of.
BEST TIME TO FISH: Mid- or late May should be grand.

Below a small but impassable waterfall in the village of Montour Falls, Shequaga Creek is essentially a straight-as-a-string flood control channel that's barely worth fishing. Above the natural barrier, 8 miles of water classified as trout-friendly make Shequaga a must-fish proposition. Wild brown trout, some in the 14- or 15-inch range, are the prize catches in this stream, which ranges between 20 to 35 feet across. There's a big jump in stream volume about 4 miles up from the waterfall, thanks to the confluence with an unnamed tributary at that point. To get to Shequaga Falls, take Route 414 south in Watkins Glen. The creek is paralleled by this road upstream to Moreland and Beaver Dams.

May is the perfect month to explore upper Shequaga Creek because the rainbow run downstream is over with and the neighbors have let out a collective sigh of relief. If you want to ask for permission to fish, you'll never find the recipients of your request in a better mood.

TOMPKINS COUNTY

When I think of Tompkins County trout fishing, a postcard-perfect image flashes instantly before my eyes. Here's a hint—it's across the street from the local high school but it is *not* the homecoming queen. It is, rather, that roaring, mist-shrouded natural wonder of Central New York, the Ithaca Falls. Students at Ithaca High School take it for granted, sometimes, but awed anglers wading thigh-deep in slippery Fall Creek struggle to watch their step and pay attention to their bobbing strike indicators instead of just admiring the incredible scenery. They wouldn't be doing the balancing act, however, if the fishing was no good.

FALL CREEK

RATING: ★★★ (3 stars)

NOTEWORTHY: One of a handful of regional streams with three kings of trout—brown, brook, and rainbow—Fall Creek also has runs of landlocked (Atlantic) salmon in spring and fall.

BEST TIME TO FISH: Late April or early May.

The huge pool at the base of the falls, which to my eye looks about 150 feet across, is populated by seasonal runs of rainbow and brown trout plus landlocked salmon, and it can be a magical place to fish in April or November. However, as the focus of this book is on year-round trout fisheries, I'll postpone further discussion of lower Fall Creek for now and zero in on the water above the falls. There's plenty to talk about, for Fall Creek is born in the Cayuga County town of Sempronius, then picks up tributary

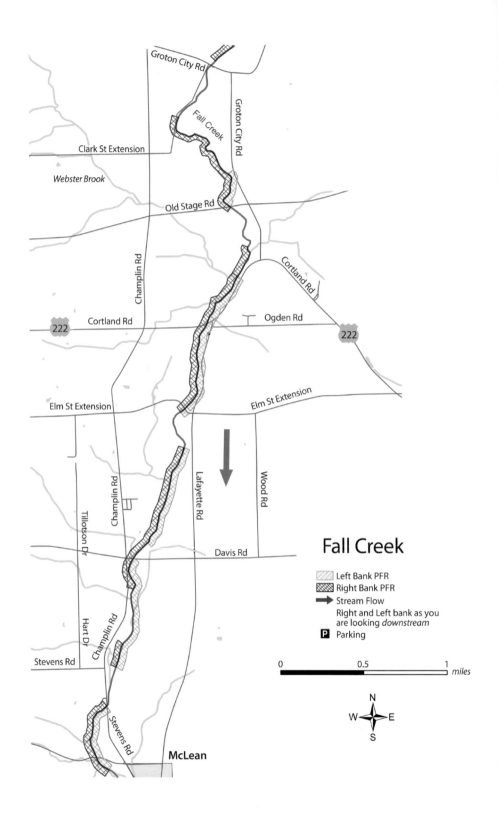

Groton City Rd

Groton City Rd

Fall Creek

Clark St Extension

Webster Brook

Old Stage Rd

Champlin Rd

Cortland Rd

222 Cortland Rd

Ogden Rd

222

Elm St Extension

Elm St Extension

Champlin Rd

Lafayette Rd

Wood Rd

Tillotson Dr

Davis Rd

Hart Dr

Champlin Rd

Stevens Rd

Stevens Rd

McLean

Fall Creek

Left Bank PFR
Right Bank PFR
Stream Flow
Right and Left bank as you
are looking *downstream*
P Parking

0   0.5   1
                              miles

N
W   E
S

flows as it heads south. It crosses the border into Tompkins County near Groton City, and proceeds to McLean and Freeville before taking a big right turn toward Ithaca. In all, the creek winds and twists more than 30 miles by the time it plunges over the famous falls.

From the headwaters near Iowa Road in Sempronius downstream to Lake Como and Groton City, Fall Creek is a narrow, alder-choked stream that's stocked with 8- to 10-inch brook trout. Native brookies live in this section, too, but heavy beaver activity has warmed the water to temperatures that have been marginal for trout in recent years. Your best prospects for catching a few brook trout, native or stocked, are in the most overgrown and darkly shaded pools. In the spring, temperatures are down and flows are up, which means anglers who are determined to catch a couple of fish may need to wade in up to their belts and fish downstream, flipping a worm or Panther Martin spinner as they go.

Brookies are the main target of fishermen from Groton City to McLean, too, but as the creek widens and bank cover decreases in this stretch, brown trout start to take over. The DEC has likely encouraged this trend in recent years by stocking two-year-old browns along Champlin Road, just above McLean. From there down to Freeville, the creek is 40 feet wide in many places, and the gradient increases, too. This is an interesting place for fly fishers, with a variety of in-stream cover and fairly

The author with a nice brown trout from Fall Creek, Tompkins County.

heavy Hendrickson mayfly hatches in early to mid-May. Smallmouth bass and chubs compete with trout for your imitations, which is not necessarily a bad thing.

Where Route 13 crosses the creek, just past Etna, you'll see the second most impressive pool on Fall Creek. (You already know the first, right?) Early in the season, before the water warms, bait fishers have fun with stocked trout and smallmouths in the Route 13 pool. Unfortunately, swimmers and beer drinkers enjoy the place, too.

The DEC has a total of 5.7 miles of public fishing rights on Fall Creek, from McLean upstream to the Tompkins–Cayuga county line.

WEBSTER BROOK

RATING: ★★ (2 stars)
NOTEWORTHY: You could easily drive right by this brook trout stream, thinking it is part of Fall Creek.
BEST TIME TO FISH: After a spring shower.

As happens to be the case with many small brook trout streams, Webster Brook is a bit difficult to pinpoint, but worth the effort when your timing is right. The brook is posted in some spots, but permission to fish is readily secured at other locations. Your best bet, as always, is to be polite, friendly, and hopeful of a happy outcome.

Webster Brook, a tributary of Fall Creek, is about 10 to 15 feet across in most sections. It has a bottom of cobblestones and smooth bedrock, which can be waded most efficiently with boot soles fitted with metal studs. The streambank is lined with high grass in some places and clumps of alders in others.

A 10-incher is a nice native in Webster Brook, and when conditions are right, a small spinner will entice such fish to strike. Work your lures as close as possible to overhanging cover.

To get to Webster Brook, drive upstream on Champlin Road, cross Old Stage Road, and take your next left, which will cross the brook almost immediately.

SIX MILE CREEK

RATING: ★★★ (3 stars)
NOTEWORTHY: Wild browns and brookies, too.
BEST TIME TO FISH: The month of May is hard to beat, for bait, lure, or fly.

Commuters who live in the Dryden–Richford area and drive west on Route 79 to jobs at Cornell University get frequent glimpses of Six Mile Creek, coming and going. It looks like an easy route to the Ivy League school's campus, and it is, but finding fishable areas of the stream can be a challenge. Although Cornell is about as cosmopolitan as can be, Six Mile Creek takes a winding course through a rural section of Tompkins County. The reward, once you have navigated a logical route, is good fishing for wild and stocked brown and brook trout. April is the ideal time for scouting the stream because the foliage comes on gradually during the month, and fishermen who try some cautious rubbernecking then can get a good look at bank cover and the stream itself. As May arrives, the leaves sprout in a hurry, but warming water temperatures mean better fishing is at hand.

Six Mile Creek flows through Cornell property and spills over a steep falls in the city of Ithaca. Downstream of the falls, it is about half a mile to Cayuga Lake, but fishing for lake-run rainbows and browns is not particularly good, in part because bare-hook snaggers and other poachers do their foul deeds in the shallows. Above the falls, the creek runs through several small reservoirs where fishing is prohibited. Access is available via Cornell properties and unposted stretches between Brooktondale and Slaterville Springs, but this section is not as productive as the steep, rippling stretch of water along Irish Settlement Road. Wild browns dominate there, but the farther upstream you go, the more brook trout you are likely to encounter. Get in shape before you tackle this part of the creek, however. Although much of it is owned by Cornell and open to the public, it has swift currents, a slick bottom, and dense bank cover in some locations.

The width of Six Mile Creek varies from 10 feet along some of Irish Settlement Road to 20 feet or more below Slaterville Springs. The creek is stocked with approximately 1,600 brown trout annually, including 200 two-year-olds.

CASCADILLA CREEK

RATING: ★★ (2 stars)
NOTEWORTHY: Wild browns are the main course, with brookies for dessert.
BEST TIME TO FISH: Cool summer mornings.

Cascadilla Creek is in the next valley to the north of Six Mile Creek, and at one point it passes through the Reynolds Game Farm, where pheasants are raised for the DEC's ringneck stocking program. It crosses Game Farm Road and Ellis Hollow Road in the town of Dryden. For a map reference, look for these bridges north of Route 79.

Cascadilla, like several other trout streams in and around Ithaca, tumbles over waterfalls—in this case, several medium-size cascades rather than one major drop. Although Cascadilla Creek meets Cayuga Inlet a short distance upstream from the south end of Cayuga Lake, it does not draw any significant number of spawning rainbows or salmon. Instead, the best fishing in Cascadilla Creek is upstream from its vertical descent. The sought-after fish there are stream-bred brown and brook trout. Of the two, browns are the larger and more numerous residents.

The greater share of properties along Cascadilla Creek are owned by Cornell, and anglers should obtain permission from the university if they encounter any NO TRESPASSING signs or if there appears to be any conflict between fishing and other uses.

More Tompkins County Trout Streams

In addition to the waters just described, anglers living in Tompkins County or desirous of making a pilgrimage to the area's scenic streams might reserve some time for exploring a couple of state parks that have modest populations of brown trout. They are **Buttermilk Falls Park**, which is just off Routes 13 and 96B on Ithaca's south end, and **Treman Park**, off Route 13 in Newfield. The former park has a modest population of brown trout above an impassable falls; the latter offers the same benefit above a falls on Enfield Creek.

Mud Creek, in the town of Dryden, has a modest population of brown trout, but be advised that these fish are protected by an almost-impenetrable curtain of alders. The bedeviling plant that shields **Peg Mill Brook** from anglers is the multiflora rose. Peg Mill's nasty cover enables its resident brown trout—and a few spawning rainbows, which swim up Owasco Inlet in April—to eat and wax fat in comparative safety. This brook is a tributary of the inlet, which slips under Chipman Corners Road just north of the village of Groton. Depending on whether you are one of those proverbial gluttons for punishment, you can fight your way upstream through the rose thorns to the small plunge pools. Don't try it if you are on a prescription blood thinner, however.

Why bother? Because Peg Mill Brook has a decent fishery for resident browns up to 15 or 16 inches long, and is also inhabited by a few brook trout. The rainbow run is a bonus.

TIOGA COUNTY

The lay of the land in Tioga County is quite convenient for fishermen. The best trout streams in the county first appear on a map in the vicinity of Dryden and Virgil, then head south and cross the Dryden and Harford town line. At that point, the East Branch and West Branch of Owego Creek proceed downstream, no more than 3 to 5 miles apart in most places. After each has traveled through more than 20 miles of creek channels, the two branches come to a rather abrupt merger, near the hamlet of Flemingville; from there the bulked-up Owego Creek is just about 4 miles from the village of Owego, which perches on the mighty Susquehanna River.

Aside from Cayuta Creek, which is covered in the Chemung County chapter because its best fishing can be found in that jurisdiction, Tioga County has only a handful of reputed trout streams—the branches and main stem of Owego Creek, Catatonk Creek, and Miller Brook, according to my research.

EAST BRANCH OWEGO CREEK

RATING: ★★★ (3 stars)
NOTEWORTHY: Excellent dry-fly fishing and easy access.
BEST TIME TO FISH: The last week of May and the first week of June, when the green drakes usually hatch.

Due to the one thing no fisherman can control—namely, the weather—dry-fly action on the East Branch of Owego Creek may vary considerably from one year to the next, but when the skies over the stream are calm and the bugs are frantic, it's game on for serious fly fishers. In the spring of the year, the East Branch has thousands upon thousands of mayflies and caddis crawling or burrowing in its silt and gravel pools. If you have a couple of artificials that look a lot like the main item on the trout's list of daily specials, make sure you tie a new tippet to your leader, and check that your fly reel's drag is working smoothly. Assuming you have correctly tuned your tackle, and a killing fly is at the end of the rig, you are ready to pick out a riser, and cause your artificial to drop gently to the surface and float drag-free toward a hungry trout.

The prime segment of the East Branch is from Richford downstream to Berkshire. Below the latter community, the summer water levels drop considerably, and temperatures climb into the low 70s, forcing trout to migrate to springs or other cold-water influences. Trout in the Richford–Berkshire area usually are able to survive, if not quite thrive until September weather comes to their rescue.

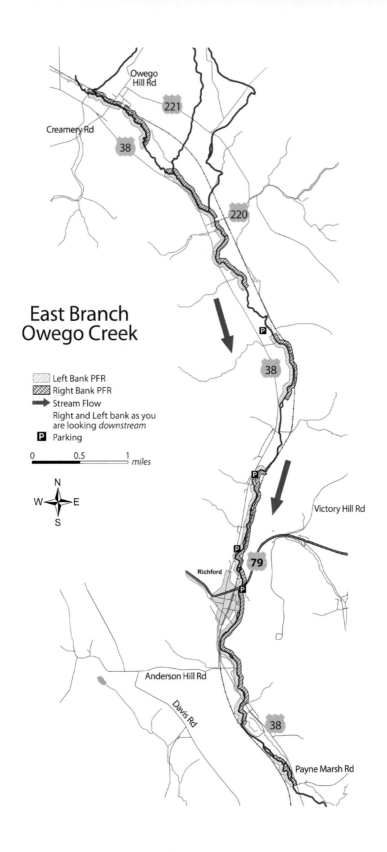

East Branch
Owego Creek

Left Bank PFR
Right Bank PFR
Stream Flow
Right and Left bank as you
are looking *downstream*
P Parking

0   0.5   1
━━━━━━━━━━━━━━ *miles*

N
W ✦ E
S

Owego
Hill Rd
221
Creamery Rd
38

220

P
38

P

P
Victory Hill Rd

P
Richford   79

P

Anderson Hill Rd

Davis Rd
38

Payne Marsh Rd

From mid-April until at least July 1, a succession of insect hatches keeps upper East Branch trout at the surface. It all begins with blue quills and continues with the appearance of Hendricksons, which keep on coming until about May 15. The Hendricksons are overlapped by March browns, and by the last few days in May, anglers start seeing big, clumsy-looking green drakes. The duns have veinated wings with a bright-olive tint and black markings, but the trout don't bother much with them, anyway. They are sometimes ravenous, however, for the green drake spinners, called coffin flies because of their funereal black speckled wings and chalky white abdomens. Imitated by floating patterns tied on size 8 or 10, 2XL hooks, the coffin flies that fall, spent, onto the stream surface just before full darkness attract vicious rises from the largest trout in the creek. We are talking genuine 18- to 20-inch browns, here.

The green drake hatch generally lasts until the first weekend in June or thereabouts, but good dry-fly fishing continues until the end of the month or longer, depending, as always, on the weather.

One definite plus for the East Branch is its mixed bank cover. It has something to pique the interest of any angler. During a full day of fishing, anglers who stay on the move will be challenged to cover surface rises over knee-deep runs and riffles, sharp bends, gravel bars, and even man-made pool diggers and other current-deflecting, hideout-creating structures. There is ample room throughout the East Branch for competent casters to try different rod-and-reel combinations or even learn how you or one of your other fishing companions.

While brown trout dominate the Richford–Berkshire reach of the creek, the headwaters of the East Branch and some spring holes and tributaries also provide decent living conditions for native brook trout. Anglers who explore the water in the vicinity of Harford should be able to find a few.

WEST BRANCH OWEGO CREEK

RATING: ★★★ (3 stars)

NOTEWORTHY: Cover, the more tangled the better, is the key to fishing success on the West Branch.

BEST TIME TO FISH: Autumn provides great opportunities to tangle with spawning browns and brookies.

Having fished the West Branch of Owego Creek under conditions good and bad, I am convinced that the trick to success on this stream is finding places where trout can hide well enough to elude predators of any kind.

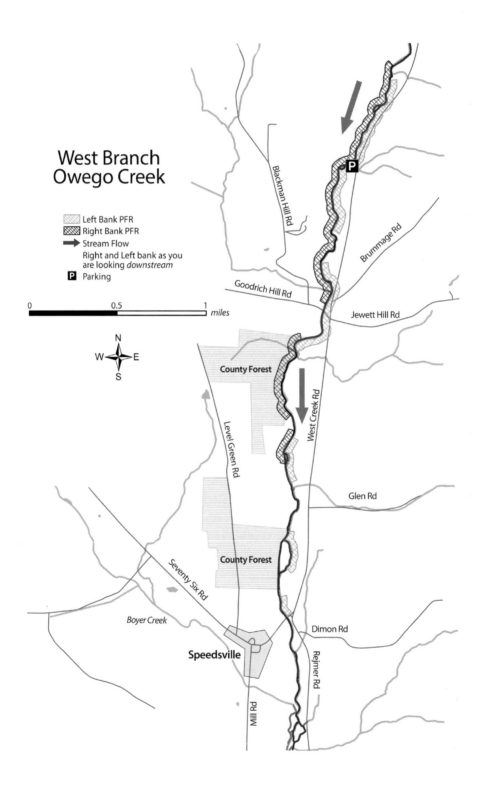

West Branch
Owego Creek

Left Bank PFR
Right Bank PFR
Stream Flow
Right and Left bank as you
are looking *downstream*
P Parking

0   0.5   1
                          miles

N
W ⊕ E
S

Blackman Hill Rd

Brummage Rd

Goodrich Hill Rd

Jewett Hill Rd

County Forest

Level Green Rd

West Creek Rd

Glen Rd

County Forest

Seventy Six Rd

Boyer Creek

Dimon Rd

Speedsville

Rejmer Rd

Mill Rd

And that is a lot easier than it sounds. Affiliates of the county Soil and Water Conservation District gave West Branch trout—and trout fishers—a big boost when they built a series of stream improvement structures in the jungle that borders the creek along West Creek Road below Route 79. Using live bait to fish as close as possible to the log-and-wire structures—or what remains of them after three or four decades of creek-wrecking floods—I have hooked and landed several browns in the 1½- to 2-pound class.

Even more interesting, at times when stream flows were well below normal in midsummer, I have seen large browns and even a couple of better-than-average brook trout in hiding right next to the aforementioned dams and wing deflectors. Most surprising was the general absence of trout from natural hiding places, such as deadfalls and undercuts, which were very close to the man-made cover.

From Caroline downstream to Speedsville, the West Branch of Owego Creek is the eastern boundary separating Tompkins and Tioga Counties. Coincidentally or not, Speedsville is the line of demarcation between water that's cold enough for summer trout and water that's not. If you go very far below Speedsville in July, you have headed in the wrong direction.

Owego Creek, West Branch.

OWEGO CREEK (MAIN STEM)

RATING: ★★ (2 stars)

NOTEWORTHY: Below the junction of East and West, you never know what might grab your lure.

BEST TIME TO FISH: Early to mid-May, when trout compete with much bigger critters.

By the time the East and West Branches of Owego Creek meld midway between Owego and Nichols, their water has warmed considerably, and most fishermen would probably be astounded to know that the main stem of Owego Creek holds some big fish—trout as well as other, piscivorous species. *Piscivorous*, in case you didn't know, means "inclined to eat fish at every opportunity." Holdover brown trout of 4, 5, or more pounds fit that definition, and so do walleyes, smallmouth bass, tiger muskies, and pure-bred muskellunge, among others. The lower Owego has all of the above, and very few people bother to fish it.

Suffice to say, any of the 3,600 or so brown trout—some 515 two-year-old browns among them—that are stocked in the Owego will either eat or be eaten. They might as well latch onto a stickbait, lipless crankbait, or whatever else has been collecting dust in somebody's tackle box.

CATATONK CREEK

RATING: ★★ (2 stars)

NOTEWORTHY: A little of this and a little of that are this creek's "usual."

BEST TIME TO FISH: Whenever you can find a young boy or girl to take along.

You never know what you will reel in next when fishing Catatonk Creek, so why not mentor a young angler when you feel like dunking a line in this pseudo-trout stream?

Catatonk Creek is accessible from Route 96 between Owego and Spencer. It's a very rural stream that meanders through farm country. Recently it has been stocked at the rate of 1,400 brown trout a year, but the hatchery evictees share the water with walleyes, panfish, and both largemouth and smallmouth bass.

If you do take a kid fishing in Catatonk Creek, keep a watchful eye, for it's a wide stream, up to 100 feet across, and has some pools that can be 15 feet deep at normal levels.

MILLER BROOK

RATING: ★★ (2 stars)

NOTEWORTHY: Wild browns a possibility, not a promise.

BEST TIME TO FISH: Opening day or as soon after as you can manage.

A bit of a long shot, Miller Brook is no longer is stocked but still has a reputation for holding some wild browns. The lower half of this 10- to 12-foot-wide stream has excellent bank cover, season-long cool water, a clean gravel bottom, and some access off Fisher Settlement Road, north of the hamlet of Spencer.

BROOME COUNTY

In terms of trout fishing, you could say Broome County hasn't got much, but what it does have is pretty good. The county takes in but three trout streams, two of the put-and-take variety and one that would make any angler proud to have made its acquaintance. Let's look at that one before we talk about the also-rans.

OQUAGA CREEK

RATING: ★★★★ (4 stars)

NOTEWORTHY: As a tributary of the West Branch of the Delaware River, Oquaga Creek definitely has connections.

BEST TIME TO FISH: The last week of April can be awesome, some years.

Picture overwintering trout, both rainbows and browns, that are feeling hungry now that the water and weather are finally warming up a few degrees. To jump-start the fun, three or four species of aquatic insects (blue quill and Hendrickson mayflies and some early black stone flies, at a minimum) are popping through the surface like kernels of Orville Redenbacher's best.

That's the sort of panorama that is imagined by anglers who fish Broome County's finest trout stream, Oquaga Creek. In Deposit, where the West Branch of the Delaware and Oquaga mingle their silt and gravel, anglers from Central New York and the Catskills symbolically shake hands and, merely by splitting their bill at the local Wendy's or identifying an unfamiliar bug on the water, perpetuate a grand angling heritage.

Oquaga Creek is a prototypical Central New York trout stream that fits right in with its Catskill neighbors, too. Home to wild and stocked browns and lesser numbers of native brookies, it is of moderate size, averaging 20 to 25 feet across. Hip boots are adequate for wading most,

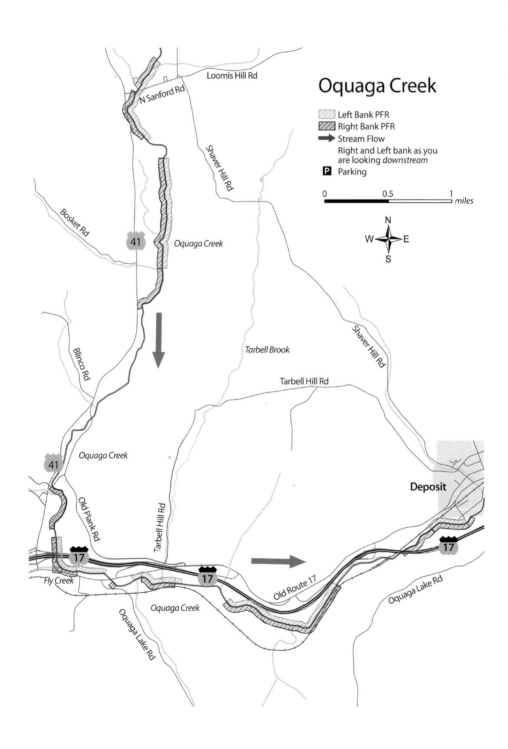

Oquaga Creek

Left Bank PFR
Right Bank PFR
Stream Flow
Right and Left bank as you
are looking *downstream*
P Parking

0   0.5   1
                     miles

N
W   E
S

Loomis Hill Rd

N Sanford Rd

Shaver Hill Rd

Bosket Rd

41

Oquaga Creek

Blinco Rd

Tarbell Brook

Shaver Hill Rd

Tarbell Hill Rd

Oquaga Creek

41

Deposit

Old Plank Rd

Tarbell Hill Rd

17

17

Fly Creek

17

Old Route 17

Oquaga Lake Rd

Oquaga Creek

Oquaga Lake Rd

if not all of the creek, which has numerous 2- to 4-foot-deep pools as it tumbles southward. The streambed consists primarily of gravel and cobble rock from its origins near Arctic Lake through the hamlet of Sanford and on to McClure, where it goes under Route 17 and hangs a sharp left toward Deposit.

The entire length of the creek is approximately 15 miles. DEC public fishing signs are posted on 4¼ miles of the stream, and many landowners who have NO TRESPASSING posters along the creek will grant permission on request.

Above McClure, the creek runs along Route 41, mainly through farmlands and clustered housing developments. From McClure down to its mouth, the creek plays peek-a-boo with anglers on Route 17 who are straining to get a look at it. The surroundings on this last leg of the creek's journey feature a mix of brushy, forested areas and actively farmed property. This homestretch, if you will, is managed with special regulations. From the Old Route 17 bridge (east of McClure) for 3 miles downstream to the new Route 17 bridge just west of Deposit, the creek is subject to year-round catch-and-release fishing, using artificial flies or lures only.

Oquaga Creek is stocked with about 3,900 brown trout annually, including 400 or so two-year-olds.

NANTICOKE CREEK

RATING: ★★★ (3 stars)

NOTEWORTHY: Not as good as it looks from the road, but locals fish it
   fairly hard for stocked browns.

BEST TIME TO FISH: With fairly heavy fishing pressure to consider, early to
   mid-April is where the smart money goes.

From Route 26, which traces long, lazy curves through the surrounding pasturelands, Nanticoke Creek has a seductive look. The stream has one nice undercut bend after another, or so it seems at a distance. Close up, experienced anglers might recognize the signs of frequent flooding—mud cast up on the creekbank, trash washed into whirlpools, and very loose gravel that washes out from under your boots as you cross the creek. A general shortage of shade cover suggests warm temperatures would threaten the survivability of stocked fish, and that is indeed the case. Yet Nanticoke Creek is fished hard by Broome County residents, and the state accommodates the inevitable crowding by planting about 4,000 trout in the stream every spring. About 800 of the stockers are two-year-olds that, though not as pretty as wild fish, put up a strong fight and taste good, too.

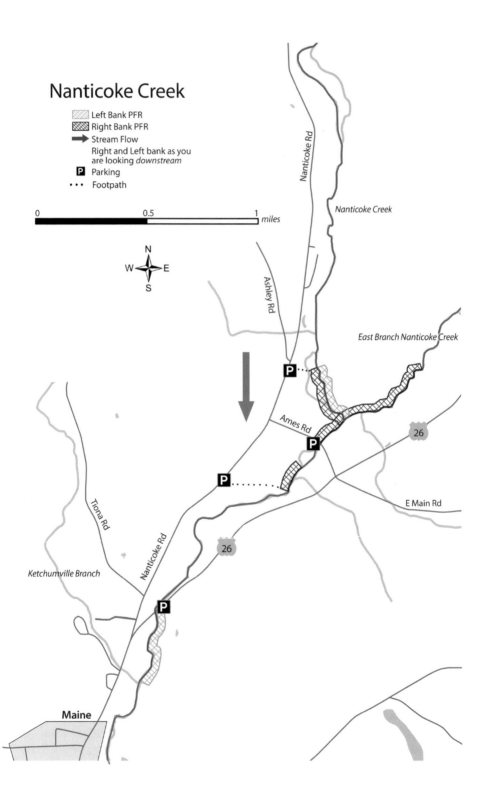

Nanticoke Creek

Left Bank PFR
Right Bank PFR
Stream Flow
Right and Left bank as you
are looking *downstream*
P Parking
••• Footpath

0   0.5   1
miles

N
W ← → E
S

Nanticoke Rd

Nanticoke Creek

Ashley Rd

East Branch Nanticoke Creek

Ames Rd

26

E Main Rd

Tioma Rd

Nanticoke Rd

Ketchumville Branch

26

Maine

Nanticoke Creek is worth fishing in the early part of the season from just below Whitney Point downstream to Glen Aubrey and the village of Maine. It is reassuring, in this age, to encounter a decent trout stream that has so few KEEP OUT signs.

DUDLEY CREEK

RATING: ★★ (2 stars)

NOTEWORTHY: A small tributary of the Tioughnioga River with mediocre fishing for brown trout.

BEST TIME TO FISH: Do you happen to have a stocking schedule?

This creek was sprinkled with 400 browns of 8 to 9 inches last spring, but they vanished in a hurry and most wound up in the stomachs of local fisherman. Dudley Creek will never be routinely mentioned in the same sentence as any of New York's famous trout rivers, but the stream does provide some healthy recreation to anglers living in the Lisle–Whitney Point area. It's about 15 feet across, in most spots, but inconsistent water levels tend to make it mainly a put-and-take area, at its best early in the morning and early in the season, too.

You can judge it for yourself, of course. To get a close-up, take Route 79 east from the hamlet of Richford—which itself is part of the headwaters of the East Branch of Owego Creek—and slow down or stop occasionally to examine the stream on your right. That's Dudley Creek, and you are heading downstream on it. It keeps going until it enters the Tioughnioga near the hamlet of Lisle.

CHENANGO COUNTY

Did we save the best for last? No, although Chenango County's trout streams are worthy of more attention, from local anglers as well as traveling sportsmen. The smaller creeks have a lot going for them, including very good water quality and excellent bank cover, but public access in the county is quite limited. Any readers who might be planning a special trip to scout for a couple of honey holes that they could revisit in the years ahead are putting the creel before the reel—unless they are scouting the county's premier stream.

GENEGANTSLET CREEK

RATING: ★★★★ (4 stars)

NOTEWORTHY: A no-kill section that is bypassed by anglers on their way to the Catskills is all yours on many evenings.

BEST TIME TO FISH: Late May or early June.

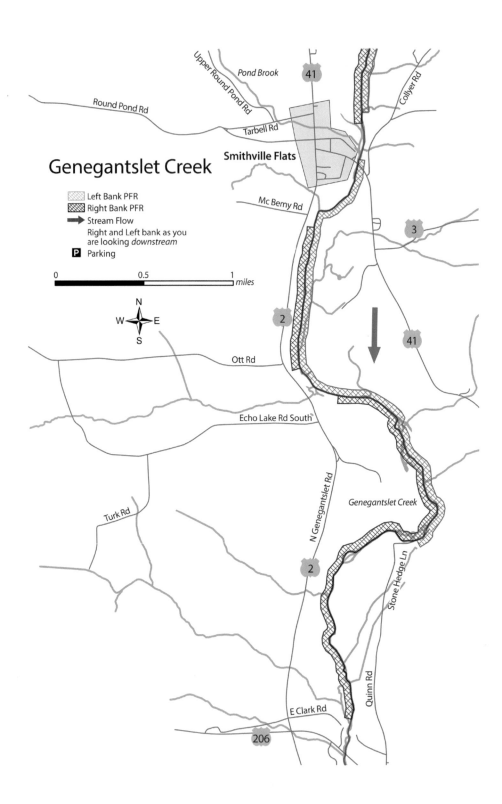

Genegantslet Creek

Smithville Flats

Legend:
- Left Bank PFR
- Right Bank PFR
- Stream Flow
  Right and Left bank as you are looking *downstream*
- P Parking

0   0.5   1 miles

N
W—E
S

Pond Brook

Upper Round Pond Rd

Round Pond Rd

41

Collyer Rd

Tarbell Rd

Mc Berny Rd

3

2

41

Ott Rd

Echo Lake Rd South

N Genegantslet Rd

Turk Rd

Genegantslet Creek

Stone Hedge Ln

2

Quinn Rd

E Clark Rd

206

To be frank, Chenango County's small streams are not the sort of drawing cards that will readily entice fishermen to wander from farm to farm in search of easy access. The main attraction nowadays is a 20- to 30-foot-wide stream called Genegantslet Creek. Known to many area residents as "the Genny," its popularity can be attributed, in part, to the 10½ miles of its banks that are decorated with PFR signs. The Region 7 DEC staff announced last year that a major landowner has agreed to sell 8/10 mile of additional public fishing rights, downstream of Route 220 in McDonough.

The new public section is just a couple of casts south of a good-looking if rather lightly trafficked no-kill section. A small angler parking area on Route 220, northeast of Smithville Flats, points the way upstream to the catch-and-release area that is approximately 1 mile long. It features several deep pools, along with some knee-deep riffles and bank retention structures that slow erosion and provide shady cover for the creek's browns and brookies. On the whole, this looks like a very productive piece of water, and it is.

A wide variety of mayflies hatch in the Genny's no-kill, among them some size 14 and 18 sulfurs (*Ephemera invaria* and *E. dorothea*) and the much larger green drakes, which can be expected on or about June 1. The slightly tea-colored creek assumes fishable proportions and is adequately cold for trout near the intersection of County Roads 8 and 10 in East Pharsalia. Fishing is fair to good from there all the way downstream to the creek's junction with the Chenango River near the village of Greene.

Route 8 follows the Genny south through the town of McDonough, and numerous side roads lead to the creek, which is about 16 miles long.

While the no-kill gets the good press from most outdoors writers, the water immediately downstream from there probably has better fishing overall. It is open to bait, lure, or fly and hides some impressive fish.

DEC Region 7 fisheries manager Dave Lemon has vivid memories of two large brown trout he encountered during work and play below the no-kill area. The first fish he mentioned in an interview about the Genegantslet was about 19 inches long. Lemon spotted it on the bottom of the creek while he was snorkeling during a stream survey. Trout number two grabbed Lemon's spinning lure during a day off. He couldn't be sure because the fish broke free before it could be measured.

"I can't prove it, but I think it was better than 24 inches," he said.

BOWMAN CREEK

RATING: ★★★ (3 stars)
NOTEWORTHY: State forests provide ample access.
BEST TIME TO FISH: Early May, when wild browns and brookies are
  on the feed.

No public fishing rights? No problem! Bowman Creek is a good example of
a stream that is overlooked because the DEC does not have any PFR—yet it
is fished quite adequately from state forest lands in its upper reaches, in the
town of McDonough. It flows southeast from Bowman State Park before
joining the Chenango River about 5 miles downstream from Oxford.

Wild browns and native brookies coexist in this creek.

More Chenango County Trout Streams

You might, indeed, bump into a black bear or two if you fish **Bear Brook**,
which is found in the town of Oxford and spills into the Chenango River
near South Oxford. But you will need permission to trespass first. The
wild brown trout in **Shapley Brook**, a tributary of Bear Brook, are a better
bet as their pools are on state forest lands. Look for the state signs along
Coventry Road.

Landowner permission is critical for those who yearn to try **Kelsey
Brook**, which has good numbers of wild brown and brook trout, for
there is no public fishing area (but quite a few NO TRESPASSING signs)
over its entire length. The stream originates in the town of Oxford and
meanders through Bainbridge and Afton en route to its meeting with the
Susquehanna River.

PART II

Tactics for Taking Central New York Trout

CHAPTER FOUR

Of Worms and Rainy Days

Anybody out there who thought I was one of those fly-fishing purists should know by now they were dead wrong. The truth is, while I do enjoy fly fishing more than any other means of catching trout, I am not ashamed to admit my enthusiasm for other means, including spin fishing and bait dunking. While I am determined to match a heavy mayfly hatch by floating a well-constructed dry fly down a glassy flat, I often resort to turning up logs and pulling cornstalks when water and weather conditions tell me that worms are going to outfish flies by a wide margin. The aspect of fishing that I love best is catching fish, so long as it can be done legally and ethically. Some fly fishers, the so-called purists, labor under the illusion that their version of angling is inherently superior to other methods. However, I would remind them that long rodders are just as capable of chicanery and rudeness as any other "sportsmen," especially when they think nobody is watching them.

That's enough scolding for the time being, but we'll revisit the issue of angler behavior near the end of this book.

Meanwhile, the next time your favorite TV weather guru is predicting "scattered thunderstorms" or, better yet, "that rain our farmers have been asking for," gather up a can of lively worms or an assortment of streamers and bucktails or even a box of spinners and spoons. Make haste lest you miss out on one of the season's best fishing days.

When I was a young boy, trout fishing and worms were pretty much synonymous. Few adult anglers who visited Nine Mile Creek or most other Syracuse-area streams in those days did much fly fishing. In retrospect that seems strange, because most of the grown-ups I saw in action used

Late May on Oriskany Creek.

fly-fishing gear to drift worms or salted minnows through trout feeding lanes and hiding places. My father, for instance, used an 8-foot fly rod with a fly reel that was loaded with a level fly line. Instead of a tapered leader he used a 6- or -7-foot length of 6-pound monofilament. He added one or two split shot to his leader, about 8 or 10 inches above the size 4 hooks he preferred. With a swing-and-drop kind of lob cast, my father could put his night crawler or garden worm exactly where he wished, time after time.

Spinning tackle was increasingly popular with anglers in pursuit of bass, walleyes, and other species, especially those living in lakes, but in the late 1950s and early '60s fly rods remained the implements of choice for the average trout fisher in Central New York. That was true even when the "hatch" could be matched perfectly by anyone who was flexible enough to survey a freshly mowed and watered lawn after dark, with a flashlight and a tin can in hand. Back in the day it was nothing for me to "pick" 100 or more night crawlers in the short grass in our yard or in front of the Methodist church across the street. The contents of the large can stored in our family's cool cellar would last for at least several days. Naturally, the better the fishing, the more worms we would need.

Eventually, my young friends and I learned through trial and error or reading books resembling this one that streamer flies or nymph patterns could also be fished effectively after a downpour. However, then as now nothing outperformed a lively worm on those spring and summer days when heavy rains pumped up the currents in our favorite trout waters.

The tackle has changed quite a bit through the decades, but the same tactics that worked well 20 or 30 years ago still stir the blood of trout and anglers, alike.

It is no mystery why trout fishing is so good after a substantial rainstorm. The stream flow quickly increases, washing all sorts of trout food off streambanks, drooping tree limbs, and other streamside cover. Along with garden worms and night crawlers, aquatic nymphs and larvae are carried along in the swollen currents. After a few minutes of rain, hungry fish take advantage of the cloudy cover by sneaking out of their clear-water hideouts and beating the competition to the choppy riffles at the upstream ends of deep runs and pools. The biggest trout in the vicinity usually stake out the top ends of these chow lines, where they can readily gorge themselves on whatever gifts nature funnels their way.

Whether you tend to assemble your favorite bait rig, stick to your fly boxes, or eagerly fan cast deep pools with an ultralight spinner under these conditions, you can be confident of having some excellent sport when rain muddies the water. I am torn between bait and fly these days, and have learned to reach for both kinds of tackle when the latest weather forecast tells me that a long dry spell is about to make way for a cloudburst. Bait fishing should be deadly during the storm and afterward, when it begins to drop and clear again. At such a crossroads, Central New York trout streams can change dramatically, and I would not wish to pass up many of these eruptions of life, hunger, and satisfaction. Anglers who have been too long at the office or assembly line are invigorated by a long-anticipated storm; and until your hookset abruptly changes their mood, the fish themselves seem downright giddy.

I am sure even the most faithful of fly fishers would admit that rising, muddy water is made to order for a wriggling night crawler, rather than a wet fly, nymph, or streamer. Having caught many post-storm trout that had 40-plus garden worms and night crawlers in their gullets, I am positive trout and other game fish relish these land-born food sources and may well prefer them to minnows, nymphs, and other aquatic organisms. That is not the same, however, as saying worms are the only way to fish in rainy weather.

One of my pet Central New York streams, Skaneateles Creek, flows from the outlet dam at the north end of Skaneateles Lake to the Seneca River just north of the village of Jordan. The creek features an extensive no-kill stretch, from which no fish may be creeled. In the 1970s and '80s, when the stream was not yet under special regulations, it produced many large browns up to 20 or 22 inches long. Worms were a sure bet in those glorious times.

However, when catch-and-release rules were promulgated over approximately 90 percent of the creek's length, many anglers were mystified.

Although the DEC did not conduct any before-and-after survey pertaining to the impact of the new rules, any of us regulars could tell that fishing pressure was greatly diminished following the changes. The separation was particularly painful among bait fishermen. Many, having never tried much fly fishing, decided to continue their bait dunking at some other venue. The rest of the old Skaneateles Creek gang just drove up and down the roads that carried heavy automobile traffic between Skaneateles Creek and fished as usual, with flies that were offered for sale at three area fly shops, one each in Camillus, Jordan, and Skaneateles. And do you know what happened? Yep, every time it rained hard in Skaneateles Creek, fly fishers began to clobber their quarry. Forced to be both patient and innovative in order to seduce rainy-day trout with flies, I soon found myself slipping a net under 15 to 20 browns and rainbows during an average rainy morning or afternoon. My secret? I didn't really have any that would account for all the fun I was having, unless it was a general scarcity of other anglers along the creek. On those dripping wet days, I seldom bumped into another fisherman, and I always figured that privacy gave me a few extra shots a day at pools that would have been flailed constantly if they were located on other, more famous streams.

When I look back at those days, I realize how much they taught me about trout and trout fishing.

Forced by regulations to fish with flies or lures only, I learned to improvise ways to deliver streamers and nymphs to likely-looking tongues of current that often were no more than 10 feet away. Skaneateles Creek has a few stretches where anglers can do some conventional fly casting, but not many. Because the stream is narrow and the banks are thickly vegetated, I had to fish on those rainy days by flipping sidearm, roll casting, and steeple casting. More often than not, I had to start retrieving the second my offering hit the water, to avoid tangling in the rocky shallows. The only remedy for the plague of snags I suffered was frequent retying of leader tippets and the replacement of one lost fly with another. The fishing was so good at times that I learned *not* to come in from the rain unless I absolutely had to change clothes, get a sandwich, tie more flies, or—most likely—dig another can of worms.

My method of bait fishing for trout can be explained in a few words, and it's not even close to difficult. Like my father, I drift my worms with a fly rod and reel, but unlike Dad, I favor a long rod—10 or 11 feet from tip to fighting butt extension—compared with the 8-footer he preferred to use, and I spool my single-action reel with clear monofilament line, all of it 4-pound test. I like the setup because the light line and light-action rod are so super sensitive that I can constantly feel every little bounce, bump, or bite. I don't miss very many of the trout that try to peel a worm from my size 4 or 6 hook. The long stick is helpful when I'm playing a trout, too, as it bends deep and acts as a shock absorber when I connect with a big Finger Lakes rainbow, among other fish. One more point in favor of the big stick is the way I can employ it to reach way out from a creekbank and, with the assistance of two or three size 3/0 split shot, drop a worm tight to a trout feeding lane with amazing ease. On most parts of most Central New York streams, although not all, I can cast from bank to bank without getting my feet wet.

Even more important than my somewhat unconventional worming tackle is my purposely slow-motion means of getting to and through trout water. Some fellows—more than a few, actually—spoil their chances of catching trout consistently by thumping their feet on the ground as they walk along a stream and splashing as they wade in places that would have room to hold more trout if they weren't already occupied by your very own hip boots! As rain washes worms into a stream, the increased current

Chittenango Creek brown, caught using the author's usual bait-fishing rig consisting of a single-action reel, the spool loaded with 4- or 6-pound clear monofilament, and a rod that is 11 feet long.

gradually turns the water into some shade of gray or brown. The roily currents embolden fish that normally flee from their own shadows, and even the biggest, baddest browns in your favorite streams will slide into shoreline eddies and ankle-deep riffles to get first crack at the storm-fed smorgasbord. Unfortunately, they will also vanish in a Syracuse second when a wading angler puts a boot down in the vicinity of the chow line.

Too many fishermen are big walkers, as well as big talkers. They wallow around like water buffalo when they would be wise to move in slow motion, like a great blue heron.

CHAPTER FIVE

Spin Fishermen I Have Known

Although I have been a somewhat indifferent spin fisherman during most of my angling career, it has been my great pleasure to fish on numerous occasions with several expert hardware hurlers. I'm talking about fellows who can catch trout with spinners, spoons, jigs, and stickbaits as if their lures came from the local tackle shop with favorite game fish attached. Three such anglers come to mind whenever I am asked about the effectiveness of spinning lures and tactics to take wild or holdover trout. Bill Thomas of Fulton, Fred Neff of Baldwinsville, and, of course, one of my frequent companions on stream or lake, John "Kid" Corbett of Syracuse have much good advice for their brother angler. Their tips are so valuable, in my estimation, that fly fishermen and bait users can also benefit from their experience and wisdom.

Thomas has fished plenty in Onondaga, Oswego, and other Central New York counties, but he also has deep roots in the waters of our state's western region, and particularly in Wyoming County's Wiscoy Creek and East Koy Creek. Thomas honed his spinning skills in those two streams, but he will attest—and I will add a hearty amen to his declaration—that his methods are deadly on Syracuse-, Oswego-, and Auburn-area creeks, too. What struck me about him during a combination interview and on-stream research session a few years ago was the speed at which he fished. Thomas flipped his favorite weighted spinners (Mepps, Panther Martins, and others) as far as he could within the confines of a stream corridor, then retrieved at a furious rate. He covered each likely trout hideout or feeding station with one or two casts, then proceeded to the next promising spot. Most impressive, to me, was the fact that three-quarters of his casts were

On the South Otselic River.

directly *upstream* and the same three out of four retrieves were directly *downstream*. The retrieves, with few exceptions, were carried out as fast as humanly possible. I mean to tell you, during many of Thomas's retrieves, his left hand was practically a blur.

Often, the reel handle would rotate only four or five times before a 12- or 13-inch brown trout clobbered the lure.

"I don't want to give them a lot of time to look the lure over, especially in fast water," Thomas said. "A fast retrieve makes them think the lure is a fleeing minnow."

Hungry trout don't often let a panicky baitfish go unmolested, it seems.

Neff, a retired engineer, grew up fishing the trout streams of Pennsylvania, and he had misgivings about moving north to New York to work on national defense projects, but he got more optimistic in a hurry when he discovered how many enchanting trout streams flowed in view of backwoods roads and suburban commuter highways. The abundance and variety of Central New York waters included many medium-size and small creeks that sheltered brown trout in the 15- to 20-inch range.

Although he was (and is) a skilled fly fisher, Neff's meat-and-potatoes trout rig has been a spinning rod and reel that he uses to seduce those hook-jawed browns.

His favorite lures for such trout are stickbaits of 2 to 4 inches in length. In deep pools, he is likely to flip fast-sinking or "count-down" Rapalas. Shallower water calls for floaters that will run just under the stream surface. But no matter what lure he attaches to his 6- or 8-pound spinning line, it won't work its magic unless an accurate caster is running the show. Neff can drop his lure within an inch or two of his target, time after time. The only way to attain such proficiency is try, try, and try again. That means countless hours of "practice," which may or may not be fully appreciated by employers or family members.

Kid Corbett is a crafty, methodical angler who keeps diaries of his fishing trips and prowls area tackle stores in search of the exact item he needs to close the circle on the trout he specializes in pursuing. Wild brook trout are his passion, and Corbett stops to make a few casts at any bridge or culvert pool that even hints at harboring a fat native. Such places are not necessarily in the boondocks; during his more than three decades on the Syracuse police force, Corbett occasionally caught natives in the inner-city tributaries of Onondaga Creek.

Like Neff, Corbett is an exceptional caster, but what sets him apart from most anglers with spinning stick in hand is his attention to detail. I suspect the outcome of the late-night raids Corbett's Special Investigations Unit planned hinged on that ability to focus on the little things. Whether the job taught him the importance of details or his meticulous shopping for fishing lures carried over into his job, I can't say, but the fact that Corbett excelled at both work and play doesn't strike me as coincidence.

For instance, just as a police task force must account for every participant's location and safety when planning a drug bust, an angler must take pains to tie a snug knot and adjust a lure so it runs true. Corbett likes Palomar knots, which can be tricky to use but almost always last the day when he is working upstream through heavy cover. Under overcast skies or in a downpour, he takes the extra time to tie precise knots, even as his companion hurries through the procedure and gets the mediocre results that might be expected from his lazy attitude.

When I am that companion, I have been known to find a curlicue of monofilament where my knot slipped and a big trout abruptly changed its mind about joining me in a prolonged game of tug-of-war. To his credit, Corbett has never reproached me for my poor knots, and I thank him for that. If a lesson is painful enough, there's no reason to rub it in.

Not a few fly fishers speak ill of spinning-gear specialists, in good measure because they think those in the "hardware business" catch their trout by simply casting and cranking as far and as fast as possible. On the surface, Thomas might appear to fit that description, but his casting is on the money even in tight corridors like the alder thickets that guard resident brown trout in Wyoming County's East Koy Creek; and his ripping retrieves would be useless if he hung his hooks on every other limb he ran into. Nor would he or any other good spin fisher pick lures at random. Rather, they would all have some very specific tools in their kit when they hit the water.

Corbett's basic battery of trout takers, carried in a canvas creel or a shirt-pocket box, includes spinners, spoons, and jigs, but his not-so-secret weapon is a small floating stickbait. His go-to lures include 5-centimeter-long Rapalas in four paint patterns. The hues he finds most effective include brown trout, rainbow trout, black and silver, and black and gold. When creek flows have crested and are beginning to clear up, however, he goes for something a little more garish.

A careful approach is key to spin-fishing success.

"These are the best possible conditions for the kind of fishing I'm talking about," said Corbett. "And I have found I do my best then by tying on a chartreuse-and-silver Rapala."

Once the streams have their normal clarity, he switches back to his more subdued, natural color patterns.

In-line spinners, such as those sold under the Mepps and Panther Martin labels, are in Corbett's second tier of trout lures but are Thomas's old reliables; and Neff uses slightly bigger lures than they do because they have rewarded him with big fish. Who's wrong? None of them, as far as I can tell. Although spinning experts don't get to solve the daily puzzle of hatch-matching that so many fly fishers have come to enjoy, they do their own kind of detective work as they wonder which lure will work best the next time they go after the big ones.

CHAPTER SIX

Hatch-Matching Made Easy

Many angling wizards, including the majority of outdoors writers who take a whack at the subject, make the identification of mayflies and other aquatic species seem a lot more complicated than it really is. The most important aspect of hatch-matching is managing to be on the water when there's a hatch to match. You know that old saying about not being able to catch a fish unless you have a line in the water? Well, it's true, and there aren't many shortcuts. You have to be there, and the only ways to be in the right place at the right time are to tag along with somebody who knows when large numbers of aquatic insects are likely to hatch on various streams, or to assemble that trove of knowledge on your own.

All other factors being equal, the more time you can spend on the water, the more you will learn about hatch-matching.

The very best way to obtain your unofficial matcher of hatches degree is to pick the brains of other fishermen who have already passed the course with flying colors. Don't be shy about it, either.

Let's say you left home late, got to the water even later, and then watched in helpless frustration as the trout ignored your flies but ravaged whatever pattern the two fellows 100 yards downstream were using. The whooping and hollering made it clear the hatch was hot and heavy below. Where you stood, however, the only sounds to be heard were the blips and splashes made by feeding trout—some of which looked pretty big.

As the sun slipped below the surrounding hills, you could tiptoe away from the water and peel rubber getting out of the parking lot to make sure nobody heard about the skunking you just endured. Or you could stick around awhile and learn something.

The next time the trout swim wide circles around your flies, reel in a few minutes ahead of your usual quitting time, so you can get back to the angler parking area before the other guys show up. When they step into the clearing, say hello and then wait until they are struggling to get their chest waders off. Now you have a captive audience. Politely ask them how the trout were hitting, whether they caught any big ones, and, most important to your hatch-matching studies, what time the fish started rising and when they stopped.

You could follow up by asking what fly patterns drew all those strikes, but be aware that some will answer that one truthfully, but others will fudge a bit and a few will lie through their teeth. The ones you should make every effort to know better are those friendly folks who insist you put a couple of their favorite flies in your box before you leave for home.

Free flies or not, resolve to be on the water at the recommended time when you make a return trip.

The next time you try that spot, make the most of the advice you have accumulated by taking a few deep breaths and studying the water before you get your boots damp. While you're still on the streambank, look and listen for any signs of rising trout. You may hear a little splash or two before your eyes detect any swirls, spreading concentric rings or other trout calling cards. Do your best to zero in on at least one decent-size fish—but when you find that trout, don't cast to him right away. Instead, watch that fish come to the surface two or three more times. Between rises, look a short distance upstream, and try to determine roughly how many insects are floating toward "your" trout in a minute's time. Is the fish taking every bug that comes close to him, or are there so many that he obviously can't eat fast enough to get them all? Are some mayflies leaving the water before any fish get to them? At this point, look up, to see if swallows, cedar waxwings, or other birds are flying patrol over the water. If a high percentage of fluttering mayflies and caddis are dodging the birds long enough to reach the sheltering trees, you are looking at what is potentially a very heavy hatch. Plenty of trout will be rising, and you must quickly ID the insects they're after or miss out on some great fishing.

If you are seeing numerous insects with upright wings that make them resemble little sailboats, you will know you're observing mayfly duns, which in a few hours or days (depending on species) will metamorphose into ready-to-mate "spinners." At this time, though, the duns are hard to miss. Glue your eyes onto a little cluster of duns and watch closely what happens to them. You may observe several taking off from the stream surface, but within a few minutes you likely will see one or two floaters disappear amid spreading concentric circles. That's the confident rise form made by a nice trout as it engulfs a dun too wet to get airborne.

Having verified that the trout in front of you are zeroed in on mayfly duns, your next step is to capture a specimen or, better, several specimens. If you're lucky, one of the targeted insects will float or fly within reach of your free hand. More likely, you'll have to slip downstream 30 or 40 feet from your chosen fishing spot to catch a couple of bugs without disturbing any trout. Wade out a bit and use a small aquarium net—available anywhere goldfish are sold—to scoop a couple of samples from the surface.

If you can't identify your captives by genus and species in Latin, take note of their shape, size, and color, in that order of importance. Pick a close look-alike from your arsenal of dry flies, and you are ready to get in on the fun!

Sometimes, the trout you are dueling with aren't eating duns, but are taking swimming nymphs, spent-winged spinners, or something totally unexpected—like tiny cinnamon ants or beetles that are on the water as a result of gusting winds. Regardless of surprises, the same procedures I just outlined will lead you to the land of many hookups. Look the water over to detect fish activity, capture a specimen or, better, several specimens, notice their shape, size, and color. This always works, unless the trout have their fill before you decipher their menu.

Now and then, the stream surface will reveal not just one, but several mayfly species, and possibly a couple of caddis or stonefly species, too. On such an occasion, the hatch-matcher's skills are put to a graduate-level test. As a rule, the larger the stream, the more likely you are to find more than one aquatic insect hatching at once. In Central New York, Oriskany Creek in Madison and Oneida Counties and the Cohocton River in Steuben County are two sizable streams that have mixed hatches to decipher on a regular basis. The only way to determine which bugs are important and which can safely be ignored on a given day is to watch what the trout are doing, capture a few samples, and rule out the possibilities until just one remains. If, after all that, you don't have an artificial fly to sub for the real thing, you will just have to make a detour to a nearby tackle shop or stow a fly-tying kit in your fishing car.

To make certain you have at least a reasonable facsimile of whatever seems to be tickling a trout's fancy the next time you're enjoying a Central New York stream, organize your personal supply of drys, wets, and nymphs to include the following regional hatch chart.

Central New York Mayfly Hatches

Approximate Dates	Popular Name	Dry-Fly Hook Sizes	Notable Location
April 1–30	Blue-winged olive	18, 20	Skaneateles Creek
April 10–20	Quill Gordon	12, 14	W. Br. Tioughnioga R
April 15–30	Blue quill	16, 18	Owasco Inlet
April 25–May 15	Hendrickson	14	Butternut Creek
May 20–June 20	Sulfur	14	Nine Mile Creek
May 25–June 25	March brown	12	Chittenango Creek
May 28–June 10	Green drake	8, 10	W. Br. Fish Creek
June 1–30	Pale evening dun	16, 18	Oriskany Creek
June 5–15	Yellow drake	10, 12	Chenango Canal
June 15–July 15	Dun variant/Iso	10, 12	Nine Mile Creek
July 1–Sept. 30	Tricos	22–24	Cohocton River
Aug. 25–Sept. 10	White fly	12, 14	Chittenango Creek

CHAPTER SEVEN

Down Below with Nymphs and Wet Flies

My father was the best bait fisherman to tramp the banks of Nine Mile Creek, but he never knotted a trout fly to his leader until one summer in the late 1960s. At the time, I was a know-it-all college student who really knew very little about life, and Dad was still auditing one or two classes a semester at the School of Hard Knocks. He was skeptical about many things that other small-town folks like us accepted without question, but he was also pretty set in his ways and firmly convinced that he could still fish rings around his eldest son, if anybody wanted to make a contest on that score.

When I began urging him to leave his ever-reliable can of garden worms at home a couple of times and try his luck with a few of my hand-tied nymph and wet-fly patterns, he replied with snorts or guffaws. But as the July heat made his baits less attractive to local trout, I regaled him with colorful but true-life reports. Dad continued to scoff at my use of sunken flies, until the day he saw me jotting a fishing report in my streamside journal while my catch of the day glistened in the kitchen sink. He could no longer conceal his admiration for the slippery stack of brook trout. The smallest of the four natives measured 10½ inches long and the biggest was a foot-long male with a handsome kype.

"Where did you say you caught those?" he asked me.

I told him again that the trout I had creeled, and another five or six that I caught and released, all came from the swift runs and shaded pools between the Martisco railroad crossing and Big Bill's Bridge, the same hole that had produced a 4-pound brown trout for me 9 or 10 years before.

"And those flies you used," Dad said. "I'd have to borrow a few."

Apparently he had been listening to my reports, after all, because his last question cut to the heart of the matter.

"And basically all you're doing is fishing them as if you had a worm on your hook," he said. "Cast up and let them drift downstream, isn't that about it?"

To be sure, there is a little more than that to fishing with nymphs and wet flies, but not as much as an inexperienced angler might think. After my father came home that evening with several nice brookies and browns resting on a bed of ferns in his wicker creel, Nine Mile's trout were truly in a pickle. Dad still dug a can of worms when conditions plainly called for it, such as early in the season or following a warm-weather thunderstorm, but after he'd tried it a few times, he swore to anyone who cared to listen that there was no better way to catch trout than using those nymphs his son had tied for him.

Not surprisingly, after a couple of seasons spent fishing with nymphs and winged wet flies, Dad was not only the best bait fisherman in town, but one of Nine Mile Creek's most proficient fly fishers, as well.

Nymph-fishing experts, and the small number of modern fly fishers who still enjoy swinging a multiple-hook "cast" of wet flies down and

These exoskeletons of Isonychia nymphs on a rock prove this species has been hatching lately. In Central New York these "dun variants" appear from about mid-August to mid-September.

across a swift riffle, sometimes exaggerate the difficulty of mastering these dark arts. Sometimes, I have to shake my head when I hear a couple of young fly fishers solemnly informing a beginner who has found his way into their circle that he should learn how to fish a dry fly effectively and concentrate on surface-fishing techniques before he even attempted to understand the theory and mechanics of subsurface methods.

And that, of course, is pure hooey, for the fastest way for a neophyte fly fisher to catch trout consistently is to start plunking an artificial nymph upstream of his wading or walking position. Pinching a size B or BB split shot on the leader will help get the fly down near the bottom, and the addition of a small bobber—which we fly rodders prefer to call a "strike indicator"—makes it easier to keep track of the fly as the current takes it for a ride. Watch that bobber and develop a twitch that causes you to raise your forearm sharply the very instant that float dives, jumps half an inch, or just acts sort of funky and you are well on your way to becoming a successful nymph fisherman. Reminds you of bait fishing, I'll bet. Suffice it to know this works, and very well.

I know because I taught several friends how to fish for trout in this manner, and none of them failed to catch at least a couple of nymph nibblers during their first lesson. They needed to follow up the outing with backyard casting practice, but the most difficult aspect of nymph fishing—strike detection—was essentially mastered right away. The key was to respond with a quick lift of wrist and forearm at the slightest hint of a strike. In other words, when in doubt, yank it out! After several on-the-water coaching sessions, most of my pupils were doing this almost reflexively.

Wet flies are a slightly tougher nut to crack. You would best begin your first lesson on wets by doing some historical research. Specifically, the rookie wet-fly fisherman should go to the public library, locate the fishing section, and start scanning the pertinent shelf or shelves for dusty tomes with yellowing pages and cracked spines. I say this because the wet fly's heyday came to an end in the 1950s, with the retirement of great angling writers such as longtime *Outdoor Life* fishing editor Ray Bergman and John Alden Knight, who developed the Solunar Tables to track the positions of moon and sun to calculate the times when trout and other fish were most likely to bite on a given day.

Wet flies in Bergman's time were generally a bit overdressed and therefore difficult to sink more than a couple of inches unless you knew a few tricks to make winged patterns run deeper. One of those maneuvers called for overcasting, so that you had about 10 feet more line on the water than appeared to be necessary. From this position, you could mend the line in the upstream direction to slow the drift and give the fly more time to sink. Alternatively, you might mend line with a downstream wrist roll, causing the fly to speed up. Because wet flies were the "old reliables" that most serious fly fishermen carried everywhere they went in that era, many anglers developed their own tactics to try whenever conditions were difficult.

Tackle shops across the United States, as well as Herter's and other mail-order catalogs, appealed to imaginative trout fishermen by offering dozens or even hundreds of wet-fly patterns for sale. Although some of these subsurface baits at least vaguely resembled real mayflies, caddis, or other food sources, the majority were flights of fancy, more likely to entice shoppers than trout. Think of the old brook trout flies, for example, like the Parmachene Belle, the Silver Doctor, or the Montreal. They were pretty to look at and undoubtedly caught many fine fish, back in the day when brookies were widespread and abundant, but few fishermen of this era bother carrying even a sparse assortment of so-called attractor wet flies such as these. This is the case even though some of the wets relied on by Bergman and his many admirers were drab in color and hackled in such a way that they seemed to live and breathe in river currents.

Even the more sober and insect-like wet fly patterns had their fall from grace, and it was not because of any dramatic flaws in their appearance or design. Rather, the wet fly's fade from America's fly boxes was due to the spectacular splash of the artificial nymph upon the fly-fishing scene. The great Edward Ringwood Hewitt, dean of the Neversink River in the Catskills, started it off when he wrote extensively of his experiments with lacquered-body nymph patterns in the 1930. Bergman himself probably contributed to the demise of his own favorite wet flies (and dry patterns, too) by touting some Hewitt-style nymphs in the color plates that appeared in his widely read book, *Trout.*

But Bergman was not alone in popularizing nymph imitations and nymph-fishing methods and tactics. To the contrary, giants in the fly-fishing world climbed on board the nymphing bandwagon one after the other in the years following World War II. *Field & Stream* fishing editor A. J. McClane, the internationally popular freelance outdoors writer Joe Brooks, and fly-fishing wunderkind Ernest Schwiebert (author of *Matching the Hatch*) were among those who touted the comparative advantages of nymphs over wet flies in the 1950s and '60s, and few among angling's rank and file would raise a voice in protest.

Fortunately for all of us, the wet fly never quite made it to oblivion. Even as nymph fishing became more and more popular, a few visionary anglers chose to refine classic wet-fly patterns, and the methods of fishing them. In 1941, a modest and unassuming fly fisher named Jim Leisenring wrote a pocket-size book called *The Art of Tying the Wet Fly*, which was decades ahead of its time in that it emphasized patterns, many without wings and featuring spun fur and wispy hackles, picked and plucked for the specific purpose of imitating the movements of hatching caddis or mayflies. Leisenring's most effective flies were sort of a cross between nymphs and wet flies, which were popularly referred to as "flymphs." Three decades later, a fly tier named Sylvester Nemes gained a sort of cult following by introducing soft-hackle wet flies. His patterns were somewhat reminiscent of Leisenring's but had even more movement due to Nemes's artful deployment of delicate hackles to suggest wings and legs.

I assure you, trout fishers in Central New York, where I live, have kept up with the times with regard to nymphs and wet flies. Among the many Syracuse-area anglers who regularly carry and cast all manner of sunken patterns, one who stands out in my mind is Mike DeTomaso, who manages the White River Fly Shop in the Auburn Bass Pro Shops store. I have shared the water with him on Nine Mile Creek, Skaneateles Creek, and other area streams—although not as often as I'd like—and although he loves to tie on a dry fly when a good hatch is under way, he is also very adept at swinging a soft-hackle pattern, such as a Partridge and Green, down and across a riffle or run. He catches some beautiful trout this way, and so will anyone who correctly copies his method.

You don't need to exactly mimic another fisherman in order to hook his share of browns, brookies, and 'bows, but we can all learn from others. It is even possible, once in a lifetime or thereabouts, for a father to glean something from his obnoxious son.

CHAPTER EIGHT

Streamers and Big Trout Are Like Bogie and Bacall

First, if there are any readers out there who don't recognize the names in this chapter's title, I feel sorry for them, because Bogie (that's Humphrey Bogart) and Bacall (Lauren) very likely had more chemistry, heat, smoldering passion, or whatever film critics might call it now than any other leading man and leading lady in Hollywood history. Doubters can check this out by Googling the details, if necessary. For now, suffice to say Bogie and Bacall were both marvelous actors on their own, but their star quality really kicked into gear when the plot called for one to notice the other. They were even better, hotter, if you prefer, than Tracy and Hepburn or Gable and Gardner.

If you aren't on the same page with me yet, just imagine, if you're a male of the species, how great it would be if you somehow managed to show up at your high school class reunion with J-Lo draped on your arm. Ladies, sub George Clooney for J-Lo. Even now we're not in the same league as Bogie and Bacall, but you get the idea.

Now, all you anglers, picture a big trout, maybe a 20-incher that weighs about 3 pounds, and imagine you know right where it lives and have just signed up for a trout-fishing derby to be held on that very stream. It's a one-fly contest. The rules specify that if you break off on a snag or the fly is lost for any other reason, you're eliminated. Furthermore, the biggest trout wins. It doesn't matter how many you catch; only your big fish of the day will count. Finally, in addition to $1,000 in cash, the winner will receive a night on the town with J-Lo, or George.

I bet I know what kind of fly you would choose!

Streamers and big trout go together like Bogie and Bacall, or J-Lo (or George) and you. If I were entering the one-fly, I'd opt to fish a black-and-olive Woolly Bugger, tied on a 2X-long size 8 hook. The Bugger doesn't look much like a minnow; in fact, it strikes me as a dead ringer for a retreating crayfish with snapping claws. But you'll find it listed among streamer patterns in most angling catalogs. The more I think about it, this fly is one of the more versatile critters that ever emerged from a fly-tying vise. You can drift it downstream, then twitch it back up to tease and intimidate the bigger fish in any river. You could work a little fly flotant into the Bugger's spiraled hackle, so that the fly will skim along just under the stream surface as it drifts from Point A to Point B. Or you could put a small split shot on the leader just an inch or two above the fly. That simple tackle adjustment permits you to retrieve the Bugger with a quick jigging motion, but you probably wouldn't want to try that in a one-fly contest, as you are bound to get your share of the river bottom. Anyway, I suspect you have a mock minnow of your own, maybe even one as radical as a Woolly Bugger, which you save for use when nothing else is working.

If that's the story, no wonder J-Lo keeps checking her watch!

Think of streamers as submarine sandwiches and other types of trout flies as popcorn, pretzels, or some other salty snack. Experience has taught you (and large trout) to appreciate foods that that can fill up an empty stomach, fast.

Other trout tidbits, whether they come in the form of aquatic insects or garden worms or any other little yum-yums that an old brown may depend on for its calories, are tasty but scattered throughout the fish's world. Trout forced to survive on them take huge chances, day after day. Feeding in the open, in plain view of ospreys, herons, otters, or other predators, is an extremely hazardous lifestyle. Its odds of attaining old age improve considerably if the trout we're monitoring can hide in a secure location—for example, under a shadowy creekbank or in the nooks and crannies created by a thick logjam—and dart out, now and then, to grab a belly-filling chub, shiner, or sucker minnow.

The baitfish itemized here can be thought of as the trout's version of hefty hoagies, and fishermen who are both lucky and skilled enough to use streamer flies on a regular basis are going to get their share of big fish, year in and year out.

Many anglers would have raised a hand by now to ask whether a certain spinning lure—perhaps a copper-colored Phoebe or a gold-and-black Rapala or whatever lure comes to mind—might be even more effective than a streamer pattern on whopper browns and rainbows. If we were talking in terms of big water only, the comparison might be valid. After all, no fly caster can cover a 100-foot-wide river as thoroughly and efficiently as a spin-fishing specialist can probe with a compact lure and an ultralight rod and reel, harnessed with 4-pound-test monofilament. However, I am moderating this discussion, and I am not limiting it to sprawling, western-style rivers, of which Central New York has very few. We're talking brooks, creeks, rivers, and every patch of moving water in between, and for everyday action in all sizes of streams, a fly that looks like a small fish (but not too small) will outperform spinning lures in many situations, if not quite all of them.

In particular, I would like to attest to the Woolly Bugger's all-around usefulness. With or without weight built into the fly or pinched on the leader, a Bugger can be flipped or roll cast up across the stream you are working. Most of the time, nothing more than a couple of quick mends will be required to keep the fly coming your way. By slightly changing your casting position as you work your way up the stretch you are exploring, you should be able to cover virtually every potential hiding place for a plus-size trout. In high water, I like to change directions and tactics now and then, casting ahead of me as I wade downstream along the stream's edge. In this way, I can manipulate the fly so it acts remarkably like a cray-fish, scuttling from one half-submerged boulder to the next. To make this tactic pay off, I raise the rod just enough to ease the fly over a large rock or around a deadfall, then drop the tip to lower the fly into a pocket or eddy. The trick is to use your imagination without losing your focus on the task at hand.

On those frustrating days when trout of any size are hard to come by, you may at least get a few nice ones to follow your fly. These should not be thought of as wasted trips, especially if you have the foresight to keep pen and paper handy for the purpose of sketching crude maps and noting landmarks that will help you cover the water more efficiently when you make a return trip.

Although it is very unlikely that our hypothetical one-fly trout derby will include after-dark fishing, due to liability issues, an occasional night-time expedition centered on the use of meaty-looking streamer patterns could reap some amazing results for a skillful trout fisher.

It so happens that big browns do their best work between sunset and sunrise. A delightful book on the topic of tussling with such fish under pitch-black skies is the late Jim Bashline's *Night Fishing for Trout*, which has been in print for more than 40 years. Not many fishing books last anywhere near that long. Bashline's slim little classic owes its staying power to the author's enjoyable writing style and his use of vivid anecdotes to simultaneously inform and entertain his readers. Every paragraph seems to contain at least one piece of instruction, on subjects ranging from the parts of a stream most likely to hold the largest fish to the names and patterns of flies that are at their trout-taking best under the cover of darkness.

Bashline was an advocate of the KISS school of trout fishing—"Keep it Simple, Stupid"—whether he was on the water before or after fog and gloom had settled in for a few hours. He was not very secretive about the location of fishy pools, probably because he knew that only a fraction of anglers, even in his own trout-crazy state of Pennsylvania, would ever give night fishing a thorough try, let alone succeed at it.

My night outings have become more common with age, partly because I do not relish being crowded by other fishermen during daylight excursions. Although my best late-night browns have barely exceeded the 16-inch mark, I have hooked and lost some larger fish on a couple of occasions. I've had my best luck on nights that are moonless or nearly so. It is worth remembering, when you plan your late-hours adventures, that the best fishing can be expected on the darkest nights. Calm weather is preferable only because gusts and steady blows, alike, make fly-casting quite difficult whether the stream surface is gloomy or illuminated by a full moon. Given the opportunity to pick and choose from weather forecasts, I would go hunting for trout at night only when the water was a few degrees cooler than the air, the moon was hidden by dense clouds, and a light drizzle peppered the stream surface. Each of those conditions would embolden the larger residents of any stream to slowly cruise the shallows or move from a hiding place to the head or tail of a deep pool.

I have stuck mainly to short-line, down-and-across presentations at night, and been rewarded with jolting strikes on occasion in my home waters of Nine Mile Creek and Skaneateles Creek. Still, I prefer to do most of my trout fishing during the day, and I think that applies to 95 percent of my fellow anglers. Why? Because I like to see what I'm doing—and where I'm about to step.

At this point, I am quite certain most readers would admit that streamers are extremely practical flies that can be used in a variety of angling scenarios, especially those that involve big fish on the prowl for little or medium-size fish. I have also suggested that streamers are superior to most other types of trout flies for finding and catching large salmonids. Going a bit farther out on a limb, I have declared that streamers outperform most spinning lures—including in-line spinners, spoons, and jigs—when hunting specifically for large trout. The most difficult aspect of casting and retrieving spinning lures is the avoidance of in-stream snags. In contrast, if you are crafty and coordinated, you can vary the pace of retrieves in such a way that hanging up on rocks, sunken branches, and similar hook-grabbers is an occasional annoyance, rather than a maddening problem.

The one arena in which streamer flies are less effective than minnow-like spinning lures, in my opinion, is at the surface of a stream. In that location, a floating stickbait, such as a Rapala floater in rainbow trout colors, may well be easier to cast and retrieve than a streamer. In low-light conditions, stickbaits are apt to draw vicious strikes from trout in the 20-inches-and-change category. Streamers can also be fished with deadly effect at the surface, but some fly patterns will work better than others. Of course, some streams are more likely than others to hold big bait or big trout, too.

One of my favorite creeks, Owasco Inlet in Cayuga County, seems at times to have a large brown—say, one of 16 inches or better—in every pool. But there are other times when these same pools appear to be barren. If I can hit that very-much-underrated stream immediately after a heavy summer rain, I have a good chance of confirming the presence of one or two lunkers. The best way to settle the issue is to use night crawlers or a big, breathing, pulsing streamer fly. You might not catch every one of the fish that swirls at your bucktail, but you will hook some of them, including some dandies.

A quick, darting retrieve often draws nasty strikes when the water is up and colored after a recent rainstorm, but under clear-water conditions, dead-drift tactics are more productive. I am not positive about this, but it strikes me that the drifting streamer is much less intimidating to slow-water trout than a more aggressive presentation.

Feeding line downstream from your position by raising your rod and shaking its tip to let out some slack is a good method for attaining a nearly motionless drift. For starters, this little trick will give indecisive trout two enticing peeks at your fly, once on the way downstream and again when it's retrieved. The first view is of a "dead" or dying minnow, floating or faintly struggling as it breathes its last. Any trout that misses a bite of that free meal or, worse yet, lets another fish snatch it before his very eyes, will want first dibs on any goodies that happen to come his way a few minutes later. That is where the retrieve, or "return trip," becomes critical. When you are ready to bring the fly back to you, pause first with your streamer hanging in the current, then begin a series of quick, foot-long line strips. Let the fly hang in midstream for 30 seconds or so while you take a couple of deep breaths and try to anticipate how you should and will react if the target trout grabs your fly. Look for a shallow place, close to the bank or in a snag-free part of the creek bottom you are fishing. It you see a flat patch of sand or gravel that's just close by, picture yourself steering your well-hooked trout in that direction. On the other hand, if the bank is lined with dense vegetation or irregularly shaped boulders, you might want to keep your landing net handy. Keep your composure and carry out your well-designed game plan for besting these particular trout. Be confident, yes, but don't take any foolish risks to cut down on fight time.

As I indicated earlier, not all of the spots you presume to be lunker hotels actually hold big trout. Any cold-water stream this side of New Zealand holds more small and medium-size trout than whoppers. You can't get rid of them, and why would you want to, anyway? Think of your average fish as sparring partners getting you ready for a boxing main event. Eventually, as you zero in on the pools within pools that really do shelter 20-inchers, all the practice fishing you've been doing with streamers will pay off, big-time.

CHAPTER NINE

Filling Up Your Fly Box

On those infrequent occasions when the trout are refusing to cooperate with my recreational program, I look around for another humble and perhaps slightly bored angler. When I find such a fellow, sitting on a rock and rummaging through his vest for something that might wake the fish up, I make him a proposition.

Specifically, I ask this stranger if he would mind letting me check the contents of his fly boxes. In return, he would be welcome to browse through my nymphs, wets, drys, and streamer patterns, too.

This proposal has never been refused. Curiosity gets the best of a good fly fisher every time, and why shouldn't it? This simple exchange of information, which usually takes no more than 5 or 10 minutes, always yields a little something for both participants to chew on.

One thing that the fly-box comparison makes obvious is the individualism of your average angler. You might think that two fly flingers who regularly fish the same water would be likely to carry similar patterns in their vests. But in fact, my experience is that any fly fisher I meet along a Central New York creek or river will have his own, distinct ideas as to what flies he ought to take along on a trout trip.

My own A-list of trout takers follows below, and it is still a work in progress. Be mindful that these dependable patterns are not meant to match specific insect hatches, for the most part. Instead, I think of them as flies that will keep my rod bent between hatches, and enable me to catch a few trout before and after area streams are blanketed with bugs.

If you'd like to tie some of these fishy-looking concoctions but aren't sure about the ingredients in a couple of the recipes, look for me the next time you're on the water. Who knows? I might have a couple of extras you can transfer from my arsenal to yours.

Part of the author's rainbow fly assortment which he always brings along to Naples Creek and other streams that are fished heavily during the spring rainbow run. Shown are large nymphs, San Juan worms, and trout egg cluster imitations.

A CENTRAL NEW YORK FLY BOX

Nymphs and Wet Flies

- Hendrickson nymph, size 14 hook. Whether or not you tie them with a body of reddish-brown seal's fur and make legs and tails of feather barbs snipped from the longest tail feather of a cock ring-necked pheasant, Hendricksons of two species (*Ephemerella subvaria* and *E. invaria*) are abundant in many Central New York trout streams.

- Hendrickson Snowshoe Emerger, size 14. Substituting a swatch of glossy fur from the foot of a varying hare for the more traditional bunch of wood duck feather barbs results in a deadly pattern to use during the exciting sulfur hatches on Nine Mile Creek, Chittenango Creek, and even the upper end of the West Branch of the Delaware River at Deposit.

- Beadhead Caddis, assorted colors, sizes 14 through 16. Once a revolutionary concept, the simple addition of a metal bead to a caddis larva pattern creates a fly so simple to make and deadly to fish that every angler should carry a couple of dozen at all times.
- Whitlock Red Fox Squirrel Hair (RFSH) nymph, sizes 8 through 16. Dave Whitlock's pet nymph looks like anything you want it to, but to me this killer fly is the perfect copy of a cranefly larvae, which trout eat by the dozens during spring downpours. During a hatch of green drakes, an RFSH that's dressed with your favorite fly flotant is a perfect imitation of an emerging nymph or a nymphal shuck.
- Nine Mile Scud, sizes 14 through 18. My friend Jake DeCapio invented the Nine Mile Scud during a fly-tying session at the Wayfarer tackle shop in Camillus. If its light tan body and silver beadhead look at all like the scuds in Nine Mile Creek, I can't see the resemblance, but the fly works in Nine Mile and every other stream where I've tried it.
- Cased Caddis Larva, sizes 10 through 14. This is a pattern to fish with confidence in any stream whose silty edges are alive with caddis. Skaneateles Creek, to name one example, is loaded with tan and olive caddis that have little take-along houses made of decaying leaves, twigs, and bits of sand and gravel.
- Queen of Waters wet fly, sizes 12, 14. In April and May, I often fish a two-fly rig, with one of the aforementioned nymphs serving as my tippet fly. The Queen of Waters wet fly is affixed to a 3- or 4-inch dropper line set about 2 to 3 feet above the tippet pattern. I came to rely on the Queen of Waters because I caught a fair number of Nine Mile Creek

Brown trout, Nine Mile Creek.

browns on it, many years ago. The local trout seem to go for orange-bodied flies, in general.

- Dun Variant nymph, aka *Isonychia*, sizes 10, 12. The late, great Art Flick, who was the guru of anglers who fished Schoharie Creek in Greene County, came up with this one. *I. bicolor* nymphs are strong swimmers that often, but not always, move into rocky shallows to wriggle free of their exoskeletons. Look for them in mid-June and July, and again in late August through September.

Streamers and Bucktails

- Blacknose Dace, sizes 4 and 6, 4X to 6X long. Because it is extremely common, just the right size for a growing trout to eat, the blacknose dace is in jeopardy whenever a nice brown trout is thinking "fish" for supper. Be sure to use dace patterns that have an obvious black stripe on their sides. The layered wings may be made of strands of hair from a deer's tail, synthetic fur, or calf-tail clumps, just so long as they are colored white, black, and brown.

- Woolly Bugger, sizes 4 through 8, on 4X long hooks. I can't say for sure that the Bugger in my favorite all-black or black-and-olive color schemes is meant to resemble small fish, but it works extremely well when retrieved through muddy water after a heavy shower.

- Badger Streamer, sizes 4, 6, and 8, all 4X long. Created by the late Poul Jorgensen, the Badger combines silver tinsel, badger saddle hackles, and colorful wood duck side feathers. The fly is highly visible yet natural looking, and it fishes well in low, clear water.

- Little (brook, brown, rainbow) Trout series, sizes 4, 6, 8, on 6X-long shanks. Designed by the legendary Pennsylvania outdoors writer Sam Slaymaker, Little Trout are a lot like their real-life counterparts, which also are apt to wind up in the gullet of a big, cannibalistic brown.

Dry Flies

- Haystack (dark, medium, light), sizes 10 through 18. The original Haystack came from the vise of Adirondack fly tier Fran Betters, to be followed eventually by the slimmed-down Caucci-Nastase Comparadun series. Every fly fisherman needs to carry a few Haystacks,

Comparaduns, or both, because their splayed deer-hair wings look great on the water and float like corks.

- Ausable Wulff, sizes 10 through 16. An attractor pattern with the same orange body color that is so effective in the Queen of Waters wet fly. Try it at dusk on Nine Mile Creek or Oriskany Creek.

- Elk-Hair Caddis, sizes 12 through 20. Caddis often rocket through the surface, and trout weary of the chase will sometimes blast a high-floating imitation so hard that they hook themselves. You want an imitation that floats all day? Then keep a few Elk-Hair Caddis handy.

- Foam Beetle, sizes 10 through 18, regular shank. Some days, the water just doesn't seem to be spitting up any aquatic insects. But unless there's still snow on the ground, one bug or another is always falling off a tree limb and into the water.

- Rusty Spinner, sizes 10 through 22. Yes, you read those hook sizes correctly. A basic spinner pattern, consisting of four to eight strands of dun-colored Microfibetts for tails, a dubbed body of dark rust-colored polypropylene, and spread wings made of white poly, will match most mayflies in their spinner stage, in a wide range of sizes.

Miscellaneous

- Diamond Braid Egg Sac, sizes 8 through 12. Anything that imitates either a single salmon egg or a cluster of trout eggs will draw bites from brown, rainbow, or brook trout during or after spawning runs in spring or fall. Diamond Braid "egg clusters" the size of an average pinkie fingernail are also effective, year-round, in Spring Creek, at the state fish hatchery at Caledonia.

- Griffith's Gnat, sizes 16, 18, 20. Many of the anglers who have difficulty seeing tiny midge flies, let alone knotting them to a leader, can side-step the problem by obtaining some Griffith's Gnats. Made to resemble a cluster or swarm of gnats, they help middle-aged anglers who have trouble seeing midge patterns on the water, or knotting a tiny imitation to a hook.

Mike Brilbeck of Syracuse fishing in the hatchery section of Spring Creek.

CHAPTER TEN

Hail to the Natives

Brook trout always held a position of honor in our household. Nobody had to tell me that when I was growing up, for it was plain to see in the excitement on my father's face as he led us through the minor rituals that occupy trout fishermen when winter is about to make way for spring.

Dad and Grandpa Kelly acknowledged the change in seasons in late March by poking through a cut cornfield with their spade forks. If the soil was thawed and the sun was warm enough, they would shake the soil from the dried-up corn plant roots and then use their fingers to pluck fat worms from the dirt and deposit them in empty vegetable cans.

Dad could fill an empty Prince Albert tobacco can with wriggling garden worms in 10 minutes or less. My sister Anne and I had to look hard even to see the bait mixed in with the soil, but we got better with practice.

In those much simpler times, the statewide trout season opened on the second Saturday in April. The sole exception applied to the tributaries of the Finger Lakes, where fishermen were permitted to try for spawning rainbow trout beginning on April Fools' Day. By the early 1960s, when I regularly accompanied my father on his opening-day trips, the April 1 start-up was in force on most trout streams in the state. That meant the Finger Lakes feeder streams were less crowded than in the past, but thousands of anglers still opened their season on Catharine Creek and other tributaries. Not the Nine Mile Creek crew, however. My father and his friends took advantage of the rule change by visiting their favorite brook trout spots on April 1. Brookies could be counted on to feed hungrily on opening day, and we were delighted to share a few worms with them.

Flipping through old trout-fishing diaries, both my father's and my own, I am immediately struck by the dominance of brook trout in Nine Mile Creek, in those long-ago seasons.

For example, on April 12, 1952, Dad started the second-Saturday opener by creeling five native brookies from 10 to 12½ inches long. He did not kill a brown trout of any length until April 17, on his fourth outing of that season.

The 1953 season started on April 11. Dad stuffed a limit of 10 trout in his basket, including 8 natives between 8½ and 13 inches. The day after that, he creeled eight more natives, the biggest a 14-incher. Other notable catches listed that year in his steno-pad journal included a creel-load of eight brookies, all measuring between 9 and 11 inches. That 1953 season must have marked the modern-day zenith for Nine Mile's natives. Out of 96 trout Dad kept that year, 73 were brookies, and most of those were at least 10 inches long.

I should point out that few anglers in those days adhered to catch-and-release principles, nor even thought to limit their catch instead of catching their limit, as Trout Unlimited's credo requests of modern sportsmen. No, in the 1950s my father and all my relatives, for that matter, had vivid memories of the Great Depression and appreciated trout as, above all their other attributes, a good source of protein. Dad put back more trout than most of his friends did, but he had a bigger family, and ate more fish, too.

THE GLORY DAYS WEREN'T ALWAYS GLORIOUS

During Central New York's brook trout era, the first day of the season was frequently a test of endurance, since April was just as brutal then as now. Snow or rain was a factor more often than not, and no fishermen stayed out for long if they hadn't first covered themselves in multiple layers of clothing and hip boots that were more or less intact.

This seems as good a time as any to tell older readers, and remind the younger ones, that New York's only native trout—and the official state fish, at that—is not really a trout at all, but a char. Lake trout are char, as well, not that there's any likelihood that the drab, bottom-hugging laker will ever be a state fish. Brookies, on the other hand, have stunning good looks and a natural charisma. How could we not name them our state's piscatorial ambassadors?

Nothing in nature is more beautiful than a brook trout, born and bred in the wild. The dorsal surface of a native is dark olive, but spattered with worm-shaped squiggles and random dots that are a very pale yellow. As your eyes work south across the brook trout's flanks, the saffron splotches make room here and there for red dots framed by sky-blue halos. The belly of a hen brookie is creamy white but the male's pectoral, dorsal, and anal fins are trimmed with black and white.

Unfortunately, brook trout can't get by on their looks alone, and many streams that were full of them not that many years ago now have declining populations of natives, or none at all.

This does not mean that our beloved brookies will soon be gone from our watery landscape, but all of us who love the thumping strikes and stubborn battles typical of the species will have to work harder than ever to stay connected with the New York's state trout in the foreseeable future.

Generally speaking, folks who want to catch wild brook trout these days must do some detective work first. Meanwhile, we will all have to give them some serious help, if they are to overcome several looming problems, including destruction of habitat by beavers, highway reconstruction, competition with other salmonids, overfishing, and climate change.

- **Pollution.** My home water, Nine Mile Creek in Onondaga County, was battered by chronic pollution for many years, thanks to inadequate sewage treatment measures and the discharge of industrial waste into the stream. The creek's saga of survival took a tragic turn, however, in 1963 when a pollutant of unknown origin caused a massive fish kill. Within hours, thousands of trout were suffocated and cast ashore between Marcellus and Camillus. Restocking began a year later, but while brown trout made a fairly rapid recovery, the natives never regained their prominent position on Nine Mile's food chain.

- **Beavers.** Nothing in nature, not even hurricanes or tornadoes, is more routinely destructive to brook trout habitat than *Castor canadensis*, the flap-tailed, buck-toothed, ever-industrious beaver.

   Beaver dams plug stream channels and slow currents to the point where they become too warm and too low for trout to survive. Their ponds also act as silt traps, and the mud that collects behind them can smother aquatic insects and trout eggs, alike.

- **Highway reconstruction.** Transportation engineers used to butt heads with Trout Unlimited and like-minded environmental organizations as a matter of routine, but modern highway departments often do the best they can to save any pools or riffles jeopardized by bridge replacement, streambank stabilization, and other highway projects. In one case, the New York Department of Transportation's engineers carefully replaced a scenic bridge at the Route 174 crossing over Nine Mile Creek at Marcellus Falls. Bridge planners opted for a natural-arch bridge that left the popular fishing hole beneath it virtually unchanged.

- **Trout versus trout.** In late 2013, researchers from the DEC Fisheries Bureau and the U.S. Geological Survey confirmed the widely held belief that native brook trout populations have a tough time competing with brown trout. The study was designed to evaluate the effectiveness of the state's trout-stocking methodology.

  USGS project leader James McKenna said the study proved there is "great potential" for browns to compete with natives for feeding lanes, overhead cover, and spawning sites in places considered for inclusion in programs to restore historic brook trout populations.

- **Overfishing.** During a fishing trip to Maine in the late 1990s, my friends and I traded fish stories with an old-timer who was watching us fly casting on the Kennebec River. The brook trout fishing there was "no good anymore," the sage lamented. He blamed that old, reliable enemy of anglers everywhere, known as "the state."

  "Heck, before the state ruined it, my friends and I used to routinely take home limits of nice brookies," he said. "And the limit was 15 in those days."

  Enough said.

  It's okay to eat a native now and then, provided your catch comes from streams that have strong populations of brook trout and aren't subject to extensive fishing pressure. But if you don't know, let them go.

- **Climate change.** Since Central New York residents were just digging out from one of the coldest winters in the last half century as I wrote the first draft of this chapter, I'm not quite ready to concede that we are seeing the results of "global warming." However, I'm willing to admit that some sort of climate change is constant and inevitable. We are better off bracing against its undesirable consequences than trying to stop it from ever happening. Brook trout lovers can do their part by planting willows to increase shade and stabilize streambanks, with the aim of maintaining the cold temperatures that are essential to the survival of *Salvelinus fontinalis*.

Plainly, the future of brook trout is precarious, and we should use the resource wisely. The days of greedy creel limits are gone forever, but that doesn't mean we can't explore untapped brook trout water or revisit old haunts in search of survivors.

Finding your own secret brookie waters is not as hard as you might think. There are numerous streams that continue to have thriving populations, despite man's best unintentional efforts to mess things up. Central New York has some streams where robust brook trout are holding their own, but not many. The outlook for natives is sufficiently worrisome that I am not willing to lead anglers directly to the banks of streams that may not be able to tolerate extra foot traffic. I'd prefer that fishermen who would like to hunt for natives use this chapter to gather basic information, and then follow the clues until they strike gold.

Brooks that are too small or hold too few natives to warrant expanded fishing pressure may be mentioned now and then, but I will not give specific directions to such precarious places.

If I were on a stream-scouting safari in quest of native brookies, I'd start pretty close to home, then extend my exploratory journeys to the next county, and then the one after that, until I had exhausted all the possibilities or, more likely, became exhausted, myself. The hunt for natives usually involves much walking, as well as the occasional stumbles and flat-on-your-face falls.

The best time to check out a stream that is supposed to hold natives is when the fish happen to be biting. I have no crystal ball in my tackle closet, so I can't give you dates or times, but brook trout feeding frenzies usually happen after a soaking rain or during a blizzard hatch of mayflies or caddis. I'm thinking here of the period from early May through mid-June, when aquatic insect hatches peak in most Central New York trout streams.

Downpours are much appreciated by bait fishermen because they wash worms and terrestrial insects and larvae into small streams, and trout quickly line up along current edges to take advantage of the situation. Frequently, storm-water runoff coincides with hatches of aquatic insects, and until the currents become so chocolate-colored that the trout can't see what they're doing, native brookies can be counted on to eat like insatiable little pigs.

Fishermen in search of good brook trout water should keep handy a copy of the Yarmouth, Maine–printed *New York State Atlas & Gazetteer*, as well as a practical but not overly technical global positioning system navigation unit, stowed under a car seat or in some other safe spot. Another great asset to prospecting brookie fishermen is the trove of stream maps available on the DEC's website. One winter when the snow and cold temperatures around Syracuse had left me even more stir-crazy than usual, I spent weeks making printouts until I had filled five loose-leaf binders with the state fishing maps protected in cellophane sleeves. They're divided in alphabetical order for storage and easy reference work when I'm writing and need to find a map in a hurry.

When I'm planning to fish a certain stream or perhaps several streams on a dawn-to-dark brookie chase, I start by retrieving any maps that would be of use. If I have not done so already, I will use a highlighter or fluorescent yellow or green pen to trace the meandering of streams across the DeLorme pages. Those that later prove to hold brookies are marked with the tiny black letters ST, the fisheries biologist's abbreviation for "speckled trout."

Perhaps the selection of that terminology is a bit sneaky on my part. *Speckled trout*, you see, is the common vernacular term for brookies or natives in the Adirondacks, but most fishermen in Central New York don't use it at all.

Before traveling any distance to try a purported brook trout stream, I endeavor to save as much time as possible by looking over any paper maps I have that are pertinent to the quest, then identify the best route there using my TomTom GPS unit.

Start your examination of a potential new (to you) brook trout spot by trying any public fishing sections that are indicated on your collection of DEC stream maps. Then, pick out a friendly-looking landowner whose name appears now and again on area POSTED signs and politely inquire whether he will allow you to fish on his property. If he's receptive, say thank you as sincerely as you can and clarify whether his invitation is good for the season. Don't forget to ask if you can bring a friend along now and then. Before moving on, be sure to ask if the landowner has any rules pertaining to fishing, besides the DEC's general regulations.

If the owner isn't home or is home but not persuaded that he should let you fish, look for bridge crossings. Most rural roads are maintained by local, county, or state DOT crews, and the exchanges of rights-of-way between jurisdictions may leave access questions up to the pertinent road commissioner. Since culvert fishermen tend to be unobtrusive, usually pick up after themselves, and seldom stay at a spot for more than half an hour, few public officials are inclined to kick them out of a roadside pool. At least, that has been my experience. However, it's important that you park your car in a safe place and do not jeopardize yourself or passing motorists by blocking part of the road.

Don't forget to prospect on state forests and other public-accessible property. Many brook trout waters in New York run through state land for a mile or two.

CHAPTER ELEVEN

Fishing the Rainbow Run: Somewhere Today, Elsewhere Tomorrow

The most challenging aspect of catching rainbow trout during their tradition-rich spring spawning run in the Finger Lakes tributaries is figuring out where the fish are hiding on any given day. Big fish, 'bows weighing 4 to 8 pounds or even more, swim up Catharine Creek, Cayuga Inlet, and other spawning grounds every year, but many of them hurry upstream, quickly fulfill their nuptial obligations, then get out of Dodge as fast as they can. Intercepting fish when they are constantly on the move can be a frustrating endeavor.

Fortunately, there are a couple of ways you can put yourself in the right place at the right time to chase rainbows. First, you can aggressively search for trout by walking long distances along a stream until you see what you are looking for in the water or on somebody's stringer. Or, if your time or mobility is limited, you can find a pool that has a reputation for holding the big boys, plunk a bait on the bottom, and wait—sometimes for hours—until an unseen rainbow finally decides to bite.

Which of these approaches better suits your temperament?

Personally, I rely on a combination of the two strategies. If the fish have been biting well—and this can be determined by consultation with the clerks at area bait shops and your fellow fishermen—my inclination is to fish through small pools at a fairly quick pace. For example, let's say a fisherman I trust tells me he has recently seen fish caught in several locations but has yet to come upon a spawning bed. This intelligence leads me to believe that there is a fresh run of rainbows in the stream I'm targeting, and, with their spawning barely under way, these fish are spread out and should be in-stream for days if not weeks. Consequently, a fast pace should allow me to show my bait or fly to numerous fish during a morning or afternoon trip.

On the other hand, my expert source might inform me that the creeks are low and clear, but most fishermen aren't seeing many fish, on their hooks, their stringers, or anywhere else. I am further informed that the egg-laying hens appear to have been hard at work. There are spawning beds here and there, but each one seems to have been deserted by its recent occupants. More ominous, the few hen 'bows that have been caught were spent, or "spawned out," when captured. They have no eggs to lay and are likely hurrying to finish their duties, vacate the tributaries, and resume their fat and happy lives in the lake. If you and I are lucky, these "drop-back" trout will pause for a bite to eat now and then on their way home.

TO FOOL 'EM, YOU HAVE TO FIND 'EM FIRST

When the water is low and clear, out-migrating rainbows will most likely hide in the deepest, darkest pools they can find during daylight hours, then resume their lakeward journey in the pitch dark. I'll try to fool them by fishing deep water patiently, often spending half an hour or more in a single hole. You could catch these fish regularly at night, by the way, but state regulations in general do not allow fishing for rainbows and other salmonids in Finger Lakes tributaries between sunset and sunrise. The best time to give the rainbows a try, legally, is at sunrise, when they have not been harassed by fishermen for a few hours.

Your reward for being the first angler to fish through a prominent pool on Naples Creek or Grout Brook could be an instant hookup. Then again, you could be looking for your first strike and starting to nod off by midmorning. You never know.

Spawning rainbows are receptive to bait, lure, or fly when the mood strikes them. Oh, certain weather and water conditions (a quick but heavy shower, an overnight warm-up that raises stream temperatures into the 50s) may trigger a flurry of action, but you can't count on it. That's why the most successful rainbow trout fishermen are those who put in the most hours on the stream. As more than a few old-timers with big rainbows in their creels have reminded younger and less successful stream-walkers, you simply must pay your dues.

LOOKING BACK, PEEKING AHEAD

The rainbow spawning runs in Finger Lakes tributaries have lured anglers from afar for more than a century. It was 1897 or thereabouts when a shipment of little 'bows was turned loose in Cold Brook, the main feeder stream of Keuka Lake. DEC records on this and other subjects were rather sketchy back then; however, there is significant documentation for the subsequent plantings of California-strain rainbows in other lakes. Brad Hammers, the DEC Region 8 trout biologist, dug into the subject a bit to help me with my previous book, *Fishing the Finger Lakes*. He concluded that rainbows were thriving in several lakes in the chain after a series of stockings in 1917 and 1927. By the 1940s and '50s, anglers from throughout the nation had heard about the annual spring spawning runs in Catharine Creek, and why shouldn't they, for some of the fish that made those epic swims weighed between 12 and 16 pounds!

Today, a rainbow of 5 pounds or more is considered a good one, although the electrofishing surveys that Hammers and his colleagues conduct in late March to give area anglers a public-relations-rooted peek at their opening-day prospects frequently turn up a 10-pounder or two.

Because the steelhead found in Lake Ontario tributaries these days are much larger and more numerous than those that spawn in the Finger Lakes feeders and can be targeted year-round, to boot, it's easy to see why one chain is gaining popularity and the other is not. However, while the Finger Lakes rainbow is not the icon it used to be, the major spawning streams in the chain still muddy up with the boots of hundreds—maybe even thousands—of anglers who wouldn't think of fishing anywhere else on the opening day of trout season, April 1.

My own love for the spring runs is rooted in tradition, but as a practical matter I do not join the April Fools' Day mobs. Instead I fish for brown and brook trout in other streams on opening day, then make my pilgrimage to Naples Creek a day or two after that. By that time the crowds will have thinned out considerably, but many trout will remain in the deep pools. There, they will be frightened half to death but can still be coaxed into hitting a mesh egg sac, consisting of five or six salmon eggs wrapped in a 2-inch square of bridal veiling and held together with elastic thread. As the fish settle down and forget the trampling hordes that whipped the water to a froth on opening day, they can be tricked into grabbing a night crawler or an artificial nymph as well as the ever-reliable egg sac.

DOING THINGS THE RIGHT WAY

Small numbers of spawned-out rainbows will linger in streams well into May, providing some surprisingly good sport for anglers with an extra atom of determination in their body chemistry. I once landed and released a 21-inch rainbow well into the upper reaches of Grout Brook in late June.

It caught me off guard not only because of the late date, but because I was fishing for brown trout.

Whether you swear by bait or fly, you can be confident that any rainbow that enters a tributary to spawn will grow hungry at some point. There is no need to play dirty with one of these spotted submarines by lifting him. *Lifting* is a euphemism for yanking a bare or baited hook into a fish body part, rather than enticing the fish into actually biting. Such shenanigans are blatantly illegal, and the epitome of laziness, to boot. The perpetrator deserves scorn. Nobody, with the exception of a person who is blind or paralyzed on his casting side, has a valid excuse for engaging in foul-hooking activity. Keep a sharp eye out for outlaws as you fish the tributaries and don't hesitate to turn them in to your regional environmental conservation officer.

Meanwhile, you would not be foolish to expect strong rainbow runs and improved fishing in coming seasons, as tighter regulations and expanding food supplies have their impact on various bodies of water in the Finger Lakes chain. The most notable rule change was adopted and implemented on October 1, 2013, when the creel limit for rainbows in tributaries of Hemlock, Canadice, Canandaigua, Keuka, and Seneca Lakes was reduced to one per day, and 15 inches. The limit had been three per day. Region 8 biologists lowered the limit to one 'bow daily in response to growing angler complaints about dwindling numbers of trout in both the lakes and their tributaries. They hope the one-rainbow rule will result in more fish being returned to the water, with surviving trout spawning multiple times over the course of a longer average life span.

I would not be surprised if the one-keeper rule prompts many tributary anglers to let *all* of their rainbows swim away after they are caught and unhooked. That is exactly what happened when the steelhead limit on Lake Ontario was cut back to one a day, and catch rates improved greatly as the no-kill ethic spread throughout the region. There is no reason I can think of why the end result in the western Finger Lakes should be any different.

Curiously, anglers partial to tributaries in the eastern (DEC Region 7) end of the Fingers weren't complaining all that much, so a three-rainbow limit still applies in those parts. Yet some important changes seem to be taking place beneath the surface of Owasco and Skaneateles Lakes, and these ecological shifts have the potential to rejuvenate or stifle future rainbow runs. In Owasco, biologists blamed several years of declining rainbow catches by participants in the state's Angler Diary Program on stocked walleyes, which grew fat by gobbling down every juvenile rainbow they could catch up to. Lake trout consumed plenty of baby 'bows, too, but DEC experts were convinced that walleyes did the heavy-duty eating. They decided to halt walleye releases indefinitely to see if that might jump-start rainbow spawning and recruitment. In fact, angler diaries indicate that rainbow populations have started to increase in the lake already, and tributaries are beginning to come back, too.

CHAPTER TWELVE

Trout-Fishing Manners and Ethics

My father, who sometimes had a difficult time deciding whether to reach for his putter or his fly rod, often used golf to make a point about fishing, and vice versa. Not all of his advice was sagacious, but a good deal of it proved to be on the money. The parental wisdom that stayed with me centered on modern anglers who, in Dad's opinion, did not have good manners and demonstrated little or no awareness of sporting ethics, aside from the trendy adherence to catch-and-release trout fishing.

Not one to start arguments with strangers or casual acquaintances, Dad would steer clear of any fisherman who was obviously inconsiderate of others. Yet if he happened to walk past the obnoxious fellow on his way back to the parking area, he would politely inquire, "How are they biting?" More than once I watched and listened as Dad turned a potential nemesis into a fast friend by giving him an effective fly or even a fat trout from his own creel.

"You take this brown and that nice native you just caught and you've got yourself a great supper," Dad would say. "And give that nymph a try. My son gave me a few and the trout go crazy for them."

Later in the season, he might bump into that angler again, and if the opportunity arose he would offer a few kind suggestions about proper etiquette on trout water. The topics covered included the importance of being friendly toward our fellow anglers, giving a bit of advice if requested, picking up bits of litter along the stream, and wading as little as possible to avoid ruining another's sport. These notions were not inscribed on stone tablets. Rather, they were handed down, from father to son, one generation to the next.

Keep a tape measure handy to keep yourself honest.

To underline a point, Dad frequently turned to his other favorite form of recreation.

"You don't cross the creek upstream from another fisherman, without his permission, unless there is no other way to get to where you are going," said my father. "It's like dragging a golf bag across a green. You just don't do it."

As I was a beginner at both golf and fishing at that time, I barely had a clue about behavior on the greens, but the importance of crossing a stream without disturbing the water to preserve another angler's chances of hooking a trout made perfect sense to me. Eventually, I learned much about the maintenance of golf courses (it would be impossible to tally the number of occasions on which I was reminded to "replace that divot, Mike"), but I never did get the hang of whacking that little white ball down the middle of a fairway. I was blessed, however, to have a fairly loud voice, and I became quite proficient at yelling "Fore" just soon enough for my playing partners to duck yet another errant shot.

Fishing was much easier than golf—at least I thought so—and the etiquette of the sport struck me as being both logical and familiar as I grew up and began to spend countless hours on trout streams in the Syracuse area. It dawned on me, after a while, that the informal rules most sportsmen followed when interacting with others were essentially spun off from the Golden Rule: Do to others as you would have them do to you. The specific rules Dad passed along and I matter-of-factly adopted for inclusion in my own coda included the following:

- Never crowd a fellow angler. If you feel there are too many other anglers working the water to have an enjoyable day, let those who got there first have it to themselves.

- If you are fishing your way downstream, give the right-of-way to the fellow angler who is fishing upstream, so you won't muddy the water or spook each other's fish.

- Whether you are wading or walking the bank en route to the next pool, always give other anglers a wide berth. Do not cast a shadow on the water or send waves ahead of you.

- If at all possible, cross a river or creek well below any other angler you spot ahead of you.

- Don't be a pool hog. If other anglers are passing you regularly, you have stayed in a place too long and should invite the next fisherman you encounter to give "your" spot a try. This does not necessarily apply to a large stream, such as the Scottsville section of Oatka Creek, if numerous anglers are fishing it. In that scenario, which often unfolds during a major mayfly hatch, a lone angler should give others a reasonable amount of room, perhaps 50 feet on either side, then ask if there is room for one more person just beyond that distance. If the answer is no, the prudent thing to do is to look around for another pool, as patiently as possible.

- Be generous with fishing tips and advice. Remember, you were a beginner once.

- Never trespass on posted property without the landowner's permission, lest his signs become bigger and more emphatic. Many landowners will give polite sportsmen a go-ahead.

- Take care of the stream and its surroundings by picking up litter, even if all of it was left behind by somebody else. It doesn't matter if you are on public or private land. You can't change the way others behave on the water, but you can always take a few minutes to pick up a plastic-bag-ful of trash on your way to the car.

Etiquette for trout fishing is mostly common sense, but the concept of ethics can be confusing at times. For example, is it more ethical to fish with artificial flies than it is to use worms, minnows, or other live bait? No doubt many fly fishers in this era would say yes, but the answer to this question is more gray than black or white. If a fly fisher puts back every trout he catches in a no-kill fishing area such as those on Genegantslet Creek or Skaneateles Creek, he is merely obeying the law. On the other hand, if a bait fisherman spending an afternoon on a stream with no special regulations uses a pinched-down barb on his size 6 worm hook to minimize injuries and even takes a few minutes to revive trout that have fought unusually hard and are weak as a result, that angler is a genuine sportsman, whether or not he keeps a couple for the pan.

Similarly, the angler who sees another exceeding the legal creel limit or otherwise breaking the environmental conservation law is an ethical sportsman if he promptly reports the violation to a conservation officer. And what if the same witness doesn't bother to file that complaint, for whatever reason? Then he is just a windbag who needs to take a long look in his mirror before he resumes criticizing other fishermen.

Stocking Quotas for Central New York Trout Streams, 2014

Unless indicated otherwise, the following trout stocking totals are made up of yearling brown trout measuring 8 to 9 inches long. DEC hatchery crews and citizen volunteers stocked approximately 320,000 trout, including 23,000 two-year-old browns, in spring 2014. Meanwhile, the Onondaga County hatchery raised and stocked (all in county waters) another 75,000 trout, almost 20,000 of them being two-year-olds. The figures here are for streams only and do not include stocking numbers for lakes and ponds.

MONROE COUNTY
- Irondequoit Creek—10,560 brown trout, including 1,600 two-year-olds measuring 12 to 15 inches.
- Oatka Creek—4,300 browns, including 700 two-year-olds.

ONTARIO COUNTY
- Canandaigua Outlet—7,555 browns, including 319 two-year-olds.

LIVINGSTON COUNTY
- Little Dansville Creek—440 browns.

YATES COUNTY
- Keuka Outlet—1,020 browns, including 400 two-year-olds.

ONONDAGA COUNTY

- Butternut Creek—6,837 browns, including 2,725 two-year-olds; also 1,411 brook trout.
- Limestone Creek—9,119 browns, including 4,175 two-year-olds; also 2,500 brookies.
- Nine Mile Creek—20,840 browns, including 5, 900 two-year-olds; also 6,300 brook trout.
- Onondaga Creek (Tully)—500 browns.
- West Branch Onondaga Creek—970 browns including 255 two-year-olds.
- Carpenter's Brook—2,465 browns, including 600 two-year-olds; also 125 brookies.
- Fabius Brook—2,800 brookies.
- Geddes Brook—1,080 browns, including 275 two-year-olds.
- Spafford Creek—1,140 browns, including 275 two-year-olds.
- Furnace Brook—400 brook trout.
- Harbor Brook—150 browns, including 50 two-year-olds.
- Skaneateles Creek—2,150 rainbows.
- Pools Brook—125 brown trout and 550 brookies.
- Highland Forest Brook—90 browns and 150 brookies.
- Tannery Creek—100 brookies.
- Bear Trap Creek—125 browns.
- Cold Brook—125 browns.

CAYUGA COUNTY

- Fall Creek—2,500 brook trout.
- North Brook—1,410 browns.
- Owasco Inlet—3,120 browns, including 400 two-year-olds.
- Owasco Outlet—790 rainbows.
- Salmon Creek—1,820 brown trout, including 150 two-year-olds.

MADISON COUNTY

- Beaver Brook—2,120 browns.

- Canaseraga Creek—1,360 browns.
- Canastota Creek—570 browns.
- Chenango River—3,910 browns, including 350 two-year-olds.
- Chittenango Creek—15,780 browns, including 1,940 two-year-olds.
- Cowaselon Creek—1,140 browns.
- Limestone Creek—1,050 browns.
- Chenango Canal—1,140 browns.
- Oneida Creek—2,210 browns.
- Payne Brook—790 browns.
- Sangerfield River—3,000 browns, including 190 two-year-olds.
- Stone Mill Creek—1,050 browns.
- Tributary 32 of East Branch Tioughnioga River—480 browns.

CORTLAND COUNTY
- East Branch Tioughnioga River—5,350 browns, including 700 two-year-olds.
- Merrill Creek—530 browns.
- Otselic River—3,455 browns, including 555 two-year-olds.
- West Branch Tioughnioga River—4,395 browns, including 485 two-year-olds.

OSWEGO COUNTY
- Black Creek—440 browns.
- North Branch Salmon River—3,800 brook trout.
- Rice Creek—359 browns.
- Salmon River—1,050 brook trout and 910 rainbows.
- West Branch Fish Creek—1,410 browns.

STEUBEN COUNTY
- Bennett Creek—790 browns.
- Canaseraga Creek—3,850 browns, including 550 two-year-olds.
- Canisteo Creek—3,780 browns, including 400 two-year-olds.

- Cohocton River—12,490 browns, including 2,300 two-year-olds.
- Meads Creek—3,020 browns, including 300 two-year-olds.
- Post Creek—1,260 browns, including 200 two-year-olds.

CHEMUNG COUNTY
- Cayuta Creek (Chemung section)—9,300 browns, including 1,550 two-year-olds.
- Newtown Creek—955 browns, including 75 two-year-olds.
- Post Creek—1,650 browns, including 250 two-year-olds.
- Sing Sing Creek—1,340 browns, including 150 two-year-olds.
- Wyncoop Creek—350 browns.

TOMPKINS COUNTY
- Buttermilk Creek—940 browns.
- Enfield Creek—12,555 rainbow trout and 2,000 browns.
- Fall Creek—5,930 browns, including 300 two-year-olds.
- Salmon Creek—2,870 browns, including 150 two-year-olds.
- Six Mile Creek—1,610 browns, including 200 two-year-olds.
- Virgil Creek—2,270 browns, including 200 two-year-olds.

TIOGA COUNTY
- Catatonk Creek—1,410 browns.
- Cayuta Creek (Tioga County section)—1,960 browns, including 330 two-year-olds.
- East Branch Owego Creek—5,750 browns, including 650 two-year-olds.
- Owego Creek (main stem)—3,675 browns, including 515 two-year-olds.
- West Branch Owego Creek—5,165 browns, including 555 two-year-olds.

BROOME COUNTY
- Dudley Creek—400 browns.
- East Branch Nanticoke Creek—350 browns, including 50 two-year-olds.

- Nanticoke Creek—3,740 browns, including 5,509 two-year-olds.
- Oquaga Creek—3,980 browns, including 400 two-year-olds.

CHENANGO COUNTY
- Genegantslet Creek—4,715 browns, including 255 two-year-olds.
- Otselic River—10,710 browns, including 1,130 two-year-olds.

Central New York Trout-Fishing Regulations

The state's standard creel limit of five trout a day, including no more than two that measure longer than 12 inches, applies to most Central New York streams, but there are some notable exceptions. The following special regulations were listed in the 2013–14 edition of the state's fishing regulations guidebook, which is available to all license buyers at no cost from town clerks, tackle shops, and other vendors.

MONROE COUNTY
- Oatka Creek—From Bowerman Road upstream for 1.4 miles to Union Street and from Wheatland Center Road upstream for 2.5 miles to the mouth of Spring Creek, fishing is catch-and-release only, with artificial lures or flies (bait prohibited) from October 15 through March 31.

  Also, from Union Street upstream for 1.7 miles to Wheatland Center Road, fishing for trout is catch-and-release, artificial lures or flies only (bait prohibited), year-round.

- Spring Creek—From April 1 through October 15, the limit is two trout of 12 inches or longer. From October 16 through March 31, the creek is catch-and-release, artificial flies or lures only (bait prohibited).

LIVINGSTON COUNTY
- Spring Creek—In that part of Spring Creek on the fish hatchery property in Caledonia, fishing is permitted from 8 AM to 4 PM. It's artificial lures or flies only (no bait). The fishing is catch-and-release from October 16 through March 31. From April 1 through October 15, the limits is two a day, 12 inches or longer.

YATES COUNTY

- Keuka Outlet—Subject to Finger Lakes tributary regulations from its mouth near Dresden upstream to the first impassable barrier for spawning fish from Seneca Lake. From there upstream to Keuka Lake, the limit is five trout, any size, all year.

ONONDAGA COUNTY

- Skaneateles Creek—From the Old Seneca Turnpike bridge just north of Skaneateles village for 10.2 miles to the Jordan Road bridge in the village of Jordan, trout are for catch-and-release fishing only. The season on the creek runs from April 1 through October 15, and it's for users of artificial lures and flies only. No bait allowed.

- Spafford Creek—Although it is a Finger Lake tributary (Otisco), Spafford Creek has no rainbows, and so has a season from April 1 through October 15; its angler may creel five trout per day, including two that are longer than 12 inches.

- Limestone Creek and Butternut Creek—Both are open to trout fishing year-round from U.S. Route 20 north to their mouths.

CAYUGA COUNTY

- Salmon Creek—From April 1 through October 15, the creel limit is five trout a day with no more than two longer than 12 inches. Bait is okay. However, from October 16 through March 31, this part of the stream is catch-and-release, and only artificial lures or flies are permitted (no bait).

MADISON COUNTY

- Chenango Canal from Route 46 to Oriskany Creek at Solsville—Year-round fishing, limit of two trout longer than 12 inches daily, and artificials only.

- Chittenango Creek from U.S. Route 20 north to Conrail tracks—Year-round fishing, creel limit of five per day of which only two may be more than 12 inches.

- Chittenango Creek from the line between the towns of Fenner and Sullivan at mile marker 1219 on Route 13 to the mile marker 1237 south of the village of Chittenango line—Catch-and-release trout fishing year-round, artificial flies and lures only.

- Oneida Creek from Peterboro Road (Route 34) to the Thruway—Trout fishing all year, creel limit of five trout including no more than two of 12 inches or more.
- East Branch Tioughnioga River and Otselic River in Madison County— Trout fishing from April 1 through October 15, creel limit of five a day but no more than two longer than 12 inches; from October 16 through March 31, trout fishing is catch-and-release.

CORTLAND COUNTY
- East Branch Owego Creek, East Branch Tioughnioga River, West Branch Tioughnioga River, Otselic River—Trout fishing is legal year-round, with state-standard creel limits between April 1 and October 15, but catch-and-release and artificials only from October 16 through March 31.

STEUBEN COUNTY
- Cohocton River—From the north boundary of the Veterans Administration facility in Bath to the Route 415 bridge and from the north boundary of the village of Avoca upstream to the mouth of Neil Creek, the trout creel limit is two, both of which must be 12 inches or longer, and fishing is with artificial flies or lures (no bait), year-round. In other parts of the Cohocton, the limit is five a day, any size, year-round.
- Mill Creek—The entire length of Mill Creek is open to trout fishing year-round, with a creel limit of five a day, including no more than two that exceed 12 inches in length.

SCHUYLER COUNTY
- Cayuta Creek—In the Schuyler County section of Cayuta Creek (known as Shepherd's Creek to some locals), anglers may creel five trout a day, of which no more than two can exceed 12 inches. Bait, lures, and flies are permitted at all times.

TOMPKINS COUNTY
- Fall Creek—From the Route 38 bridge at Freeville upstream to the bridge at Groton City, trout fishing is allowed all year, with a daily limit of five to include no more than two that are 12 or more inches long.

- Salmon Creek above Ludlowville Falls and the county segment of the West Branch of Owego Creek—Trout fishing is allowed year-round. From April 1 through October 15, the limit is five, of which no more than two can be longer than 12 inches. From October 16 through March 31, trout fishing in both these places is catch-and-release and bait fishing is prohibited.

TIOGA COUNTY

- Cayuta Creek—In the Tompkins County stretch of this creek, trout fishing is permitted all year, with a creel limit of five, including no more than two longer than 12 inches.

- Owego Creek and its East Branch and West Branch—trout fishing is allowed year-round. From April 1 through October 15, the creel limit is five, of which no more than two can exceed 12 inches in length. From October 16 through March 31, fishing is catch-and-release, with artificial lures and flies only (no bait).

BROOME COUNTY

- Oquaga Creek—From the old Route 17 bridge east of McClure downstream for 3 miles to the new Route 17 bridge east of Deposit, trout fishing is catch-and-release, artificial flies and lures only, all year.

CHENANGO COUNTY

- Genegantslet Creek—From first Route 220 bridge north of Smithville Flats upstream to the mouth of "Five Streams," the season for trout is year-round, and regulations are catch-and-release, lures and flies only (no bait).

- Otselic River—The Chenango County section of the Otselic River is open to trout year-round. From April 1 through October 15, the creel limit is five trout per day, of which no more than two can be longer than 12 inches. From October 16 through March 31, the river is catch-and-release, and only artificial lures or flies may be used.

East Branch of Owego Creek.

Index

Abraham, Bill, xiv, 15
Albright Creek, 110
Amber Brook, 59
Archer, Leon, 95
Art of Tying the Wet Fly, 189
Arthur, George, 38
Atlas & Gazeteer, 207
Ausable Wulff fly, 201
Austerman, Pete, 5, 18, 21, 131,
    134, 137

Badger Streamer, 200
Bait fishing outfit, 172
Barbagallo's Restaurant, 119
Bashline, Jim, 193
Bass Pro Shops, 73, 189
Bass, 88, 113, 133
Beadhead Caddis, 199
Beadhead nymphs, 80
Bear Brook, 166
Bear Swamp Creek, 71
Beaver Creek, 93
Beavers, 69, 71, 72, 205
Bennetts Creek, 134

Bergman, Ray, 187
Betters, Fran, 200
Big Bay Creek, 121
Bishop, Dan, 70
Blacknose Dace, 200
Blue Creek, 94
Bowman Creek, 166
Bradley Brook, 94
Bridge crossings, 208
Brilbeck, Mike 18
Brook trout, 12, 111; appearance of,
    204; native, xvi, 5, 72, 101
Brooks, Joe, 188
Brown Cow, 64
Brown trout, 12, 64, 73, 79, 89, 104,
    113, 126, 133, 147
Buck Settlement Creek, 138
Bucktails, 200
Buttermilk Falls Park, 152
Butternut Creek, 52, 226

Caddis, Cased, 80, 129; Elk Hair, 129
Caddisflies, 11, 64, 80, 183
Caitlin Mill Creek, 145

Caledonia hatchery, 21

Campbell Creek, 138

Canandaigua Outlet, 19

Canaseraga Creek, 25, 93, 135, 139

Canastota Creek, 93

Canisteo Creek, 133

Canoga Creek, 5

Carpenter's Brook, 51

Carrington Creek, 138

Cascadilla Creek, 151

Cased Caddis Larva, 199

Catatonk Creek, 158

Catch-and-release (no-kill), 43, 47, 163

Catharine Creek, 141, 143

Cayuga County trout streams (more), 73

Cayuta Creek (Shepherd's), 139, 227, 228

Cayuta Lake, 140

CDI Fly Fishers, 99

Central New York "Slam", 13

Chamberlain Creek, 138

Chandler, Leon, 99

Char, 204

Chemung River, 140

Chenango Canal, 82, 226

Chenango County trout streams (more), 166

Chenango River, 88, 165

Chittenango Creek, 76, 226

Climate change, 206

Clockville Creek, 93

Cochran, Rod, 100

Cohocton River, 124, 227

Cold Brook, 107

Cold Spring Brook, 75

Coleman, Carl, 11

Constantia hatchery, 81

Corbett, Kid, 112, 120, 177

Cornell University, 151, 152

Cortland County trout streams (more), 107

Cottrell Brook, 121

Cowaselon Creek, 93

Creel limits, xiv, 212, 218

Crown Woolen Mill, 42

Cryder Creek, 139

DeCapio, Jake, 90, 199

Decker Brook, 67

Deer hunting, 123

Delaware River, 159

Delayed Harvest regulations, 92

Dennison, Tony, 56

DeTomaso, Mike, 73, 189

Diamond Braid Egg Sac fly, 201

Dresserville Creek, 65

Dropper line, 199

Dry Creek, 100

Dry flies, 200

Dudley Creek, 163

Dun Variant nymph, 200

Dutch Hollow Brook, 70

Dyke Creek, 139

Dykeman Creek, 121

Eelpot Creek, 13

Egg Sac fly, 201

Elk Hair Caddis, 201

Fabius Brook, 55

Factory Brook, 95

Fall Creek, 147, 227

Fat Nancy's Tackle Shop, 110

Feeding line, 195

Fish Creek, West Branch, 121
Fish kill, 38
Fishing the Finger Lakes, 211
Flick, Art, 41, 200
Flint Creek, 29
Fly Box, Central New York, 198
Foam Beetle, 201
Franklin Square, 58
Furnace Brook, 60

Ganargua Creek, 18
Geddes Brook, 43
Genegantslet Creek, 163, 228
Genesee River, 8
Goff Creek, 137
Gold Ribbed Hare's Ear, 129
Greek Peak Ski Center, 109
Green drakes, 155, 165
Green Gulf Brook, 26
Green, Seth, 5, 21
Gridley Creek, 109
Griffith's Gnat, 201
Grimes Creek, 16
Grout Brook, 104

Haight Gulf, 110
Hammers, Brad, 9, 141, 211
Happy Valley WMA, 121
Hatchery trout, xiii
Hatches, mixed, 183 (*see also*
    Mayflies); 184
Haystack fly, 200
Hector Falls Creek, 145
Hemlock Creek, 74
Hemlock Lake, 23
Hendrickson mayflies, 7, 10, 40, 64,
    84, 88, 127, 150, 155, 159
Hendrickson nymph, 198

Hendrickson Snowshoe Emerger,
    198
Hewitt, Edward R., 188
Highway construction, 205
Homer Rod and Gun Club, 106
Honeoye Inlet, 18
Hunter, Rod, 44, 56

John O'Hara Brook, 117
Jorgensen, Poul, 200

Kelsey Brook, 166
Keuka Lake Outlet, 27, 28, 226
Kingsley Crook, 94
Knight, John Alden, 187
Kowalski, Tony, 44

Labrador Creek, 110
Lake Como, 66
Leisenring, Jim, 189
Lemon, Dave, 165
Lifting, 212
Limestone Creek, 54, 226
Limestone springs, 42
Little Dansville Creek, 26
Little John Wildlife Management
    Area, 121
Little Mill Creek, 26, 135
Little Sandy Creek, 121
Little Trout flies, 200
Livingston County trout streams
    (more), 26

Mad River, 117
Madison County trout streams
    (more), 93
Malinda's Tackle, 110
Marcellus *Observer*, 36

March browns, 10, 11, 129, 155
Martisco Paper Co., 42
Matching the Hatch, 188
Maxwell Brook, 138
Maybury Brook, 110
Mayfly hatch, 40, 64, 84, 182,
    184
McClane, A. J., 188
McCorn Creek, 141
McKenna, James, 206
Mepps spinner, 175, 179
Merrilly Creek, 108
Mill Creek, 19, 129, 227
Miller Brook, 159
Morgan Hill Brook, 110
Mud Creek, 18, 152
Munger Creek, 94

Nanticoke Creek, 161
Naples Creek, 13
Neff, Fred, 175
Neil Creek, 135
Nelson Swamp, 79
Nemes, Sylvester, 189
New York State Outdoor Writers
    Assn, 94
Newtown Creek, 141
Night Fishing for Trout, 193
Night fishing, 193
Nine Mile Creek, 34, 186
Nine Mile Scud, 199
North Brook, 72
Nymph patterns, 170, 172
Nymphs, 186, 198

Oatka Creek, 7, 225
Onandaga County trout streams
    (more), 59

Onandaga County Fish Hatchery,
    51
Onandaga Creek, 57
Onandaga Creek, West Branch,
    59
Oneida Lake, 93
Oquaga Creek, 159, 227, 228
Oriskany Creek, 84, 226
Orwell Brook, 116
Oswego County trout streams
    (more), 120
Otselic River, 89, 108, 227, 228
Overfishing, 206
Owasco Inlet, 4, 61
Owasco Lake, 70
Owaskantisco Anglers, 47
Owego Creek, 158, 228
Owego Creek, East Branch, 153, 227
Owego Creek, West Branch, 155

Pale Evening Dun, 87
Palomar knot, 177
Panfish, 133
Panther Martin spinner, 175, 179
Pardee Hollow Creek, 26
Park Station Lake, 141
Peel, Bob, 31, 44, 56
Peg Mill Brook, 152
Pike, 88; northern, 102
Pine Hollow Brook, 74
Pocket water, 79
Pollution, 58, 205
Pool's Brook, 60
Post Creek, 142
Powder Mills Park, 11
Public Fishing Rights (PFR), 66
Put-and-take streams, 92
Putnam Brook, 75

Queen of Waters wet fly, 199

Rahme, Dave, 31
Rain, effects of on fishing, 171, 172, 207
Rainbow trout, wild, 39; non-migratory, 65; spawning, 210
Rapalas, 177, 178
Reeder Creek, 5
Region 7 Conservation League, 71
Regulations, fishing, 23
Reservoir Creek, 17
Retrieve, fast, 175, 195
Reynolds Game Farm, 151
Reynolds Gulf Brook, 26
Rising trout, 182
Robins, Jeff, 69, 75
Rogers Nature Center, 89
Roscoe, NY, 3
Rusty Spinner, 201

Salmon Creek, 74, 226, 228
Salmon River, North Branch, 112; East Branch, 114
Salmon, 4, 107, 116, 147; landlocked, 27
Sanderson, Matt, 11
Sangerfield River, 92
Schwiebert, Ernest, 188
Scottsville, 8
Scriba Creek, 81, 121
Shapley Brook, 166
Shepherd's Creek, 140
Shequaga Creek, 146
Shopping Cart Pool, 101
Shove Park, 45
Sinclair Creek, 138
Sing Sing Creek, 142

Six Mile Creek, 150
Skaneateles Creek, 47, 171, 226
Skaneateles Lake, 106
Slate drakes, 80
Slaymaker, Sam, 200
Snail Hole, 80
Snail, amber ovate, 80
Spafford Creek, 59, 226
Spawning run, 209
Spin fishing, 9
Spinner fall, 10
Spinners, 175, 179
Spinning tackle, 170
Spring Creek, 8, 19, 20, 225
Springwater Creek, 23
St. Mary's Pond, 121
State forest lands, 208
Steelhead, 4, 11, 116, 211
Steuben County trout streams (more), 138
Stickbaits, 177
Stocking quotas, 71
Stoneflies, 159, 183
Stony Brook, 139
Streamer flies, 170, 172, 195, 200
Strike indicator, 187
Sugar Creek, 27, 139
Sulfur hatch, 40, 129, 165
Syracuse *Post-Standard*, 31

Tallette Creek, 94
Tannery Creek, 17
Taughannock Falls Creek, 146
Temperature, water, 41, 79, 86, 113, 131
Terrestrials, 11, 57, 86
"The 900", 21
Thomas, Bill, 175

Tioughnioga Creek, East Branch, 87

Tioughnioga River, East Branch, 102, 227

Tioughnioga River, West Branch, 99

Tompkins County trout streams, more, 152

Treman Park, 152

Tricos, 65, 84, 126, 129

Trout (Hewitt), 188

Trout Brook, 103, 117

Trout Unlimited, 205

Tully Lake, 100

Virgil Creek, 109

Wading gear, 22, 30

Walleye, 70, 81, 88, 102, 121, 133

Webster Brook, 150

Wedge, Les, xiv, 97

Wet flies, 187, 188, 198

White Bottom Brook, 60

White River Fly Shop, 189

Whitlock Red Fox Squirrel Hair nymph, 199

Whitney Pond, 121

Winter fishing, 52, 82

Woolly Bugger, 129, 192, 200

Worms, fly gear for, 170

Wynkoop Creek, 144

Yellow drakes, 84